IIAS Series: Governance and Public Management

International Institute of Administrative Sciences (IIAS)

The International Institute of Administrative Sciences is an international association with scientific purpose based in Brussels. As a non-governmental international organisation its activities are centred on the study of public administration and providing a forum in which comparative studies – including both practical experiences and theoretical analyses of experts in public administration from all cultures – are presented and discussed. The Institute is interested in all questions related to contemporary public administration at national and international levels.

Website: http://www.iias-iisa.org

Governance and Public Management Series

The *Governance and Public Management* series, published in conjunction with the International Institute of Administrative Sciences (IIAS), brings the best research in public administration and management to a global audience. Encouraging a diversity of approaches and perspectives, the series reflects the Institute's conviction for a neutral and objective voice, grounded in the exigency of fact. How is governance conducted *now*? How could it be done better? What defines the law of administration and the management of public affairs, and can their implementation be enhanced? Such questions lie behind the Institute's core value of *accountability*: those who exercise authority must account for its use – to those on whose behalf they act.

Titles in the series include:

Eberhard Bohne
THE WORLD TRADE ORGANIZATION
Institutional Development and Reform

Michiel S. De Vries
THE IMPORTANCE OF NEGLECT IN POLICY-MAKING

Michiel S. De Vries, P.S. Reddy, M. Shamsul Haque (*editors*)
IMPROVING LOCAL GOVERNMENT
Outcomes of Comparative Research

Wouter Van Dooren and Steven Van de Walle (*editors*)
PERFORMANCE INFORMATION IN THE PUBLIC SECTOR

Governance and Public Management Series
Series Standing Order ISBN 978–0230–50655–8 (hardback)
978–0230–50656–5 (paperback)

You can receive future titles in this series as they are published by placing a standing order. Please contact your bookseller or, in case of difficulty, write to us at the address below with your name and address, the title of the series and the ISBNS quoted above.

Customer Services Department, Macmillan Distribution Ltd, Houndmills, Basingstoke, Hampshire RG21 6XS, England

---

The World Trade Organization

Institutional Development and Reform

Eberhard Bohne

Professor of Public Administration,
German University of Administrative Sciences Speyer,
German Research Institute for Public Administration

palgrave
macmillan

First published 2010 by
PALGRAVE MACMILLAN

Palgrave Macmillan in the UK is an imprint of Macmillan Publishers Limited, registered in England, company number 785998, of Houndmills, Basingstoke, Hampshire RG21 6XS.

Palgrave Macmillan in the US is a division of St Martin's Press LLC, 175 Fifth Avenue, New York, NY 10010.

Palgrave Macmillan is the global academic imprint of the above companies and has companies and representatives throughout the world.

Palgrave® and Macmillan® are registered trademarks in the United States, the United Kingdom, Europe and other countries.

ISBN: 978–0–230–23257–0 hardback

This book is printed on paper suitable for recycling and made from fully managed and sustained forest sources. Logging, pulping and manufacturing processes are expected to conform to the environmental regulations of the country of origin.

A catalogue record for this book is available from the British Library.

A catalog record for this book is available from the Library of Congress.

10 9 8 7 6 5 4 3 2 1
19 18 17 16 15 14 13 12 11 10

Printed and bound in Great Britain by
CPI Antony Rowe, Chippenham and Eastbourne

Contents

List of Figures and Tables

Figures

Tables

Preface

The World Trade Organization (WTO) has become a symbol of global economic prosperity for many students of international trade, and a symbol of exploitation and oppression of developing countries for some radical critics of globalization. This book is not about the economic and political benefits and detriments of the WTO trading system. This book is about how the WTO functions as a public formal organization and how its functioning can be improved. Thus, this study analyzes and evaluates the WTO from a public administration perspective. This perspective is largely absent from the current debate on WTO reforms. The public administration perspective has also been neglected in the general debate on international organizations which is still dominated by the traditional view that only nation states matter, not international organizations. Therefore, this study aims to contribute to a better understanding of the WTO and international organizations as public administrations, and to a realistic assessment of the practicability of WTO reform measures. Many reform proposals are derived from normative democratic or rationalistic models of decision making which are likely to fail in the real world of public administrations.

The author wishes to thank his former research assistant, Dr. Sonja Bugdahn, for her diligent work on the research project. She conducted most of the interviews at the WTO alone, and substantially contributed to the research report.

The preparation of the book manuscript was in the hands of Andrea Langlotz. Her diligence, patience, and good humor were essential for the successful completion of the project.

The author is indebted to the German Research Institute for Public Administration Speyer which funded the research.

The permission by the WTO to reprint Figures 1.1, 4.1, 4.2, and Table 6.1 is appreciated.

Speyer, March 2009 Eberhard Bohne

Acronyms

ACP	African, Caribbean, and Pacific Group of States
CHF	Swiss Francs
DSB	Dispute Settlement Body
DSU	Dispute Settlement Understanding
EU	European Union
GATS	General Agreement on Trade in Services
GATT	General Agreement on Tariffs and Trade
IATP	Institute for Agriculture and Trade Policy
ILO	International Labour Organization
IMF	International Monetary Fund
IO	International Organization
ITC	International Trade Centre
ITU	International Telecommunication Union
JITAP	Joint Integrated Technical Assistance Programme
LDC	Least Developed Country
MEA	Multinational Environmental Agreement
NAMA	Non-Agricultural Market Access
NGO	Non-Government Organization
OECD	Organisation for Economic Cooperation and Development
QUAD	Quadrilateral, i.e. country group consisting of Canada, the United States, Japan, and the European Union
TNC	Trade Negotiations Committee
TPRB	Trade Policy Review Body
TRIPS	Trade-Related Aspects of Intellectual Property Rights
UK	United Kingdom
UN	United Nations
UNCED	United Nations Conference on Environment and Development
UNCTAD	United Nations Conference on Trade and Development
UNDP	United Nations Development Programme
UNESCO	United Nations Educational, Scientific and Cultural Organization
US	United States
WHO	World Health Organization
WIPO	World Intellectual Property Organization
WTO	World Trade Organization

1
The WTO as an International Organization

I. Introduction

The Marrakesh Agreement created the World Trade Organization (WTO) in 1995 to be a new international organization (IO) with legal personality, and endowed it with decision-making processes, an institutional structure, and several distinctive functions (*Matsushita et al.* 2003: 14). The organization is not a UN organ. Although the WTO is comparatively young, it benefits from experience with trade liberalization and dispute settlement under the General Agreement on Tariffs and Trade (GATT) regime, which was established in 1947. The preamble of the Marrakesh Agreements lists the improvement of living standards and sustainable development as objectives of the new organization; however, the WTO may pursue its goals exclusively through trade liberalization.

The WTO is intended to facilitate the implementation and administration and further the objectives of the Marrakesh and other multilateral trade agreements. In particular, the WTO is to provide a forum for negotiations among its members (Art. III (2)) of the Marrakesh Agreement) and administer the Dispute Settlement Mechanism (Art. III (3)) and the Trade Policy Review Mechanism (Art. III (4)).

The vast proportion of GATT/WTO law has been legislated in trade negotiating rounds (*Steinberg* 2002: 350). The Marrakesh Agreement establishing the WTO contained, as integral part, the new GATT 1994 (the GATT 1947 was terminated), the General Agreement on Trade in Services (GATS), the Trade-Related Aspects of Intellectual Property Rights (TRIPS) Agreement, and a number of other agreements (*Steinberg* 2002: 360). Membership of the WTO automatically implies an obligation to uphold all multilateral trade agreements (single undertaking approach[1]). An exception are the two remaining plurilateral agreements that had a narrower group of signatories, the Agreement on Trade in Civil Aircraft and the Agreement on Government Procurement (*WTO* 2008: 51f.).

In 1947 the 23 founding GATT members were mostly industrialized countries, while the accession of developing countries began in the late fifties. Since the birth of the WTO in 1995, membership has grown rapidly and reached 153 member countries in 2008. This is despite the fact that accession to the WTO is a difficult and time-consuming process since countries may join the WTO only after negotiating terms of accession. In practice, a consensus of all members is required (*Matsushita et al.* 2003: 11). Developing countries now comprise about three quarters of the total WTO membership (*WTO* 2008: 109). The increase in membership at the WTO is largely attributed to an increase in developing country membership, and countries such as Brazil and India play an increasingly important role at the WTO (*McRae* 2004: 15). It should be noted that the European Union is a member of the WTO together with all of its member states.

As the WTO approaches universal membership, the share of its members in world exports and imports has also grown significantly. Between 1948 and 2005 the share of GATT/WTO members of world merchandise exports showed a steady upward trend, rising from 60.4% in 1948 to 94.4% in 2005. In the same period the share of GATT/WTO members of world merchandise imports rose from 52.9% in 1948 to 96.1% in 2005.[2] It is thus fair to say that the major share of the total world merchandise imports and exports is made under rules of the WTO. The share in exports is, however, unevenly distributed among its members. The EU-25 accounts for 39.4% of the world merchandise exports, followed by the United States (8.9%), China (7.5%), Japan (5.9%), Canada (3.5%), Brazil (1.2%), and India (0.9%). By contrast, the whole of Africa (whether member of the WTO or not) accounts for only 2.9% of world merchandise exports, with South Africa accounting for .5%.[3]

Figure 1.1 depicts the organizational structure of the WTO.

The WTO has two governing bodies: (1) the Ministerial Conference and (2) the General Council. The Ministerial Conference is composed of representatives of all WTO members and meets at least once every two years. Between these meetings, the General Council is the chief decision-making and policy-body (*Matsushita et al.* 2003: 10). It is characterized as the collective voice of the member governments and is not an independent decision-making institution (*Howse* 2001: 359). All councils and committees encompass all member states. Decisions have to be regularly taken through consensus and this promotes the use of informal

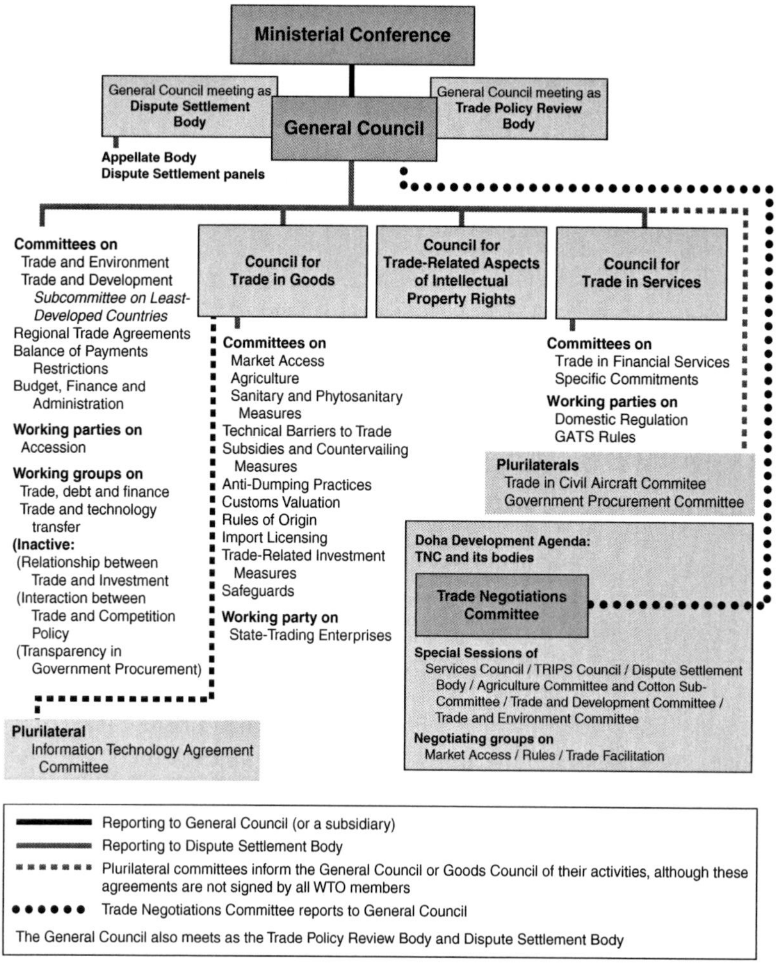

Figure 1.1 Organigram of the WTO
Source: WTO 2008, p. 103

mechanism for reaching decisions, such as smaller meetings, which may also take place outside the WTO (*WTO* 2008: 104).

The Dispute Settlement Mechanism provides an institutionalized process for the settlement of disputes between WTO member states. This is an unusual feature for an international organization, only few of which have a compulsory dispute settlement procedure, e.g. the Law of the Sea Convention (*Bronckers* 2001: 45). If a member state believes that another member is violating its commitments made under the trade agreements, it can file suit in the WTO with a dispute settlement body (DSB). The DSB establishes ad hoc panels for each case that deliberate in secret. The decision of a dispute settlement panel is binding, but the losing party can file an appeal with a standing Appellate Body. If the decision establishes that a member state has violated its commitments, the defendant is ordered to change its action. If the member state refuses, it faces economic sanctions by the winning party (*Kirshner* 2005: 496f.). The Dispute Settlement Mechanism has been identified as an example for how international organizations combine elements of centralization and decentralization. On the one hand, the WTO has centralized elements for judging trade disputes. On the other hand, its enforcement is decentralized since the organization cannot impose any sanctions, but it can authorize individual members to punish violations of trade law (*Koremenos et al.* 2001: 772). Yet, the decentralization of enforcement has not been extended so far as to enable private individuals or corporations to take member states to domestic courts for alleged violation of trade agreements. WTO law may or may not be given direct effect or be supreme, depending on the constitutional doctrine of WTO member states. As set out in Chapter 4, I, WTO law has currently neither supremacy in the United States nor in the European Union. In this regard, it differs from Community law in the European Union.

The WTO has a Secretariat with 630 staff members and a Director General, but officially the Secretariat's role is mostly limited to administrative and technical support for other WTO bodies (*WTO* 2008: 107). It is certainly a remarkable fact that the WTO in its own organizational chart omits the Secretariat. The organigram is instead focused on intergovernmental bodies. This is a reflection of the WTO's self-perception as an international arena for negotiations (see Chapter 2, I.1) rather than as an international actor (see Chapter 5, VI).

In recent years, the WTO faces problems in launching and concluding new trade rounds. Negotiations for launching a new trade round first failed in Seattle in 1999. On that occasion, several thousand demonstrators from over 1200 Non-Government Organizations (NGOs) comprising environmental groups and labor unions to human right activists and development lobbies were in the streets protesting against trade liberalization policies and decisions taken by the dispute settlement bodies of the WTO. However, views differ on whether the demonstrations in Seattle were a direct cause of the failure of negotiations. Another reason was the disappointment of developing countries with the results of trade liberalization as agreed to in the Uruguay Round and the unwillingness of industrialized states to listen to their concerns (*Das* 2000: 188). This led to the adoption of the Doha Development Agenda in 2001 at the Ministerial Conference in Doha. Promises were made that in the new round of negotiations particular attention be paid to the needs and requirements of developing countries.

However, the next Ministerial Conference in 2003 in Cancún collapsed again without any results. The reason was that developing countries aimed at achieving trade liberalization in agriculture through a substantial reduction in subsidies, to which the European Union and the United States did not consent. Instead, the European Union and the United States still tried to negotiate new trade-related agreements on the so-called Singapore Issues: competition, investment, procurement, and trade facilitation. An interesting development in Cancún was a rally of most NGOs behind developing countries and their agendas (*Cho* 2004: 235). After Cancún, the European Union and the United States agreed that the issue of new trade-related agreements be removed from the agenda.

A compromise was found at the Ministerial Conference in Hong Kong in 2005 which was to provide a basis for further negotiations. However, the WTO members were unable to respect the short-term deadlines set in Hong Kong. When it became obvious that agreement among the negotiating parties could not be reached by July 2006, trade talks of the Doha Round were suspended. Hence, the WTO negotiating machine has currently come to a halt.

The difficulty of launching new trade rounds together with the protests of NGOs against the WTO has sparked off lively discussions among scholars and practitioners on the causes for the crisis and on proposals for reforming the WTO. Proposals by scholars range from a transformation of the WTO into a World Economic Organization through a progressive widening of competencies to cover multilateral environmental and social agreements (*Guzman* 2004) to a tempering of the WTO operations through new modesty, subsidiarity, and self-restraint in rule-making and rule interpretation (*Howse* 2001: 359; also *Howse* and *Nicolaidis* 2003). Other scholars focus on procedural reforms concerning participation of the public and of NGOs (*Charnovitz* 2002a: 495ff.), or on the creation of a Parliamentary Assembly at the WTO (*Mann* 2005; *Shaffer* 2005c, see also *Petersmann* 2001).

The former WTO Director General *Supachai Panitchpakdi* reacted to the discussion by setting up a Consultative Board of eight "eminent persons" in June 2002 who delivered the so-called Sutherland Report on institutional reform of the WTO at the end of 2004 (*Sutherland et al.* 2004). The group selected to serve on the Consultative Board was close to the WTO, and failed to include any scholar, intellectual, or politician who has voiced substantial and serious criticism (*von Bogdandy and Wagner* 2005: 439). The insider character of the report was reinforced by the lack of external consultation which was in stark contrast to the drafting process of comparable expert report on UN reform (*Pauwelyn* 2005: 330). It is thus unsurprising that the Sutherland report has been criticized as "largely a defence of the *status quo* by WTO insiders" (*Pauwelyn* 2005: 329). Others view the report as providing some interesting ideas even though it appeared "as fully rooted in WTO orthodoxy and – unlike many citizens, politicians and scholars – very much satisfied with the evolutionary path the WTO has taken" (*von Bogdandy and Wagner* 2005: 447).

In the following section an overview is given over the main issues discussed in critical analyses of the WTO by scholars and practitioners.

II. Issues: Effectiveness, equity, and legitimacy

*Porte*r (2001: 8f.) distinguishes between the WTO issues of efficiency, equity, and legitimacy. These concepts offer a useful starting point for an analysis of WTO reform issues, although some adaptations are necessary: First, one should distinguish more clearly between efficiency and effectiveness. While effectiveness consists in the achievement of intended objectives, efficiency is concerned with the relationship between the achievement of objectives and the resource input required to achieve them (*Heinelt* 2002: 113). However, reliable data on the resources used by the WTO and its members for WTO-related activities are not available. The WTO budget only covers a small section of all resources used because it does not include member state resources. Moreover, the WTO budget is small compared to the budgets of other international organizations (*Blackhurst* 2000; *Barfield* 2001), and, therefore, only gives an incomplete picture of the resources needed for the negotiation and implementation of trade agreements. Consequently, *Porter* and other authors actually focus on the effectiveness of achieving WTO objectives, although they use the term efficiency.

Effectiveness, equity, and legitimacy are discussed with regard to four areas of WTO activities: trade negotiations, implementation of trade agreements, trade policy review, and dispute settlement. As outlined above, trade negotiations in the last decade have failed to lead to the conclusion of new agreements. The effectiveness of the WTO regarding trade negotiations is therefore doubtful. By contrast, dispute settlement is often regarded as being comparatively effective (*Blackhurst* 2000; *Barfield* 2001). Much less attention has been paid in the literature to the effectiveness of trade policy review and implementation.

Concerns with equity may assume different forms: A concern with equity between WTO member states and a concern with equity between economic and non-economic policy objectives are prominent issues in the debate surrounding the WTO (*Porter* 2001: 8). The WTO is criticized for offering unequal opportunities for participation of member states in decision-making procedures: its decision-making system is criticized as being intransparent and exclusive, particularly with regard to developing countries (*The Third World Network et al.* 2003; *Steger* 2004: 111). Second, the impact of the WTO on developing countries has been criticized as "overwhelmingly negative" since predicted gains from trade liberalization have proven to be exaggerated (*Bullard and Chanyapate* 2005: 21). Third, the organization is criticized for not having properly balanced trade liberalization and other non-economic policy issues. In a majority of anti-trade campaigns, the argument has been used that the WTO has sacrificed health, safety, and environmental standards for the sake of trade (*Figueres Olsen et al.* 2001: 166), and that by furthering competition it promotes a "race to the bottom" (*O'Brien et al.* 2000: 147; *Hoberg* 2001: 192).

Finally, the analysis focuses on deficiencies regarding the legitimacy of the WTO. The term legitimacy is employed in this study (see Chapter 3, I.5.c) in an empirical and not in a normative sense. It then refers to the "beliefs of persons about the proper exercise of authority" (*Applbaum* 2000: 325). Thus, legitimacy in an empirical sense is understood as acceptance of the WTO, for instance, by member states and NGOs. In literature it is claimed that outcomes of the Uruguay Round have deeply disappointed developing countries, since developed countries were able to maintain trade barriers on imports of those labor-intensive goods on which developing countries hold a comparative advantage (*Gavin* 2001: 189; *Cho* 2004: 223). However, many developing countries are still seeking to accede the WTO and it seems to be an open question how WTO member states view the legitimacy of the WTO as an institution. Apart from concerns with legitimacy of the WTO among member states, legitimacy of the WTO with NGOs seems precarious. Scholars acknowledge that public acceptance of the authority and decisions that emerge from the WTO cannot be taken for granted outside of a "close-knit trade community" (*Esty* 2002; also *Keohane and Nye* 2000, 2001).

As an organization the main objective of which is trade liberalization, the WTO has been targeted by NGOs which fundamentally doubt that trade liberalization alone can achieve sustainable development and raise the standards of living as promised in the preamble of the Marrakesh Agreement.

The issues of effectiveness, equity, and legitimacy are embedded in a controversy over the nature of the WTO as an international organization. Since the governments of member states determine the decision-making process of international organizations like the WTO, some students of International Relations consider international organizations to be merely a "tool," "arena," or "club" of nation states for organizing diplomatic activities (Chapter 2, I.1). Other authors view the WTO as a "regime" rather than an organization (Chapter 3, I.1).

The fact that the official organization chart of the WTO in Figure 1.1 omits the Secretariat with some 630 people is indicative of the notion that only member states interacting in councils and committees are relevant for the actions and decisions of the WTO. Even a large body like the Secretariat headed by a Director General is not considered to qualify the WTO as an actor of its own.

III. Research questions

There is a need for further research on the nature of the WTO as an international organization and on the causes leading to deficiencies in the areas of effectiveness, equity, and legitimacy. Therefore the main research questions are identified as follows:

- Which sort of organization is the WTO – a tool, arena, club, regime of states, an international administration, or what else?
- Which procedural and structural features promote or impede effectiveness, equity, and legitimacy of the WTO?
- Which reforms of the WTO can be devised to address deficiencies in effectiveness, equity, and legitimacy?

2
Approaches to the Analysis of International Organizations and the WTO

I. Concepts of international organizations

International organizations may be described as "any institution with formal procedures and formal membership from three or more countries" (*Willetts* 2006: 440). Those organizations in which full legal membership is officially open only to states are called "intergovernmental organizations" or simply "international organizations," which is the more frequently used term (*Archer* 2001: 1; *Barkin* 2006: 1) and, therefore, preferred here, too. They can be contrasted with "international non-governmental organizations," which may have memberships from national NGOs, local NGOs, companies, political parties etc. (*Willetts* 2006: 440).

A starting point for research into international organizations is often based on the observation that the existing international organizations are extremely diverse in many respects. Differences exist in dimensions such as membership (restrictive versus encompassing), scope (broad versus narrow coverage of issues) (*Koremenos, Lipson, and Snidal* 2001), mandate, size of secretariat or level of autonomy from government (*De Senarclens* 2001: 501) etc.

Another distinction may be made regarding the various functions performed and outputs delivered by international organizations. *Abbott and Snidal* (1998) list the following functions:

- supporting state interaction by providing negotiation forums serviced by secretariats,
- functioning as arbiters ("honest brokers") in negotiations and in resolving disputes,

- initiating collective state action (for instance, the UN Secretary General may put before the Security Council any matter that threatens international peace and security),
- pooling resources and managing operational activities (for instance, the World Bank finances massive development projects, provides technical assistance and training in many disciplines, and publishes research),
- monitoring state action (for instance, the International Atomic Energy Agency monitors safeguard agreements concluded under the Treaty on the Non-Proliferation of Nuclear Weapons).

Cox and Jacobson divided decisions of international organizations into seven categories: representational and boundary (referring to internal procedures and external relations), symbolic and programmatic (referring to the elaboration of the organization's purposes), rule-creating and rule-supervisory (referring to international law and standard-making), and operational (referring to the provision of services) (1973a: 9ff., see also *Karns and Mingst* 2004: 9). More generally, *Rittberger and Zangl* distinguish three main outputs: policy programs, operational activities, and information (2003: 153–180).

However, the discussion of nature and purpose of international organizations should go beyond a mere description of functions and outputs (*De Senarclens* 2001: 510). Generally speaking, International Relations scholars have failed to devote a great deal of attention to the analysis and reform of international organizations (for a characterization of international organizations as the "ugly duckling of International Relations," see *Verbeek* 1998). Rather, international organizations have not been perceived "as worthy of explanation" (*Nielson and Tierney* 2003). However, over a period of more than 30 years, some concepts have been developed in International Relations that shall be explored in more detail in the following sections.

1. State-centered concepts

There has been a strong presumption in International Relations that international organizations hardly matter because nation states prevail (*Reinalda and Verbeek* 1998: 3). International organizations are therefore characterized as tools, arenas, or clubs. Following the realist approach,[1] both the creation and operation of an international organization is supposed to depend on the existence of a powerful hegemon, which employs the international organization to further his own interests (*Rittberger and Zangl* 2003: 36). Therefore, realist authors regard international organizations as "state instruments," lacking in any genuine autonomy (*De Senarclens* 2001: 510), or as "mechanical *tools*" (*Ness and Brechin* 1988: 269) in the hands of the states. Also, in the neo-realist view, international organizations are unable to influence the behavior of their member states (*Klabbers* 2001: 224; *Rittberger* and *Zangl* 2003: 37).

Another state-centered view focuses on international organizations as *arenas* for intergovernmental negotiations. Again, it is the states which are seen as the "real" actors, whereas international organizations are only seen as providing the necessary framework for conference diplomacy (*Rittberger and Zangl* 2003; *Barnett and Finnemore* 2005: 162).

It has been argued that the (neo-)realist view of international organizations has little concern for questions of effectiveness. Following its own logic, states have to be blamed for ineffectiveness, not the international organization (*Barnett and Finnemore* 1999: 717). Also (neo-)realists would consider international organization as being unable to provide for equity of member states that have unequal resources and power.

Keohane and Nye (2001) have used the metaphor of *club* for developing an understanding of traditional international organizations. In the second half of the twentieth century, multilateral cooperation was organized in form of regimes that operated like "clubs" of wealthy countries. Given the fact that overarching institutions such as the United Nations were weak, cabinet ministers with responsibilities for particular issues got together and negotiated in secret agreements concerning particular issues (trade, finance, defense, etc.). Such agreements were then reported to national legislatures and the public which were usually unable to identify which bargaining positions were held (*Keohane and Nye* 2000: 26).

In the view of *Keohane and Nye*, the club model of multilateral cooperation has worked well for the past half century, but is now threatened by four key problems. First, number and heterogeneity of states in the system has increased. Developing countries are unwilling to support rules previously established by "clubs" of industrialized countries. Second, business firms, associations and NGOs have become more active participants in the multilateral policy process. Third, international organizations including their bureaucracies are faced with demands for more accountability and transparency. And fourth, regimes organized by issue-areas are in difficulty because of increasingly close linkages among issue-areas (*Keohane and Nye* 2000: 26, 30).

In the view of *Keohane and Nye* international organizations understood as traditional clubs were thus effective, whilst they successfully balanced the interests of what were then only a few rich member countries. The legitimacy of these organizations was understood as a legitimacy based on the consent of sovereign states. Today, effectiveness, equity, and legitimacy of international organizations are under threat.

The approaches discussed so-far are state-centered, in the sense that they fail to consider international organizations as autonomous actors on their own. An approach which offers a starting point for recognizing some autonomy for international organizations is the principal-agent approach. The basic idea is that one or multiple principals (in this case several states) create an agent (in this case the international organization) in order to fulfill certain functions. Benefits of delegation may be grouped in different categories: the existence of an agent with a visible mandate facilitates credible policy commitments of states. If agents develop and employ policy-relevant expertise, they may reduce information asymmetries. The operation of an agent can make detailed rule-making more efficient, and it can shift blame for unpopular decisions and policy failures (*Tallberg* 2002: 26). Principal-agent theory usually directs attention toward the problems of agents exploiting their discretion and taking action that are different from the principal's goals (*Tallberg* 2002: 32; *Barkin* 2006: 36). The approach remains state-centered in the sense that scholars frequently investigate how principals (the states) can construct various mechanisms to keep their agent (the international organization) under control.

The more interesting question is, however, what the theoretical starting point is for assuming differences in interest between an international organization and the member states that have created it (*Barnett and Finnemore* 1999). The search for autonomy requires an investigation of structures and intraorganizational processes. Therefore the following sections discuss the approach to international organization based on political systems theory by *Cox and Jacobson et al.* (1973) as well as approaches based on organizational theory developed by *Haas* (1964) and *Barnett and Finnemore* (1999).

2. Political systems theory

Cox and Jacobson et al. in their influential study "The anatomy of influence" (1973) have developed an elaborate framework for analyzing international organizations (1973a: 16f.). International organizations are conceptualized as a political system, which includes both "representative subsystems" and "participant subsystems." The most important representative subsystems are country subsystems, which are composed of individuals from various nation-based institutions such as ministries and associations that seek to influence a particular international policy. The "participant subsystem" is composed only of those individuals, which actually participate in an international organization's decision-making process. This includes delegates of international conferences and segments of international bureaucracy such as the executive head of the organization.

The framework was applied by a number of scholars to eight different international organizations. It was found that organizations such as International Telecommunication Union (ITU), International Monetary Fund (IMF), and GATT that took rule-creating and rule-supervisory decisions were usually dominated by "representative country subsystems." Governments considered these organizations as "direct instruments of policy or places where policies can be harmonized." By contrast, organizations that lacked rule-creating and rule-supervisory powers such as the International Labour Organization (ILO), the World Health Organization (WHO), United Nations Educational, Scientific and Cultural Organization (UNESCO), and United Nations Conference on Trade and Development (UNCTAD) were dominated by "participant subsystems," that is delegates, international officials and associated specialists (*Cox and Jacobson* 1973b: 426f.) Members of international bureaucracies were found to be "usually most influential in operational decisions" (*Cox and Jacobson* 1973b: 399). Conclusions reached by *Cox and Jacobson* on the limited autonomy of rule-creating international organizations have been characterized as being inspired by the (neo-) realist concept of international organizations and as being in part still valid; their systems theoretical framework is considered useful today, too (*Hazelzet* 1998: 31f., 39).

3. Organizational analysis

Another strand of theorizing about international organizations is based on concepts of organization theory (*Karns and Mingst* 2004: 58ff.). *Haas* (1964) was among the first to apply organizational theory to international organizations. *Haas* (1964: 109f.) found that the typical international organization could be decomposed into four sub-units:

- a formal bureaucracy staffed with specialists,
- groups of independent experts who are called upon to make recommendations for programming or examining organizational performance,

- groups of official experts who are appointed by governments and who do the same, and
- delegates of governments and of large voluntary organizations who represent the interests of "environmental structures."

In other words, *Haas* conceptualized member states (together with what would be described nowadays as international NGOs) to be part of the environment of an international organization. At the same time, however, he recognized that the conference of governmental delegates is an integral part of the international organization.

Drawing on an organizational approach developed by *Thompson and Tuden* (1959), *Haas* assigned specific structures and modes of decision making to each of the above listed structural features. The conference of delegates has a representative structure and takes decisions through compromise. Independent and official expert groups work in a collegial structure, taking decisions through judgment (in case of official expert groups this may shade into compromise). Bureaucracies that exhibit a hierarchical structure take decisions by "computation."

*Haa*s portrayed the role of computation within international organizations as a rather limited one. Computation, in his view, was only a suitable means for taking decisions if purely technical issues in organizations with a limited mandate were at stake (e.g. for telecommunication, postal rates, and weather information). However, computation could not work in organizations in which general objectives required amplification and adaptation in specific fields. Hence, bargaining is the dominant mode of decision making for solving conflicts between governmental delegates on the one hand and independent experts or the bureaucracy on the other hand. The only alternative would be charismatic leadership by the bureaucracy (1964: 110).

Haas has made an important contribution in so far as he has recognized the structural complexity of international organizations. However, the presentation of different structures and modes of decision making as being neatly separated is somewhat misleading. The influence of bureaucracies on intergovernmental bargaining (and judgment) and the influence of governmental delegates on bureaucratic decision making are not really discussed[2].

Barnett and Finnemore (1999, 2004, 2005) developed a comprehensive constructivist sociological approach to international organization. Their starting point is a conceptualization of international organizations as bureaucracies (2004: 17, 156), basically following *Max Weber*'s bureaucratic model. By looking at international organizations as "autonomous sites of authority, independent from the state "principals" who may have created them" (*Barnett and Finnemore* 1999: 707), states and governmental delegates seem to be conceptualized as being entirely outside of international organizations, which are reduced to civil servants working in international secretariats or other international bureaucracies.

In this perspective, international organizations derive authority – and also autonomy to some degree – from four sources: rational-legal, delegated, moral, and expert authority (*Barnett and Finnemore* 2004: 25). Drawing on Max Weber, rational-legal authority derives from four central features of bureaucracies:

- *Hierarchy* – since each official has a clearly defined sphere of competence and is answerable to superiors,
- *Continuity* – since a full-time salary offers the prospect of regular advancement,
- *Impersonality* – since the work is conducted according to prescribed rules that eliminate arbitrary and politicized influences, and
- *Expertise* – where officials control access to knowledge stored in files.

In sum, authority is derived from the fact that the rationalized organization can deliver precision, stability, discipline, and reliability (*Barnett and Finnemore* 2005: 164).

Authority of international organization is in part also derived from the moral authority generated by the mandate which usually set out that the organization is created to embody some widely shared set of principles. Moreover, international organizations tend to emphasize their "neutrality, impartiality and objectivity." The public image of international organization is thereby implicitly contrasted with the public image of states that are supposed to be guided by their own particularistic interests (see *Barnett and Finnemore* 2005: 173). Expertise is another important source of authority for international bureaucracies. It often comes in conjunction with professional training, norms and occupational cultures, and an increased reliance on expertise serves to depoliticize decisions (*Barnett and Finnemore* 2005: 174).

Barnett and Finnemore conceded that part of the authority of an international organization is delegated authority in the sense that states give the mandate to international organizations to perform certain tasks. However, these mandates are often broad and vague or contain conflicting directives. The organization's response to the mandate will thus be heavily colored through "agenda, experience, values, and expertise of IO staff" (*Barnett and Finnemore* 2005: 172).

By focusing on the importance of bureaucracies, *Barnett and Finnemore* tend to obscure that many important decisions in international organizations continue to be taken by delegates of governments. This kind of decisions is subject of their empirical analysis. Two decisions investigated by *Barnett and Finnemore* – the redefinition of tasks of the IMF and the decision of the United Nations not to intervene in Ruanda – were in fact taken by member states. *Barnett and Finnemore* argued, however, that these decisions were heavily influenced by what the bureaucratic staff did or, in the UN case, rather by what it failed to do (2004: 58, 153).

In the view of *Barnett and Finnemore*, international bureaucracies exert powers through several means: they classify and organize information and knowledge (e.g. they classify real world events as "civil war"), they define problems, craft solutions, and they fix meanings (e.g. what is development, security) and diffuse norms (2004: 29–34, 2005: 175–181). More concretely, they can influence state decisions by, for instance, setting the agenda of meetings (*Barnett and Finnemore* 2004: 178). *Reinalda and Verbeek* (2004b: 238) stressed that the power of international bureaucrats is seldom formal: most of it is rooted in forms of soft power, such as expertise, coalition building, or naming and shaming. Bureaucrats are also very careful in not "antagonizing their masters," the member states, too much.

For social-constructivists, effectiveness of international organizations is more important than for realists. The so-called dysfunctional behavior is understood "as behaviour that undermines the stated goals of the organization" (*Barnett and Finnemore* 1999: 716). While it is conceded that states can be a source of pathologies of international organizations, *Barnett and Finnemore* (1999: 717ff.) identified a number of mechanisms by which external and internal culture can breed pathologies in international organizations. International organizations may be driven more by the search for legitimacy than by the effective implementation of their goals. Moreover, official objectives may be contradictory, reflecting contradictions in the environment. Internal culture can, at least, have five pathological effects which are attributed to characteristics of bureaucracies: the irrationality of rationalization (overly dominance of rules and procedures), bureaucratic universalism (inappropriate application of experience made in one context to another context), normalization of deviance (routinization of exceptions to rules), organizational insulation (organizations that do not pursue economic goals may be insulated from environmental feedback), and cultural contestation (different local cultures within a organization may develop different views on the environment of an organization and of the organization's overall mission).

Barnett and Finnemore's bureaucratic model avoids the shortcomings of the traditional state-centered concepts of international organizations, and focuses on the role and influence of secretariats, staff and administrative activities of international organizations which may justify, in a given case, to conceive of international organizations as international actors with some independence from member states. However, the bureaucratic model does not account conceptually for the role of member states, and tends to be too simplistic. As will be shown in Chapter 5, international organizations may be different things in different task areas: a bureaucratic actor in one area and an instrument in the hands of member states in another area.

4. Network perspectives

The starting point of scholars using a network perspective is that traditional international organizations are criticized for being ineffective and undemocratic. A decade ago, *Slaughter* (1997) published an article that portrayed the United Nations, the European Commission, and the WTO as creatures of a liberal internationalist ideal that sought to establish "centralized rule-making authorities, a hierarchy of institutions and universal membership." These efforts, however, were hampered by the nation's resistance to cede power and sovereignty to international institutions (*Slaughter* 1997: 183). While international institutions are viewed as having a "lackluster record" on global problem-solving, the establishment of global governmental networks is regarded as a more appealing and effective solution (*Slaughter* 1997: 195). Moreover, the operation of transgovernmental networks may be more acceptable to conservative US politicians who demonize international organizations as the United Nations and the WTO as supranational bureaucracies that violate the national sovereignty of democratic states (*Slaughter* 1997: 185; *De Senarclens* 2001: 513).

Scholars have indeed found a trend of establishing international cooperation on a more informal basis (*Klabbers* 2001). However, *Slaughter*'s work has been criticized for overstating this trend and for downplaying the role of multilateral organizations that "cannot be simply sifted out of the picture like lumps in flour" (*Alston* 1997: 441). It is also an open question to what extent the operation of transgovernmental networks is preferable to the operation of international organizations. Some experts believe that international organizations can better reflect the principles of transparency, participation, and accountability than transgovernmental networks (*Alston* 1997: 447). In more recent work,

Slaughter acknowledged that the relationship between governmental networks and international institutions may be a complex and interdependent one, and that government networks can exist both within and alongside formal organizations in a variety of modes. However, she also claims that the formation of negotiating networks among ministers from particular countries can "breathe new life and power into the international organization itself" (*Slaughter* 2004: 152f.).

Other scholars have focused on the capabilities of private actors to enhance the effectiveness of international organizations rather than on governmental networks. Here again the starting point is that governments and international organizations often lack the ability to design and implement effective public policies, since the creation of international treaties and conventions is a slow process. The so-called Global Public Policy Networks (e.g. the Global Water Partnership) that bring together business, NGOs, international organizations, and states are found to be a more effective answer to global problems (*Witte et al.* 2000; *Stone* 2004). NGO cooperation with international organizations has not been confined to specific projects; non-governmental organizations have also been admitted to the negotiating table, for instance at United Nations Conference on Environment and Development (UNCED) conferences in Rio and Johannesburg and in the negotiations of international treaties on climate protection and biodiversity (*Mathews* 1997; *Arts* 1998).

However, the role of NGOs in international governance has not been only a constructive one. The objective of the anti-globalization movement is to make those international negotiations that lead to further national deregulation and liberalization fail, with the successful campaign against the Multilateral Agreement on Investment (1996–1998) being a first example of a continuing trend (*Metzges* 2006: 188f.).

The network approach to international organizations draws attention to the operation of transgovernmental networks or Global Public Policy networks as possible alternative or complimentary structures to international organizations. However, the network approach is unable to offer a framework for the analysis of the functioning of international organizations.

II. Studies on the WTO

1. International relations perspective

The framework developed by *Cox and Jacobson* was also applied to a study of the WTO's predecessor, the GATT, which was characterized as a "traders" club (*Curzon and Curzon* 1973). While the authors concluded that "governments remained the true actors in the forum for international trade cooperation," with the delegates being closely briefed, it was also found that, at least, one GATT Director General had been an influential figure (*Curzon and Curzon* 1973: 317f.). Though their findings are certainly interesting, a remark by Curzon and Curzon (1973: 317) illustrates particularly well that findings concerning the GATT cannot simply be applied to today's operation of the WTO: "The fact that GATT's tariff conferences are geographically isolated from domestic lobbying arenas may contribute to the quiet atmosphere of GATT's deliberations." This assessment no longer holds valid in the age of information technology.

Changes from GATT to the WTO are taken into account by *Keohane and Nye* (2001), who, however, have not drawn on the framework developed by *Cox and Jacobson*. Rather, the GATT as it operated in the Uruguay Round is seen as representative for their own "club model" (2001: 268). The fact that a small number of rich-country trade ministers controlled the agenda and made deals led to great progress in trade liberalization. However, in a dialectical fashion, club arrangements were undercut by their success (*Keohane and Nye* 2001: 269). Increasing trade made publics more sensitive to the issues of trade concessions, so that trade negotiations could no longer be held behind closed doors. Further, the proliferation of non-state agents exerted pressure on the WTO to become more inclusive, also for state agents representing interests other than free trade (environment and labor). At the same time, the growing number of developing countries was demanding greater participation. However, as *Keohane and Nye* stressed, developing countries do not seek to break up the club by pressing for a greater inclusion of, for instance environment ministers or NGOs in the operation of the WTO. Finally, the spread of democratic norms to more and more countries resulted in a questioning of the democratic qualities of many international organizations, including the WTO.

Keohane and Nye pay attention to possible trade-offs between equity and effectiveness. Thus they considered that giving NGOs the right to participate in trade bargaining sessions might obstruct consummating deals (2001: 289). Having discussed several approaches for reforms, *Keohane and Nye* (2001: 290f.) concluded that the club model requires modification, but should not be discarded entirely for the WTO. Legitimacy of the WTO and other international institutions is likely to remain shaky for many decades. One of the guiding principles is therefore subsidiarity: space has to be preserved for domestic policy processes and for allowing domestic politics to sometimes depart from international agreements. However, more attention has to be paid to questions of legitimacy, which is viewed as a complex issue resting both on effectiveness and on domestic and international processes. Accountability can be improved by involving NGOs in decision making and dispute resolution. Networks may have to play a role in that regard, and enhanced transparency is crucial to the process.

Hocking's study (2004) of arrangements of expanded trade policy consultation in Canada and the European Union has been inspired by the *Keohane–Nye* framework. In his view, some countries have moved to an adaptive "club model" by including business and labor representatives in domestic consultations. For instance, Canada and the European Union have moved to a "multi-stakeholder model" by adding another set of stakeholders, especially NGOs (2004: 12f.). *Hocking* (2004: 23) found that moving to a "multi-stakeholder model" might result in a "crisis of expectations concerning the objectives of consultation, the means through which they are achieved and the likely outcomes." There are divergent expectations among trade officials of what the objectives of consultations are, with some officials viewing it more as a briefing exercise, while some NGOs seek to redefine the agenda in a way that bureaucrats are unable to respond to (*Hocking* 2004: 26).

2. International law perspective

Traditionally, international lawyers have focused on describing the formal mandate and the formal structures of the WTO, or on various aspects of substantive international trade law (*Matsushita et al.* 2003). The problematic relationship between international law established through WTO agreements and international law derived from other sources (e.g. from Multinational Environmental Agreements, MEAs) has become a "cotton industry" for legal scholars (*Pauwelyn* 2003; *Scott* 2004). However, international lawyers have also made contributions to the WTO reform debate. Three normative models for WTO reform can be contrasted (*Barfield* 2001: 163ff.): The "Trade Stakeholders Model" (*Shell* 1996), the "Global Subsidiarity Model" (*Howse and Nicolaidis* 2003), and the "Libertarian Model" (*McGinnis* 2000). The "Efficient Market Model" (*Petersmann* 2001) and the "Integration Model" (*Guzman* 2004) may be added to the list.

Petersmann (2001) articulated strong concerns about the effectiveness of WTO law. In his view, GATT and WTO laws mainly protect the interests of governments to preserve domestic production by concurrently violating individual traders' and consumers' right to import. He also criticized the Dispute Settlement Mechanism for its state-centered design and one-sided trade orientation. *Petersmann* argued that individuals have the "human right" to engage in foreign trade and to defend this right at the domestic level, since GATT and WTO exert "constitutional functions" of limiting governments. At the same time, *Petersmann* recognized that constitutionalism requires the control of power. Therefore, he proposed the establishment of an advisory parliamentary WTO body and an advisory Economic and Social Committee.

McGinnis (2000) viewed the WTO as a kind of shield against rent-seeking national interest group that lobby against trade liberalization. However, the increasing use of national regulation works as a limit on the effectiveness of trade liberalization. *McGinnis* therefore recommended that the WTO dispute settlement bodies adopt a series of tests to invalidate national regulation that does not comply with certain procedural standards (e.g. transparency, consistency in the treatment of domestic and foreign companies, etc.).

Guzman (2004) viewed the effectiveness of WTO law from a more optimistic perspective than *Mc Ginnis and Petersmann.* In contrast to many other international organizations, the WTO has the capacity to strike package deals and it has a powerful dispute settlement system. Organizations such as the ILO, or possibly a future Global Environmental organization, could never achieve the success and influence of the WTO (*Guzman* 2004: 314). *Guzman* therefore argued that the international community should take advantage of the WTO's strength "by expanding its jurisdiction to include additional substantive issues" (*Guzman* 2004: 309). The WTO could be structured in departments, and "departmental negotiating rounds" would address issues within their respective issue areas (*Guzman* 2004: 310). Obligations that go beyond departmental authority, however, could only be established in Mega-Rounds, where any number of departments may be involved (*Guzman* 2004: 311). Dispute resolution procedures should be extended to cover other issues, and the dispute resolution system should be structured in such a way so as to have adequate expertise to address the issues at hand (*Guzman* 2004: 334).

Shell (1996) developed a "Trade Stakeholders Model" in response to the reform of dispute settlement through the Uruguay Round. The switch from arbitration under GATT to a more legalist framework of the dispute settlement, in his view, necessitates changes. The starting point for *Shell* is that the legitimacy of a norm is based on the consent of those who have a special interest ("stake") in the matter. *Shell* argued that the role of stakeholders, that is representatives of environmental, labor, consumer, human right, and feminist groups in WTO dispute settlement must be strengthened. The standing rules of WTO dispute settlement should be relaxed to include private parties. New rules should enable not only the enforcement of technical trade rules, but also of "a limited set of globally defined, international trade-related labor, environmental, safety and consumer norms," both at the international and at the domestic level. Trade dispute resolution would thus be transformed into a "wide-ranging deliberative process," by which global priorities could be set.

Howse and Nicolaidis (2003) developed their own counter-model to Petersmann and Shell (termed the "Global Subsidiarity Model" by *Barfield* (2001: 167)). In their view, both Petersmann and Shell have a "constitutional view of the WTO" (2003: 74) by advocating that WTO agreements be regarded as something higher than domestic law that is no longer contestable. However, in the view of *Howse and Nicolaidis* (2003: 74) reforms of the WTO based on "constitutionalization will only exacerbate the legitimacy crisis or constrain appropriate responses to it." Concerns about democracy, inequality, and instability affecting the empirical legitimacy of the WTO should not be dealt with by extending the coverage of the dispute settlement to other norms and/or by opening it up to non-state actors. Instead, "moderation and new-found modesty in WTO rule-making or rule-interpretation" is called for (*Howse* 2001: 359). The dispute settlement organs of the WTO should display "deference" to domestic regulatory choices and to other international regimes concerning health, labor standards, the environment, and human rights (*Howse and Nicolaidis* 2003: 75). The WTO should also encourage governments to provide for greater public and interest group participation in domestic trade policy-making (*Howse and Nicolaidis* 2003: 89).

The analysis shows that international lawyers deal with questions of effectiveness, equity, and legitimacy. However, foci, assessments, and proposals for reforms are extremely diverse. For some (*Petersmann, Mc Ginnis*), the effectiveness of WTO agreements is a major concern, while *Guzman* views the effectiveness of WTO agreements as being rather good if compared to the effectiveness of other bodies of international law. Some believe that legitimacy of the organization could be strengthened if environmental, health, and labor concerns could be negotiated and/or made subject to dispute settlement within the WTO (*Guzman and Shell*). For others, this would seriously overburden the WTO and further diminish its legitimacy (*Howse and Nicolaides*).

Hence, the scope of the reform proposals advanced by international lawyers range from sweeping reorganization of the WTO transforming it into the World Economic Organization to the advice to confine organizational scope and reach. Reform proposals cover legal (e.g. the possibility of invoking WTO law before domestic courts), structural (e.g. the creation of a Parliamentary Assembly or the creation of new rule-making departments in the WTO) and procedural issues (e.g. the right of private parties to use Dispute Settlement or procedurally oriented tests of protectionist domestic laws).

3. Organizational perspective

Until recently, studies of the WTO using an organizational perspective were lacking. However, *Xu and Weller*, two scholars with a public policy/public administration background, conducted research on the role of the GATT/WTO Secretariat "in shaping and facilitating the international trade system" (2004: 5). Negotiations of the Uruguay Round were reconstructed based on documents and interviews with officials of the Secretariat were conducted to trace the influence of the then GATT Secretariat on negotiations (2004: 17).

While *Xu and Weller* (2004: 6) do not claim that international civil servants make decisions, they emphasize that "multilateral cooperation is unlikely to reach any decisions and solutions without them." The influence of international civil servants is generally seen as coming from several sources: First is the influence that all (also domestic) bureaucrats have through the management of routines, the provision of advice, networks, etc. Second, international officials may have specific roles as "policy innovators," "bridge builders," "identity builders" and "educators" The authority of international civil servants rests on legitimacy, credibility, and competence (*Xu and Weller* 2004: 52).

Though the approach by *Xu and Weller* offers interesting starting points for research into the interaction between member states and international bureaucracies, it also suffers from a variety of deficits. First, there is a lack of an overall theoretical framework for the operation of the WTO which also takes into account external actors such as NGOs. Second, analysis is focused on the effectiveness of trade negotiations and it is further narrowed down through its focus on GATT and the Uruguay Round. Negotiations in the Doha Development Round, other areas of WTO activities (e.g. implementation, trade policy review, and dispute settlement) and broader policy concerns (e.g. environment) which feature prominently in international law writings are largely neglected.

4. Practitioners' perspective

Practitioners can be defined as those persons who have been involved in the operations of the WTO or who have been involved in the ratification and implementation of trade agreements at the national level. In discussing reforms, practitioners often rely on experiences with the operation of the WTO or the GATT, and on workaday theories. The *Sutherland Report* may be characterized to a large extent as being based on practitioners' perspectives. It discusses in nine chapters a variety of issues (the case for liberalizing trade; the erosion of non-discrimination, sovereignty, coherence and coordination with intergovernmental organizations, transparency, and dialogue with civil society; the WTO dispute settlement system, decision making, and variable geometry; and the role of the Director General and Secretariat). Other practitioners discuss, for instance, the role of domestic parliaments in WTO decision making based on their own experience with parliaments (*Mann* 2005; *Skaggs* 2005) or the adequacy of WTO decision-making procedures, based on their own experience (*Ehlermann and Ehring* 2005).

One of the advantages of readings by practitioners is that they focus on incremental reforms that are feasible, thereby refraining from developing "grand designs" that stand no chance of being realized. On the negative side, practitioners have a tendency to analyze insider problems and to defend the status quo of an organization.[3] Moreover, since insiders can draw on insider knowledge, they typically fail to systematically analyze organizational structures and procedures.

5. Conclusions

Traditional approaches of International Relations to international organizations have been state-centered by analyzing international organizations as tools, arenas or clubs. The network approach remains state-centered by advocating the replacement of international organizations with transgovernmental networks. Others advocate Global Public Policy networks which bring together international organizations, states, business, and NGOs as possible alternative or complimentary structures to international organizations.

As a result, most political scientists have neglected interactions between the bureaucracies of international organizations and its intergovernmental sections (*Liese and Weinlich* 2006: 512). The *Cox–Jacobson* framework (1973) based on political systems analysis and the organizational theory framework developed by *Haas* (1964) represent noticeable exemptions to the rule. Both frameworks take into account the structural complexity of international organizations, offering interesting starting points for research into international organizations. However, they have not been taken up, employed, or further developed by other scholars (*Reinalda and Verbeek* 2004a: 17). Surprisingly, the rather simplistic conceptualization of international organizations as Weberian bureaucracies (*Barnett and Finnemore* 1999) falls back behind the frameworks developed by *Cox and Jacobson and Haas* several decades earlier.

Against this background, it is unsurprising that the application of International Relations approaches to the WTO also has been rather patchy. While the team led by *Cox and Jacobson* performed an early empirical study of the GATT, the frameworks developed by *Haas and Barnett and Finnemore* have not been employed for empirical studies of the GATT and/or the WTO. *Keohane and Nye* (2001) have applied the club metaphor to the GATT and the WTO. However, while the club metaphor has been useful for restating problems with effectiveness, equity and legitimacy of the WTO, proposals for reform cannot be easily distilled from it. *Keohane and Nye* have refrained from carrying out in-depth empirical research of the WTO as an organization.

International lawyers have shown varying concerns with effectiveness, equity, and legitimacy of the WTO "output" (i.e. WTO agreements and dispute resolutions). Since these discussions tend to be unrelated to an analysis of the WTO as an organization, proposals for WTO reform are usually based on normative concepts, such as "constitutional functions" or "stakeholder legitimacy."

Xu and Weller have focused on the operation of the GATT/WTO Secretariat, and on its influence on the effectiveness of the trade negotiations. However, the development and application of a broader theoretical and conceptual framework, taking into account other non-governmental actors, other areas of activity, and issues like equity is lacking.

To conclude, public administration scholars have largely ignored international organization, while International Relations scholars have not used "public administration" approaches for the study of international organizations. Some interesting attempts have been made (*Haas and Cox and Jacobson*), but this has not been followed up.

3
Conceptual Framework, Variables, and Method

I. Conceptual framework

1. A public administration perspective on international organizations

Public administration as a discipline combines managerial, political, and legal perspectives on public formal organizations which are social entities and provide regulatory and service functions (*Rosenbloom et al.* 2009: 5).[1] The term "public administration" is also used to denote the sum of all public organizations as part of government.

A public administration perspective (*Rosenbloom et al.* 2009: 14ff.)[2] is characterized by

- the subject of analysis which focuses on organizations belonging to public administration,
- the application of organization–theoretical concepts (managerial dimension),
- the focus on "public" characteristics which distinguishes public administration from private organizations, e.g. public interest orientation (political dimension),
- the application of constitutional and public law concepts to public administration (legal dimension).

Public administration as the subject of analysis consists of public formal organizations. Formal organizations are collectivities (*Kieser and Walgenbach* 2007: 6ff.; *Scott and Davis* 2007: 11, 29, 60; *Rosenbloom et al.* 2009: 141f.)

- whose members are individuals and/or actor aggregates,
- which are oriented to the pursuit of relatively specific goals,

- which exhibit a formalized social structure designed to coordinate the activities of organization members toward goal attainment, and
- which strive to ensure their organizational maintenance (survival).

Goals and activities of an organization are not identical with the goals and activities of its members. Discrepancies and conflicts between goals and activities of the organization and its members may explain shortcomings in actual organizational performance.

Goals, structures, procedures, and all other organizational characteristics which are laid down in writing by the competent authority (e.g. in statutes, administrative acts, organization charts, memoranda, contracts, etc.) are called "formal" (*Scott and Davis* 2007: 22f.). All characteristics of an organization which are not captured in official documents but are concerned with its actual functioning are termed "informal." Organization theory, therefore, distinguishes between the dimensions of formal and informal organization. The latter will be explored in more detail in Section I.3.b of this chapter.

The concept of formal organizations covers private and public organizations. The characteristics which constitute the "publicness" of organizations (*Rosenbloom et al.* 2009: 7, 11) are

- their formal tasks which primarily serve the common welfare (public interest), and
- the fact that they either have the sole competence for the legitimate use of coercive physical power, or that they are set-up by an authority with said competence, and operate under its supervision.

All government authorities meet the two criteria. Problems arise with respect to private organizations. There are many private organizations, e.g. non-profit organizations, which serve the public interest but are not set up and controlled by government authorities. These private organizations may be called "public organizations" (*Rainey* 2003: 68f.; *Gortner, Nichols, and Ball* 2007: 5). However, they belong to public administration only if they also meet the second criterion (second alternative) which reflects the core characteristic of public administration: the monopoly on the legitimate use of physical power in a given territory. This element of the sovereignty of nation states distinguishes private organizations belonging to public administration from other private organizations which serve public or private interests.[3]

Finally, courts and legislatures are excluded from the concept of public administration, because they are separate social entities in constitutional states due to the doctrine of the separation of powers.

The concept of formal public organizations has only been applied to domestic public administrations. International organizations, so far, are ignored by public administration as a discipline.[4] International public administration has not gained a disciplinary identity. This is a fact that scholars of comparative public administration deplore (*Heady, Perlman, and Rivera* 2007: 607f.).

International Relations theory, as outlined above (sub Chapter 2, I.3), applies some elements of formal organization concepts to international organizations, e.g. the Weberian bureaucratic model (*Barnett and Finnemore* 2004: 16ff.; *Karns and Mingst* 2004: 56). Due to their bureaucratic structure and authority, intergovernmental treaty secretariats (e.g. the Ozone Secretariat under the Vienna Convention and the Montreal Protocol) are even considered by some authors a specific type of international organization (*Bauer* 2006: 28). The secretariats of international organizations like the WTO are, at times, termed "international administrations" which influence the actions of international organizations (*Liese and Weinlich* 2006: 503). In any event, public administration concepts are not being used in International Relation studies. The question of whether or not international organizations constitute an international public administration has not been asked by international relations theory as far as the author knows.

International organizations are generally defined as organizations whose members include at least three states and are held together by a formal intergovernmental agreement (*Karns and Mingst* 2004: 7; *Willetts* 2006: 440). Their membership, goals, structures, and procedures are formalized in documents. Thus, international organizations are formal organizations.

They also meet the criterion of "publicness." First, international organizations have formal tasks which serve public state interests.

Second, international organizations while not endowed with the monopoly on the legitimate use of physical power within their jurisdictions are set up and fully controlled by sovereign states. States have this monopoly on physical power which is limited, though, to their respective territories. However, in creating international organizations states either pool their sovereignty with respect to the organizations' task areas, or delegate certain aspects of their sovereignty to international organizations (*Moravcsik* 1998: 67; *Rittberger and Zangl* 2003: 24).

International organizations need to be distinguished from international regimes. International regimes, according to a standard definition (*Krasner* 1982: 185; *Footer* 2006: 83; *Little* 2006: 373), are identified as "sets of explicit or implicit principles, norms, rules, and decision making procedures around which actors' expectations converge in a given area of international relations and which may help to coordinate their behavior" (*Krasner*). The main point of this definition is that regimes do not have the quality of being actors like states or international organizations (*Rittberger and Zangl* 2003: 25). Regimes are merely principles, norms, rules, and procedures designed to coordinate the behavior of actors which are states and international organizations. In contrast, international organizations can make decisions independent of member states and are said to have a will of their own. Examples are the World Bank and the IMF which have separate executive boards to which member states have delegated certain powers. Within these powers World Bank and IMF make their own decisions independent of member states.

From the perspective of regime theory some authors consider the WTO a regime rather than an international organization, because "the WTO does not fulfill the requirement of an international organization that has a will of its own, separate and distinct from that of its individual members and is able to function separately from its members" (*Footer* 2006: 78). This assessment will be reviewed in Chapter 5, VI. At this place, the discussion is confined to theoretical aspects of regime theory.

Since the WTO with its complex organizational structure and other international organizations of a similar kind are more than principles, norms, rules, and procedures, regime theorists are forced to still use the term international organization besides regime in order to depict their institutional complexity (*Footer* 2006: 74ff.). This means, they must distinguish between international organizations with a will of their own and international organizations without such a will – also labeled "regimes." This distinction makes things unnecessarily complicated. This is why regime theorists have been criticized for doing no more than introducing new terminology to characterize the familiar idea of an international organization (*Little* 2006: 373).

Furthermore, from an empirical perspective, the notion of "will" is unsuitable to determine the actor quality of social institutions. The notion of "will" is a psychological characteristic of decision makers. Its content varies with decision situations. Therefore, it is not a constitutive element of an organization as a social entity. If, for example, the members of the executive board of an international organization closely follow the wishes of member states inspite of the board's limited autonomy, the international organization does not lose its quality as an actor. Or, if an organization which is considered a regime has a very active secretariat which informally influences member state decisions, this organization empirically has, so far, the quality of an actor.

In public administration theory the distinction between organization and regime is unknown, although rules, norms, principles, and procedures are pervasive in this field. The organizational structure of public administrations includes decision-making bodies which encompass all organization members[5] as well as decision-making bodies which are composed of appointed or elected officials.

In line with public administration concepts and the prevailing view in International Relations theory (*Rittberger and Zangl* 2003: 24f.), the actor quality of international organizations is empirically determined by the existence of decision-making bodies as part of the organizational structure regardless of their composition of member states, appointees, or elected officials. The extent and attributes of the actor quality of international organizations may vary considerably, and are to be identified empirically from case to case.

Public administration research integrates theoretical concepts and approaches from various social science disciplines and public law. Empirical research particularly draws on concepts of organization theory and policy analysis. The theoretical framework of this study combines the perspective of actor-centered institutionalism with the organization–theoretical concepts of focal, formal and informal organization, and elements of the governance paradigm. Figure 3.1 displays the conceptual framework for the analysis of the WTO.

2. Concepts of actor-centered institutionalism

Actor-centered institutionalism (*Scharpf* 1997: 21, 38ff., 43ff.) is an approach to policy analysis which considers institutions, i.e. legal and social rules, as constitutive for actor aggregates like international organizations and for their interactions. This approach is designed to explain policy decisions primarily on the basis of the characteristics of actors (e.g. perceptions, preferences, and capabilities) and their interactions, problem situations, the institutional setting, and the policy environment.

Figure 3.1 applies these concepts to the analysis of the WTO's task performance. According to Art. III of the Marrakesh Agreement the task

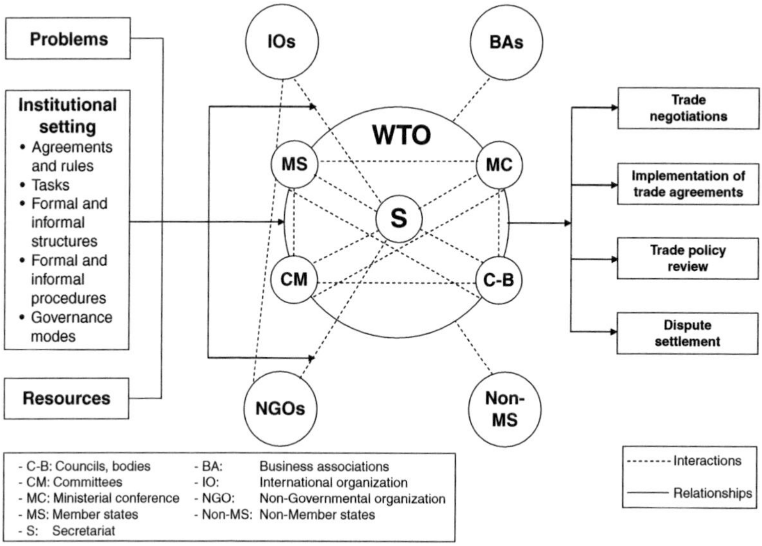

Figure 3.1 Conceptual framework for the analysis of the WTO system

areas of the WTO are trade negotiations, the implementation of trade agreements, trade policy review, and dispute settlement. The cooperation of the WTO with the International Monetary Fund and with the International Bank for Reconstruction and Development and its affiliated agencies, listed in Art. III (5) of the Agreement as another area of the WTO's responsibilities, has been excluded from the analysis due to the lack of resources and time for this research.

As Figure 3.1 indicates, it is assumed that the effectiveness, equity, and legitimacy of the WTO's task performance is influenced by intra- and inter-organizational interactions as well as by characteristics of the problem situations, the institutional setting, and available resources.

The intra-organizational interactions include the main decision-making bodies of the WTO, member states, and the Secretariat.

The analysis of inter-organizational interactions is confined to selected international organizations and NGOs, both with a focus on development policies. This criterion of selection was chosen because the great majority of WTO members are developing countries. Interactions of the WTO with other international actors like non-member states or private international organizations representing business interests are excluded from the analysis, since they play a minor role in the ongoing reform debate on the WTO. The institutional setting of interactions includes formal and informal structures and procedures of the WTO as well as legal and social rules on modes of organizational governance.

Since policy decisions are intentional actions, the perceptions, preferences, and capabilities of actors influence these decisions. Actor-centered institutionalism provides a useful typology of actors for analyzing the kind of influence which actor characteristics have on policy decisions (*Scharpf* 1997: 51ff.).

Actor aggregates like formal organizations are labeled composite actors and distinguished from individuals. International organizations are composite actors. They are subdivided into collective and corporate actors.

Collective actors are characterized by the dependence of their decisions on the preferences of their members. There are further differentiations of collective actors like coalition, movement, club, and association. In this context, the actor type of "club" deserves closer attention, since international organizations like the WTO have been labeled "clubs" in International Relations theory (*Keohane and Nye* 2001). From the perspective of actor-centered institutionalism, the collective actor type of "club" is characterized by pooling collective resources like a central budget and a secretariat, while its actions are determined by the individual self-interest of its members (*Scharpf* 1997: 56).

In contrast, corporate actors enjoy some autonomy from the preferences of their members. They have a hierarchical leadership. Their activities are carried out by a bureaucratic staff. Members are not actively involved in defining the corporate actor's course of action (*Scharpf* 1997: 56; *Maier-Rigaud* 2008: 2f.). In general, members only have the power to select and replace the leaders. Consequently, corporate actors may have identities and preferences of their own which are independent from the interests and preferences of their members (*Jansen* 1997: 202; *Scharpf* 1997: 57).

From a systems theoretical perspective, *Cox and Jacobson* (1973b: 428) have suggested for the analysis of international organizations not to only focus on how independent of states international organizations have become. Attention should also be paid "to how far they involve the effective policy-making processes of government."

Following this suggestion, international organizations are considered corporate actors if they enjoy a certain degree of autonomy from the interests and preferences of their members or if they have some influence on the preferences and policy decisions of their members.

Corporate actors are assumed, on the one hand, to perform more effectively and efficiently than collective actors (*Scharpf* 1997: 57). On the other hand, corporate actors tend to defy controls and accountability which may have negative effects on the legitimacy and equity of their actions as compared to the decisions of collective actors.

However, one should keep in mind that corporate and collective actors are analytical categories. In reality, there are likely to be many intermediate forms of corporate and collective actors.

This study will identify in which task areas and to what extent the WTO displays the characteristics of a collective actor and/or a corporate actor (see Chapter 5, VI).

Indicators for the WTO as a collective actor are decisions and actions by WTO decision bodies (e.g. Ministerial Conference, councils, committees, panels, and Secretariat) which are fully determined by the preferences and interests of member states without the latter being significantly influenced by WTO decision-making processes (e.g. initiatives of chairpersons, reports by committees or the Secretariat).

Indicators for the WTO as a corporate actor are decisions and actions by the WTO decision bodies which are not fully determined by member states' interests and preferences, or which reflect the influence of the WTO on member states' governments. This relative actor autonomy is based on the scope of the legal mandate of international organizations, on their perceived moral authority derived from common welfare orientation, political neutrality and impartiality, and on their expertise (*Barnett and Finnemore* 2004: 22ff.; *Liese and Weinlich* 2006: 505f.).

3. Focal, formal, and informal organizations

(a) Focal organization

In organization theory the concept of "organization-set" is used to study the interactions and relations between several organizations (inter-organizational analysis). An organization-set consists of a "focal organization" as the point of reference and a set of other organizations in its environment (*Evan* 1976: 119). The choice of a focal organization depends on the research question. This approach has proved to be useful in directing attention to a specific organization and examining its effectiveness of goal attainment, its strategies and degree of autonomy in decision making, its identity and internal structure (*Evan* 1976: 122; *Scott and Davies* 2007: 116).

Figure 3.1 depicts the WTO as the focal organization of a set of international organizations, NGOs, international business associations, and non-member states. Placing the WTO at the centre of the organization-set does not suggest that it is the most powerful actor. Identifying the WTO as a focal organization merely reflects the research interests of the study to exam the interactions and relations of the WTO with other organizations in its environment and to assess their influence on the WTO's task performance.

The concept of focal organization is also useful to analyze the intra-organizational relations of a composite actor.

The Ministerial Conference, councils, committees, panels, member state representations, and the Secretariat are internal actors of the WTO viewed as an interaction system. As Figure 3.1 indicates, the Secretariat is selected as the focal actor. This choice reflects the research interest in the Secretariat's role and influence within the WTO.

(b) Formal and informal organizations

As outlined above (sub I.1 of this chapter), formal organizations are collectivities characterized by a defined membership, goals, structures, and procedures which, in general, are laid down in statutes, contracts, memoranda, or in other official documents (*Kieser and Walgenbach* 2007: 6–27; *Scott and Davies* 2007: 22, 28f.).

The term "informal organization" is generally used to capture those aspects of an organization which are not prescribed by formal authority, but supplement or modify the formal organizational structure and affect how the organization operates (*Gross* 1968: 238; *Holzer et al.* 2007: 73f.; *Scott and Davies* 2007: 23). Since the 1930s when the concept of informal organization was introduced to organization theory numerous studies have revealed that the members of any formal organization follow practices and procedures and participate in group interactions which do not conform to the formal structures and procedures of the organization but affect, to varying degrees, the functioning of the organization. The explanation and interpretation of this phenomenon are controversial.

Informal behavior was first discovered in industrial organizations and explained with the human relations among workers, their personal needs and social satisfaction (*Roethlisberger and Dickson* 1939; *Holzer et al.* 2007: 74). Since informal practices and group processes threatened the authority of the formal organizational order and could negatively affect organizational performance, the informal organization was often viewed with suspicion and considered dysfunctional for the effectiveness and efficiency of organizations. However, it was pointed out very early (*Barnard* 1938: 120f.) that informal behavior is an inevitable consequence of formal structures and procedures and, to some extent, a prerequisite for the maintenance of formal organizations. Today the inevitability and functional ambivalence of informal organizations have generally been recognized.

Both are explained with systems problems of formal organizations and the potential of informal organizations to resolve or alleviate these problems (*Barnard* 1938: 122f.; *Luhmann* 1995: 30f., 244f., 285f.; *Schuppert* 2000: 230ff.; *Holzer et al.* 2007: 74; *Scott and Davies* 2007: 63; Schreyögg 2008: 13f., 47). Systems problems of formal organizations include

- the effective attainment of formal goals,
- the reduction of uncertainties and complexities in decision making,
- the resolution of internal and external conflicts,
- coping with scarce resources, and
- the adaptation to a rapidly changing environment.

Organization members tend to resort to informal practices and procedures and to the establishment of informal groups within the formal organization when formal rules and organizational structures are too inflexible, cumbersome or even prohibitive for effective goal attainment, coping with uncertain and complex decision situations, conflict resolution, cost-effectiveness, or timely adaptation to new demands from the environment. A frequently found example of informal decision practices are bargaining processes outside official channels which precede or run parallel to formal decision procedures or negotiations in order to make the adoption of formal decisions possible and acceptable to organization members. These are the positive functions of informal organizations.

However, informal practices, procedures, and structures are at odds with the implementation of formal rules designed to protect the interests of certain members or stakeholders of the organization. Informal communications and bargaining processes may be used to outmaneuver these actors in the formal decision-making process of an organization. There is an inherent conflict between informality and equal treatment.

In a similar vein, informal behavior tends to be non-public and intransparent. Therefore, informal organizations may be at odds with formal rules of transparency in organizations.

There is no criterion to determine in the abstract at what point of informality the functionality of informal organizations turns into dysfunctionality. The assessment of functionality is contingent upon the characteristics of specific organizations and problem situations. In any event, "the art of administration" largely rests on the administrators' ability to move adroitly between the formal and informal levels of organizations.

The concept of informal organization originated from research in private organizations. In organization theory the concept was later applied to all organizations including government organizations and public–private organizations. The dichotomy of formal–informal was specifically used in public administration and empirically oriented administrative law studies (*Woll* 1963; *Bohne* 1981) as well as in constitutional law research (*Schulze-Fielitz* 1984). Recently, the concept of informal governance has been applied to the analysis of the European Union (Christiansen *et al.* 2003).

Despite its widespread usage there is no generally accepted definition of the term "informal." It is usually associated with unwritten rules, organizational culture and values, or social networks (*Scott and Davies* 2007: 23). This vague notion of informal makes it difficult, if not impossible, to clearly identify informal behavior in empirical organizational analysis. The understanding of the term "informal" as being equivalent to "non-written" is, on the one hand, too wide because there are non-written communications and interactions which occur in official situations and are, therefore, considered "formal" like communications and interactions of government representatives in a political press conference. On the other hand, the equation of "informal" and "non-written" is too narrow because there are written informal interactions. For example, the results of political talks held outside official channels may be summarized in a memo. This is why the term "informal" must be operationalized more specifically for empirical research.

Helmke and Levitsky (2004: 727) define "informal institutions" as "socially shared rules, usually unwritten, that are created, communicated, and enforced outside of officially sanctioned channels." The authors then continue to describe what an informal institution is "not." This concept begs the definitional question by basically replacing the term "informal" with the notion of "not official," and by indicating what informal is not rather than saying positively what it is.

Christiansen *et al.* (2003: 7) define informal governance as "regular though non-codified and non-publicly sanctioned exchanges in the institutional context of the European Union." Earlier, *Bohne* (1984: 344) suggested three criteria for identifying informal behavior. Informal actions are

- legally non-binding and not regulated,
- based on the exchange of mutually beneficial behavior, and
- deliberately taken as an alternative or supplement to a formal action.

Both definitions concur on the first two criteria. These are the criterion of exchange and the criterion of lack of codification and sanctioning power by a public authority (*Christiansen et al.* 2003) which is another way of saying that the exchange is legally non-binding and not regulated. The criterion of informal actions serving as alternatives or supplements to formal actions in the second definition reflects the fact that the formal organization is the point of reference for informal actions. This means that interactions without any reference to the formal goals, procedures, and structures of an organization like a discussion in the cafeteria on the latest soccer results are not elements of the informal organization, but represent private or "formless" behavior. Thus, an organization encompasses three types of behavior: formal, informal and formless, or private actions.

4. Modes of governance

All organizations have to cope with the aforementioned systems problems of goal attainment, internal and external conflict resolution, scarcity of resources, and adaptation to environmental changes. Consequently, intraorganizational and interorganizational behavior must be influenced in such a way that it contributes to the resolution of these systems problems. How to influence organizational behavior is one of the fundamental issues of organization theory and the ongoing governance debate. In the past, the purposeful inducement of systems-functional organizational behavior was discussed using concepts like managing, coordinating, steering, governing, networking, and so on. Today "governance" is the name of the game. There is no generally accepted concept of governance. Its uses include governance (*Rhodes* 1997: 47) as

- the minimal state,
- corporate governance,
- the new public management,
- "good governance,"
- socio-cybernetic systems, and
- self-organizing networks.

The concept of governance is applied to interactions between organizations (e.g. governments and/or private organizations) at the global, European, and national level[6] as well as to interactions within organizations (*Fombrun* 1984). For the purpose of this study there is no need to review the manifold meanings of governance and to take sides in the definitional debate. This is because this study aims to identify and analyze the modes of influencing organizational behavior which is a focus of most governance concepts (*Rhodes* 1997: 15; *Kooiman* 2003; *Benz* 2004: 25; *Treib et al.* 2007: 4ff.), generally emphasizing non-hierarchical modes of governance.

The numerous and diverse instruments, forms, and mechanisms of influencing people's behavior in and outside of organizations can be reduced to three basic modes of governance.[7] They are

- threat or use of coercion,
- exchange of mutually beneficial behavior, and
- persuasion.

All hierarchical forms of influencing organizational behavior are based on the threat or use of coercion. The fear of enforcement actions or other imposed disadvantages make people comply with commands and prohibitions.

Negotiations, bargaining patterns, and all incentive-based instruments rest on the exchange mode. Mutually beneficial behavior includes tangible as well as intangible benefits (e.g. positive publicity).

The term of persuasion is broadly used. Its defining characteristic is the lack of trade-off relationships. For examples, it includes appeals for certain actions, warnings, recommendations, propaganda, as well as all forms of information and other unilateral services which are provided in order to influence behavior.

These modes of governance do not presuppose the existence of a single actor. They may also occur in network-type interactions. The threat or use of coercion, for example, includes prospective litigation and enforcement actions. They are frequently part of the interactions between two or more actors. In the WTO context, dispute settlement procedures and eventual national countermeasures under DSU Art. 22 (4) belong to the governance mode of coercion which may influence interaction and negotiation patterns among member states.

Exchange patterns are common features of negotiations, bargaining, and network relations.

The same thing can be said about persuasion as a governance mode which is often reflected in public relations and reporting activities.

The governance modes of coercion, exchange, and persuasion are analytical categories. In reality there are various intermediate modes of governance. In particular, the role of threat of coercion – often metaphorically referred to as "shadow of hierarchy" – for the efficacy of policy making and policy performance is of central concern in the current governance debate (*Héritier and Lehmkuhl* 2008: 3).

5. Performance criteria

The performance of the WTO is evaluated against the criteria of effectiveness, equity, and legitimacy.

(a) Effectiveness

The criterion of effectiveness depicts the extent to which the goals of an organization are achieved (*Henry* 2007: 68f.). The concept of efficiency refers to a means-ends relationship. It has two dimensions:

- minimizing costs or other resources in attaining fixed goals, and
- maximizing the extent of goal attainment while costs or other resources are fixed.

The term "efficiency" is often used loosely and interchangeably with "effectiveness." This is misleading.[8]

This study is confined to the evaluation of WTO effectiveness because data on the cost of world trade and WTO activities including their causal relationships with goal attainment of the WTO are not available. Their collection was beyond the scope and resources of this study.

For the same reason the study focuses on outputs of WTO activities like results of negotiations, compliance with trade agreements and dispute settlements rather than on outcomes like trade growth, increase or decrease of standards of living. Besides that, an examination of WTO outcomes and their causal relationships with organizational characteristics of the WTO does not seem feasible. This is because the effects of organizational variables on the world trade system cannot be isolated from the effects of a plethora of other intervening variables.

(b) Equity

The concept of equity involves the notion of fairness and equality. In organization theory, the concept has been refined to denote the ratio of outcomes and inputs of a person's membership and participation in an organization (*Gortner et al.* 2007: 305f.). Equity between organization members occurs when the ratios are equal. In this sense though without quantification the concept of equity is often applied to the WTO to denote that developing countries "are receiving a disproportionately small share of the benefits of a more liberal global trading system" (*Porter* 2001: 8).

This substantive notion of equity is complemented by procedural equity. This means that organization members have equal access to decision-making procedures which is not the case in the WTO context. One could summarize these aspects of equity under the term "equity of organization members."

There is another dimension of equity which "involves the tension between economic and non-economic objectives" (*Porter* 2001: 9). Critics of the WTO and the present free-trade system call for an equal treatment of trade concerns with social and environmental concerns under existing WTO trade agreements and in the development of new trade rules. This dimension of equity could be called "equity of policy concerns."

(c) Legitimacy

According to a common definition, legitimacy in international relations is "a property of a rule or rule-making institution which itself exerts a pull toward compliance on those addressed normatively because those addressed believe that the rule or institution has come into being and operates in accordance with generally accepted principles of right process" (*Franck* 1990: 24). This definition like many others combines empirical elements (e.g. "exerts a pull," "those addressed believe") and normative elements (e.g. "principles of right process"). The empirical and normative dimensions of legitimacy must be kept separate in order to avoid confusion (*Applbaum* 2000: 324f.; *Krajewski* 2001b: 168f.; *Steffek* 2003: 253). Empirical legitimacy is about social acceptance of domination. Normative legitimacy is about moral or legal justification of domination. The controversy over the legitimacy of the WTO tends to confound the empirical and normative dimensions of legitimacy.

The normative justification (legitimacy) of domination can only be derived from a written or unwritten legal or social norm. Social acceptance or public opinion alone is no sources of normative legitimacy. A case in point is Hitler's race laws which were illegitimate since they violated fundamental human rights, although a majority of Germans accepted them in the 1930s. From a legal perspective, the normative legitimacy of the WTO, its law and decisions, is beyond doubt because it is based on international law and national ratification acts (*Howse* 2000: 37). Critics of the WTO often claim that the institution suffers from democracy deficits (*Aman* 2004: 5; *Zürn* 2004: 260). A correct normative reasoning would require

- to demonstrate the violation of fundamental human rights by the WTO, or

- to propose a new normative concept of democracy which is applicable to international organizations despite the absence of a core characteristic of the traditional concepts of democracy; this is the existence of a community in which there is a general consensus on what makes public decisions legitimate (*Keohane and Nye* 2001: 282).

In the debate on the WTO's democracy deficit there is a tendency to employ the concepts of democracy loosely (e.g. *Porter* 2001: 11; *Stokes and Choate* 2001: 60ff.) and to maintain that WTO decisions are undemocratic because they lack transparency and the consent of those who are affected by them. However, some authors (*Cohen* 1989: 21ff.; *Krajewski* 2001b: 171f.; *Steffek* 2003: 262ff.) have proposed a new "deliberate democratic model" for international organizations which is based on public rational discourse and rooted in *Habermas'* (1996) theory on law and democracy. The characteristic feature of this model is the rational exchange of arguments which eventually arrives at a conclusion in the form of agreement (*Steffek* 2003: 263). Intransparent decision-making processes violate this normative concept of democracy. While there is a controversy over the practicability of this model in international relations, this study does not engage in the normative debate on democratic legitimacy. Rather it is confined to the analysis of empirical legitimacy.

Max Weber (1980: 122f.) was first to elaborate on legitimacy as an empirical concept. He conceives of legitimate domination as a "belief in legitimacy" by those who are subject to the domination of legal rules, tradition, or a charismatic leader. Weber's concept of legitimate domination is still the base for the present debate on empirical legitimacy. In this sense, legitimacy is an attitude of individuals or groups to accept a social order as binding and justified (*Steffek* 2003: 253).

WTO law is legally binding on member states and, through national acts of transposition, on the citizens of these states. Therefore, this study focuses on the attitudes of representatives of member states and NGOs toward the legitimacy (justification) of the WTO system.

A distinction is often made between input and output legitimacy of international organizations (*Keohane and Nye* 2001: 282ff.). Input legitimacy is concerned with the transparency, fairness, and other properties of procedures and with the structural characteristics of an organization. Output legitimacy refers to the results of organizational behavior, e.g. effective goal attainment. Thus, input and output characteristics of legitimacy are empirical factors which both influence the attitudes of members and stakeholders of an organization toward accepting its order as justified (legitimate).

Perceptions of equity and legitimacy may overlap under certain circumstances. This is because the occurrence or absence of fairness and equal treatment may be factors to accept or reject the legitimacy of a social order. However, perceptions of legitimacy are, in general, more fundamental than perceptions of equity. Instances or areas of unfairness and inequality do not necessarily call the legitimacy of a social order as a whole into question. Therefore, equity and legitimacy are used as separate performance criteria in this study.

(d) Indicators of effectiveness, equity, and legitimacy

There are no objective indicators for the effectiveness, equity, and legitimacy of WTO activities in terms of quantitative measures or fixed operationalized WTO objectives and requirements. Consequently, negative indicators are used which suggest the absence or shortcomings of WTO performance. They include with respect to deficiencies of

- effectiveness: failure and/or delay
  - to conclude implementable trade agreements,
  - to implement and/or comply with trade agreements, and
  - to make and/or comply with trade policy reviews and dispute settlement decisions,
- equity: failure and/or shortcomings
  - to balance the trade interests of all WTO members,
  - to participate in WTO decision-making processes, and
  - to balance environmental and/or labor policy concerns with trade policies,
- legitimacy: lack of acceptance by WTO members, NGOs, and the public due to perceived unfair practices and intransparency in decision making, or because of opposition to the free trade system.

In addition to these negative indicators for the absence or shortcomings of effectiveness, equity, and legitimacy the direct evaluation of WTO performance is taken into account as expressed by people who are intimately involved in WTO activities: WTO officials, member state representatives, and NGO activists who critically observe the WTO. These evaluations include the effects of informal structures and procedures.

II. Research variables

Figure 3.1 displays the sets of dependent and independent variables used in this study.

Dependent variables are actions and decisions of WTO bodies in the task areas of trade negotiations, implementation of trade agreements, trade policy review, and dispute settlement. Characteristics of these variables are form, content, and performance in terms of effectiveness, equity, and empirical legitimacy. The negative indicators listed sub I.5.d in this chapter are used to determine the absence or shortcomings of these performance characteristics.

Independent variables include characteristics of:

- trade problems, e.g. conflicts on agricultural subsidies,
- actors, e.g. WTO bodies, member states, international organizations, NGOs,
- agreements, rules and regulatory requirements like the Marrakesh Agreement, Dispute Settlement Understanding (DSU), and legal principles of consensus, neutrality, single undertaking etc.,
- informal structures and procedures, e.g. Green Room meetings, country groups like G20, G33 and the like,
- organizational systems requirements, e.g. need to resolve internal and external conflicts, to reduce uncertainties and complexities, to adapt to changing environments (see I.3.b in this chapter),
- governance modes, e.g. exchange patterns, persuasion, threat of coercion, and
- administrative, budgetary and personnel resources of the WTO and member states.

Dependent and independent variables are described and interpreted in light of the theoretical concepts explained sub I.1–5 of this chapter. Independent variables are used to suggest, where possible, explanations of WTO actions and decisions in different task areas.

III. Research methods

1. Interviews

The study is based on 21 expert interviews which were conducted between September 2005 and May 2006 in Geneva with representatives of

- the WTO Secretariat,
- permanent member state missions to the WTO,
- intergovernmental organizations, and
- NGOs.

Eight interview partners came from the Secretariat including a Deputy Director General and officials from seven divisions with responsibilities in the areas of trade negotiations, implementation of trade agreements, trade policy review, and dispute settlement.

Six interview partners represented the permanent missions of four developing countries (Brazil, India, Kenya, and South Africa), the European Union and the United States. One of these interviewees served as a committee chairman.

The interviews with inter-governmental organizations were conducted with two representatives of UNCTAD and the South Centre.

Five experts from NGOs were interviewed coming from the Center for International Environmental Law, the Institute for Agriculture and Trade Policy (IATP), the International Center for Trade and Sustainable Development, Oxfam, and the Third World Network.

The interview sample is not representative of WTO members, intergovernmental organizations, and NGOs in a statistical sense. The choice of interviewed institutions is based on their reputation for political relevance and expertise in international trade affairs. Reputation sampling is a common approach in public administration research (*Northrop and Arsneault* 2008: 225).

The interviews were conducted with the help of guidelines, taped, transcribed, coded, and evaluated with a computer program for qualitative data analysis. The duration of interviews ranged from 40 to over 120 minutes.

Furthermore, the interview partners were asked to rate the present and desired future roles of the Secretariat as a tool of member states (1) or a leader (10) on a ten-point scale.

Finally, the interview partners were presented with a matrix of 19 reform proposals (see Annex 1) and their potential impacts on WTO performance in terms of effectiveness, equity, and legitimacy (i.e. acceptance by member states and external actors). They were asked to assess the potential impacts of reform proposals on a five-point scale with +2 = strong positive effect, +1 = small positive effect, 0 = no effect, −1 = small negative effect, −2 = strong negative effect, and to fill in the matrix accordingly. Thirteen tables were returned. The means of estimated impacts are calculated, and presented in Chapter 7 if they are, at least, ± .5.

2. Survey

In fall of 2006, a questionnaire (see Annex 2) was distributed to the permanent missions (in and outside Geneva) of all member states (149 at that time). Seventy-five members (50,3%) returned the questionnaire, 70% of them are developing countries including least developed countries (LDCs). Developed countries (30%) primarily comprise EU member states, the United States, Canada, Australia, and Japan. Since about two-thirds of WTO members are developing countries (*WTO* 2008: 93), the sample can be considered broadly representative with regard to the share of developing and developed countries.

The responsibilities of respondents focus primarily on trade negotiations (90%), followed by implementation of trade agreements (62%), trade policy review (50%), and dispute settlement (41%). Hence, expertise and experience of respondents cover the relevant task areas.

3. Legal analysis and literature review

The GATT and Marrakesh Agreement, various multilateral trade agreements, the DSU, other WTO rules of procedure and guidelines, as well as relevant principles of international law were analyzed to identify the formal tasks, structures, and procedures of the WTO. This analysis required to make use of legal methods of interpretation.

The literature review focused on the WTO, international organizations, and concepts of public administration.

4. Adequacy and validity of methods

The *adequacy* of employing different qualitative, quantitative, and legal methods for the analysis of the WTO follows from the public administration perspective of the research. The managerial, political, and legal dimensions of public administration (*Rosenbloom et al.* 2009: 14ff.) require the triangulation of multiple methods and data (*Gabrielian et al.* 2008: 143). The quantitative survey of permanent missions of member states to the WTO provides a systematic and standardized description of key characteristics of the WTO tasks, structures, and procedures. The qualitative expert interviews flesh out details, and help to understand the functioning of the WTO and to interpret survey data. Legal concepts like the principles of consensus, neutrality, single undertaking, estoppel, etc. have influenced the content of the interview guidelines and the written questionnaire. Methods of legal interpretation are used to analyze agreements and rules of procedure.

The *validity* of measurements denotes the effectiveness of a research instrument (e.g. questionnaire) to measure exactly what it is supposed to measure. Theoretically, one would need an instrument whose validity is known in order to assess the validity of another instrument. While this procedure can be followed in the natural sciences, it is generally not feasible in the social sciences. Therefore, it is a common practice to rely on expert judgments, i.e. "face validity" (*Hu and Olshfski* 2008: 207), in order to ensure the validity of research instruments. In this study, the questionnaire was developed on the basis of the interviews. Ultimately, only scientific criticism and the results of other studies can prove or disprove the validity of this research.

4
WTO as a Public Formal Organization

I. Agreements, membership, and principles

The WTO Marrakesh Agreement created the WTO as a new international organization with a legal personality.[1] The objectives of the WTO are set out in the preamble of the Marrakesh Agreement, which lists raising standards of living, full employment, a large and steadily growing volume of real income and effective demand, an expanding production of and trade in goods and services (while allowing for the optimal use of the world's resources in accordance with the objective of sustainable development) and protection and preservation of the environment. In the preamble, the WTO members expressed their desire to work toward these objectives by concluding agreements on trade liberalization. The 2001 Doha Ministerial Declaration also stressed that an open and non-discriminatory multilateral trading system and the "acting for the protection of the environment" and the "promotion of sustainable development" could and had to be mutually supportive (*WTO* 2003: 3).

A package of agreements is annexed to the WTO Agreement, which becomes binding on all member states as "a single body of law" (*Matsushita et al.* 2003: 7f.). The package consists of the following WTO agreements:

- General Agreements on Tariffs and Trade 1994,
- Agreement on Agriculture,
- Agreement on the Application of Sanitary and Phytosanitary Measures,
- Agreement on Textiles and Clothing,
- Agreement on Technical Barriers to Trade,
- Agreement on Trade-Related Investment Measures,

- Agreement on Implementation of Art. VI of the General Agreement on Tariffs and Trade 1994 (Antidumping Agreement),
- Agreement on Implementation of Art. VII of the General Agreement on Tariffs and Trade 1994 (Customs Valuation Agreement),
- Agreement on Preshipment Inspection,
- Agreement on Rules of Origin,
- Agreement on Import Licensing Procedures,
- Agreement on Subsidies and Countervailing Measures,
- Agreement on Safeguards,
- General Agreement on Trade in Services, and
- Agreement on Trade-Related Aspects of Intellectual Property Rights.

A distinction can be made between WTO agreements setting out general principles (GATT, GATS, and TRIPS) and all other agreements and supplements dealing with more specialized sectors and issues that concern trade of goods and services in general (e.g. subsidies) (*Kouvaritakis et al.* 2004: 35f.).

The WTO agreements – like international treaty law in general (*Herdegen* 2007: 151) – are not directly effective in member states. Rather they put a legal obligation on member states to ensure the conformity of national laws with WTO law, Art. XVI (4) of the WTO Marrakesh Agreement. The domestic law of the state concerned determines the effect of WTO agreements on domestic law (*Herdegen* 2007: 151) – in the United States, the WTO Agreement is an executive agreement and constitutes a binding international obligation of the United States. However, it is not directly effective. In the European Union, the European Court of Justice also avoided giving direct effect to GATT and WTO agreements and WTO panel and appellate body reports (*Matsushita et al.* 2003: 98–107).

When the WTO was established in 1995, all former members of GATT were invited to join the new WTO by ratifying the Marrakesh Agreement. By the time the Agreement was signed in 1994 the GATT had 128 members. Since then, 45 governments have applied to accede to the WTO. By 2005, 20 countries had completed the accession procedure, but many others were still seeking to complete it (*Gallagher* 2005: 13f.). More than three-quarters of WTO's Members have self-elected the status of developing countries, of which 30 are least developed.

Accession to the WTO is basically a negotiated process. Following the Marrakesh Agreement, any state may accede, "on terms to be agreed between it and the WTO."[2] In practice, full acceptance of the obligations of the WTO agreements is only a first precondition. Other terms of accession are set in bilateral negotiations with WTO members, and they have sometimes been more exacting than those contained in WTO agreements (*Gallagher* 2005: 14). The Ministerial Conference shall approve the terms of accession by at least a two-third majority.[3]

International organizations have often relatively small budgets if compared to national public administrations (*Liese and Weinlich* 2006: 497). The budget of the WTO in 2008 was 185 Mio. CHF.[4] The WTO budget is usually evaluated to be very small compared to the budget of other international economic organizations. The member states' contribution to the budget is based on its – extremely divergent – share in world trade (see Chapter 1, I).[5] Hence, increases in the budget would be paid primarily by the large traders (*Blackhurst* 2000: 41ff.).

Operation of the WTO is guided by a number of important principles:

- the principle of single undertaking,
- the principle of consensus decision making,
- the principle of impartiality of the Secretariat, and
- the most favored nation principle.

The first important principle guiding WTO operations is the principle of "single undertaking." As outlined above, all of the Multilateral Trade Agreements in the Annexes to the Marrakesh Agreement are binding on all WTO members.[6] This principle had been adopted with the objective in mind to terminate the GATT "à la carte" approach under which many GATT Contracting Parties were not parties to various Tokyo Round codes (*Davey* 2005: 57). The effect of the single undertaking is that "almost every government in the world now has precisely the same set of fundamental trade obligations toward every other government" (*Gallagher* 2005: 13). There are, however, two remaining plurilateral WTO Agreements to which most members of the WTO are not parties. The principle of single undertaking is also used as a guiding principle in the negotiations of the current Doha Round. Following Section 47 of the Doha Declaration, conclusions of the Doha negotiations "are treated as parts of a single undertaking." In other words, interim results in WTO negotiations can be become meaningless since "nothing is agreed until everything is agreed." Any compromises which may be reached in specific committees cannot lead to any changes in WTO agreements unless they are accepted (and possibly amended) by membership as part of broader packages.

Central to the multilateral trading system is also the principle of consensus decision making in Art. IX (1) of the Marrakesh Agreement.

Because no decision is taken unless all member governments agree, effectively every country – from the largest to the smallest – has the formal power of veto (*Moore* 2005: 41f.). Consensus was already a common principle under GATT, but when discussions about the design of the WTO started, the initial US government position considered consensus decision making in an organization with an expected membership of more than 120 too cumbersome. Instead, the United States proposed making decisions under a majority rule or creating an Executive Committee composed of the 18 largest trading nations. However, the European Union persuaded the United States to maintain the consensus rule. One of the arguments was that legislative outcomes achieved in a consensus-based system might enjoy more legitimacy than those from a weighted or majority voting system (*Steinberg* 2002: 365).

There are a few limited exceptions[7] for majority or "weighted" voting if consensus is not possible. In these cases one country has one vote: (a) an interpretation of any of the Multilateral Trade Agreements that can be adopted by a majority of three quarters of WTO Members (Art. IX(2)), (b) the waiving of an obligation imposed on a particular member by a Multilateral Agreement through a three quarters majority of the Ministerial Conference (Art. IX (3)), (c) the decision to admit a new Member is taken by a two-thirds majority in a Ministerial Conference or by the General Council in between conferences (Art XII (2)). Finally, decisions to amend provisions of the Multilateral Agreements can be adopted through approval either by all members or by a two-thirds majority depending on the nature of the provision concerned. But the amendment will take only effect for those WTO members which accept them (Art. X (3); see *Moore* 2005: 41). So far, there have been no formal amendments of the Marrakesh Agreement or any of the annexed Multilateral Trade Agreements (*Footer* 2006: 96).

Also, there is the most-favored nation principle (MFN), which is a non-discrimination principle.[8] If a WTO member grants another member a privilege, the same thing must be done for all other WTO members. This means that WTO members cannot discriminate between foreign goods, or treat products from one member better than those from another (*Moore* 2005: 40). However, in the context of several Regional Trade Agreements advantages may be limited to the members of these agreements and not all the members of the WTO (*Kouvaritakis et al.* 2004: 36).[9]

International organizations tend to emphasize "neutrality, impartiality and objectivity" of their bureaucracies (*Barnett and Finnemore* 2005: 173). These principles are deemed vital to the functioning of any international organization (*Footer* 2006: 306). In the Marrakesh Agreement, these principles are spelt out in Art. VI (4) as the "international character of the responsibilities of the Director General and of the staff of the Secretariat."

II. Tasks

1. Trade negotiations

The WTO shall provide a forum for negotiations among its members concerning matters dealt with under the annexed agreements. The Marrakesh Agreement also provides for further agreements to be negotiated under the framework of the Marrakesh Agreement.[10] Traditionally, under GATT trade negotiations were organized in form of rounds which were named after the place in which the negotiations began or the person associated with initiating the round. Names and dates of the GATT rounds are as follows: Geneva (1947), Annecy (1949), Torquay (1950), Geneva (1956), Dillon (1960–1961), Kennedy (1962–1967), Tokyo (1973–1979), and Uruguay (1986–1994). The objectives of the early GATT negotiating rounds were primarily to reduce tariffs, with non-tariff barriers emerging as a vital concern as well. In the Tokyo and Uruguay Round, the most important objective was to reduce non-tariff barriers (*Matsushita et al.* 2003: 6). The WTO agreed on the opening of negotiations of a new round in Doha in 2001. The agenda contained a "demanding program" for negotiations which was to bring about a "further major reduction in existing trade barriers," covering agriculture, services, and industrial goods (*Grimwade* 2004: 34). In practice, the main controversial issue in the Doha Round has been the reduction of agricultural subsidies in developed countries (*Halle* 2006). The Doha Agenda had established an ambitious target for the so-called Doha Round, as it was supposed to be closed by January 2005 (*WTO* 2003: 95). However, deadlines in the Doha Round have been consistently missed, and an agreement has remained elusive so far.

2. Implementation of trade agreements and technical assistance

Member States are generally obliged under Art. XVI (4) of the Marrakesh Agreement to ensure the conformity of their laws, regulations, and administrative procedures with their obligation as provided in the annexed Multilateral Trade Agreements. The precise scope of the duties of the member states and the duties of the Secretariat is laid down in these agreements.

Three basic compliance control mechanisms of international organizations may be distinguished (*Beyerlin et al.* 2006: 362 with regard to Multilateral Environmental Agreements): reporting, assessment of reports and non-compliance procedures. There is no generally applicable mechanism or procedure for the implementation of the various Multilateral Trade Agreements. Rules differ depending on the applicable agreement. As set out under Section IV.2 of this chapter, many procedures for reporting and assessment of reports are laid down in various Multilateral Trade Agreements. However, there are hardly any procedures for the identification and handling of problems of non-compliance.

A task of the WTO closely related to trade negotiations (and also to implementation) is technical cooperation. The foundations for technical cooperation can be found in the 1994 WTO/GATT Marrakesh Declaration, in which the ministers recognized "the need for strengthening the capability of the GATT and the WTO to provide increased technical assistance in their areas of competence, and in particular to substantially expand its provision to the least-developed countries." Also, various Multilateral Trade Agreements mandate the provision of technical assistance to developing countries (*Durán* 2005: 464).

General objectives of technical cooperation which are laid down in the Guidelines adopted by the Committee of Trade and Development in 1996[11] are

- the strengthening and enhancing of institutional and human capacities in the public sector for an appropriate participation in the multilateral trading system (in consultation with the government concerned and with representatives of the private sector for capacity building),
- the improvement of knowledge of multilateral trade rules and WTO working procedures and negotiations, and
- the assistance in the implementation of commitments in the multilateral trading system and in the full use of its provisions, including the effective use of the dispute settlement mechanism.

Technical cooperation provided by the WTO shall be "fully and closely coordinated with other assistance provided by multilateral and bilateral institutions." To this end, the WTO shall enter into a close institutional dialogue with other international organizations, in particular with the International Trade Centre (ITC)[12] and with UNCTAD.[13] The WTO Secretariat has concluded a Memorandum of Understanding with UNCTAD, in which the parties agreed to cooperate for the purposes of technical cooperation, capacity-building, training, research, and analysis, both through specific interagency programs, or in other areas, or as mandated under the Doha Development Agenda.[14]

Funding of technical assistance is through the regular budget of the WTO and through the WTO Trust Fund which receives voluntary contributions by members.[15] Since the Doha Ministerial Conference technical cooperation has gained importance in the WTO. The Doha Ministerial Declaration of 2001 has put renewed emphasis on the importance of "well targeted, sustainably financed technical assistance and capacity-building programmes" to ensure that developing and especially LDCs increasingly benefit from integration into the multilateral trade system (see *WTO* 2003: 2). The General Council adopted on 20 December 2001 (one month after the Doha conference) a new budget that increased technical assistance funding by 80% and established a Doha Development Agenda Global Trust Fund. The fund has currently an annual budget of 24 Mio. CHF based on donations from WTO member countries, while 6 Mio. CHF come from the regular WTO budget.[16]

3. Trade policy review

International organizations make increasingly use of peer reviews, "the purpose of which is the examination of one state's performance or practices in a particular area by other states [...]. The point of the exercise is to help the state under review to improve its policymaking, adopt best practices and comply with established standards and principles." Recommendations resulting from such a review can help governments win support at home for difficult measures. Peer reviews originated with the Organisation for Economic Cooperation and Development (OECD), and the tool has been adopted by other international organizations such as the European Union, the IMF, and the WTO (*OECD* 2003: 1–2).

The trade policy review mechanism which the WTO is required to administer[17] can be qualified as a peer review mechanism. Its predecessor was established in 1988 under GATT rules (*Blackhurst* 2000: 42). The trade policy review mechanism enables members to examine and comment on the trade policies and practices of individual WTO members and their effects on the functioning of the multilateral trading system (*Davey* 2005: 58f.). It is regulated in detail in Annex 3 to the Marrakesh Agreement. While the purpose of the trade policy review is to contribute to "improved adherence [...] to rules, disciplines and commitments made under the Multilateral Trade Agreements," any linkages between the trade policy review and the dispute settlement mechanism are excluded. Annex 3 to the Marrakesh Agreement explicitly prohibits that information from the trade policy review be used in dispute settlement procedures or that the trade policy review be used to impose new policy commitments on Members.[18]

4. Dispute settlement

At the international level, states have increasingly chosen to delegate the resolution of disputes to tribunals rather than resolving disputes through "institutionalized bargaining." Depending on how international courts and tribunals are defined, their number ranges between 17 and 40 (*Keohane et al.* 2000: 457). However, as set out in Chapter 1, few international organizations have a compulsory dispute settlement procedure (*Bronckers* 2001: 45). The WTO dispute settlement system, which came into operation in January 1995 is considered one of the strengths of the WTO. It is arguably the most important international tribunal. It functions very much "like a court of international trade" due to compulsory jurisdiction, the settlement of disputes by applying rules of law, binding decisions on the parties and sanctions that may be imposed if decisions are not observed (*Matsushita et al.* 2003: 18). However, while WTO panel and Appellate Body reports are binding on the parties of the dispute, they are *not* interpretations of the WTO agreements, and have no legal effect on other WTO members (*Matsushita et al.* 2003: 25).

The "Understanding on Rules and Procedures governing the Settlement of Disputes" in Annex 2 of the Marrakesh Agreement lays down that the "dispute settlement" shall preserve the rights and obligations of members under the covered agreements, and [...] shall clarify the existing provisions of those agreements "in accordance with customary rules of interpretation of public international law." However, recommendations and rulings of the DSB shall not add or diminish the rights and obligations provided in the covered agreements.[19] Procedures can be opened if a Member considers that it does not receive benefits accruing to it directly or indirectly under the covered WTO agreements because of measures taken by another member.[20]

III. Organizational structure

The structure of the WTO is shown in Figure 1.1. It is set out in Art. IV of the Marrakesh Agreement. The Ministerial Conference, which is the highest decision-making organ of the WTO, shall meet at least every two years. The conference shall be attended by ministers from all WTO members (*Davey* 2005: 60). WTO Ministerial Conferences have so far taken place in Singapore (1996), in Geneva (1998), in Seattle (1999), in Doha (2001), in Cancún (2003), and in Hong Kong (2005). However, Ministerial Conferences are not always successful in reaching agreements among member states: thus, the Seattle Ministerial failed to reach an agreement among members on the opening of a new round (on its failure see *Das* 2000). The Cancún Ministerial Conference failed to reach an agreement on how negotiations of the Doha Round were to proceed (on its failure see *Cho* 2004).

In between meetings of the Ministerial Conference, the powers of the Ministerial Conference are exercised by the General Council, which is composed of representatives of all WTO members, and which meets at least every other month. It is charged with supervising the WTO's dispute settlement system and "in doing so convenes as the Dispute Settlement Body." In connection with the Trade Policy Review Mechanism it convenes as the Trade Policy Review Body (TPRB).

A number of subsidiary bodies report directly and indirectly to the General Council. First, there are three specialized councils under the General Council: The Council for Trade in Goods, the Council for Trade in Services, and the Council for TRIPS. Second, subsidiary bodies such as committees and working groups may be established under each of the councils. As a rule, standing committees with full membership have been set up under each of the Multilateral Trade Agreements. The mandate of these committees is to deal with administration and implementation of existing agreements.

However, some committees (Committees on Trade and Development; on Balance of Payments Restrictions; on Budget, Finance, and Administration; on Trade and Environment; and on Regional Trade Agreements) have a broader mandate that goes beyond the administration of a special Multilateral Trade Agreement. These committees report directly to the General Council (*Davey* 2005: 64).

For negotiations under the Doha 2001 mandate, some new bodies were created (Negotiating Groups on Market access and WTO rules). Other parts of the negotiations take place in Special Sessions of existing councils (Services Council; TRIPS Council) and Special Sessions of existing committees (Agriculture, Trade and Environment, and Trade and Development) (*Davey* 2005: 65). Special Sessions of existing bodies have the same membership as General Sessions, but they are chaired by different persons.

Negotiations under the Doha mandate are supervised by the Trade Negotiations Committee (TNC) which was established in 2002 (*WTO*

2008: 77). It is chaired by the Director General and it meets every two or three months. The task of the TNC includes supervising the scheduling of the timetables of the negotiations meeting with a view to the constraints of smaller delegations. The TNC reports to the General Council which has an overall responsibility for the whole work program as agreed at the Doha Ministerial Conference, and for preparation of all Ministerial Conferences.

For the settlement of disputes, specific organs are established. On request of a complaining party, the DSB establishes a panel on a case-by-case basis, which shall be composed of well-qualified governmental and/or non-governmental individuals,[21] and which shall issue a report to be adopted by the DSB.[22] The DSB also establishes a standing Appellate Body that shall hear appeals from panel cases on issues of law covered in the panel report and legal interpretations.[23]

Typically, agreements establishing international organizations often fail to identify concrete tasks for the organizations' secretariats (*Liese and Weinlich* 2006: 498). This is also the case for the Marrakesh Agreement, which provides for the establishment of a Secretariat headed by a Director General under Art. VI (1), but fails to assign any functions to them. The Ministerial Conference is to appoint the Director General. Following the Marrakesh Agreement, the Ministerial Conference is also to adopt regulations setting out the powers, duties, and conditions of service of the Director General, who is then to appoint members of the staff of the Secretariat, and to determine their duties and conditions of service in accordance with regulations. However, to date no such regulations have been adopted (*Davey* 2005: 71). An important task of the Director General as set out in the Marrakesh Agreement is the presentation of the annual budget estimate and financial statement of the WTO to the Committee on Budget, Finance, and Administration. The Committee is then to make recommendations to the General Council, which has to approve the budget estimate by a two-thirds majority.[24]

Tasks of the Secretariat are scattered across Multilateral Trade Agreements (Annex 1), the Understanding on Rules and Procedures Governing the Settlement of Disputes (Annex 2), the rules on Trade Policy Review Mechanism (Annex 3), and various guidelines. For instance, the WTO Guidelines on Technical Cooperation assign to the Secretariat the task of administering technical cooperation provided by the WTO.[25] The annual program for technical assistance is laid down in the annual Technical Assistance and Training Plan, which is adopted by the Committee on Trade and Development following a proposal by the Secretariat.[26] The Secretariat is to report annually on program implementation, and

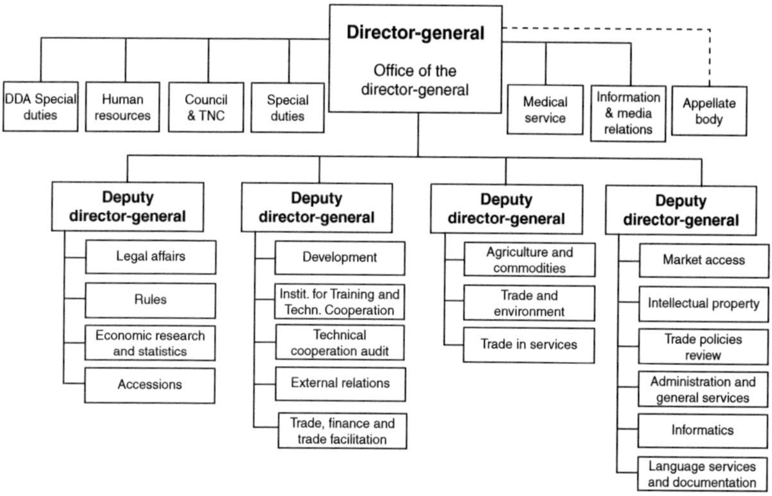

Figure 4.1 Organizational structure of the Secretariat
Source: WTO, March 2007.

the Committee on Trade and Development shall evaluate the results of the technical assistance activities.[27]

The organizational structure of the Secretariat is shown in Figure 4.1. Some of the divisions of the Secretariat are responsible for supporting particular committees. Thus the Agriculture Division assists the Committee on Agriculture, but other divisions such as the one for technical cooperation provide broader support for WTO activities (*WTO* 2008: 107).

Typically, international organizations have only a very limited number of personnel if compared against national administrations (*Liese and Weinlich* 2006: 497). The WTO Secretariat is no exception with a staff of only 630 (*WTO* 2008: 107). The conditions of service in the WTO and the personnel practices of the Secretariat together with rights, duties, and obligations of staff members are set out in the so-called Staff Regulations which have been adopted together with rules on pensions.[28]

The Marrakesh Agreement also provides for the General Council to make appropriate arrangements for consultation and cooperation of the WTO with intergovernmental organizations that have responsibilities related to those of the WTO,[29] and non-governmental organizations concerned with matters related to the WTO.[30] The Guidelines for Arrangements on Relations with Non-Governmental Organizations adopted in 1996[31] prescribe that the Secretariat should "play a more active role in its direct contacts with NGOs." The guidelines point to organizing, on an ad hoc basis, symposia on specific WTO-related issues, to making informal arrangements to receive the information that NGOs may wish to make available for consultation by interested delegations, and to responding to requests for general information and briefings about the WTO.

IV. Procedures

It has become established practice for an international organization (and by analogy for any of its principal and subsidiary bodies) to adopt its own rules of procedures (*Footer* 2006: 296). The rules of procedure for proceedings of the General Council and the Ministerial Conference were adopted first. WTO subsidiary bodies (i.e. councils and committees) have adopted separate rules of procedures, major parts of which, however, tend to be modeled on the rules applicable to the meetings of the General Council (*Footer* 2006: 296). Due to the different nature of its proceedings, different rules have been adopted for the operations of the TPRB.[32]

1. Trade negotiations

Meetings of the Ministerial Conference, the General Council and other councils and committees are guided by similar rules. While each member shall be represented by an accredited representative, he or she "may be accompanied by such alternates and advisers as the representative may require."[33] Observer status may be granted to other international intergovernmental organizations "which have competence and a direct interest in trade policy matters" or which have responsibilities related to those of the WTO.[34] Requests for observer status shall be considered on a case-by-case basis by the body concerned taking into account the nature of the work of the organization concerned. Representatives of organizations accorded observer status may be invited to speak at meetings of the bodies to which they are observers. This does not include the right to circulate papers or to make proposals.[35]

The rules of procedure assign a central role to the chairperson who shall declare the opening and closing of each meeting, shall direct the discussion, accord the right to speak etc., and, subject to these rules, shall "have complete control of the proceedings."[36] Special guidelines have been adopted for the appointment of chairpersons to WTO bodies.[37] As a rule, such appointments are based on the principle of rotation, with the term of office being limited to one year.[38] Emphasis is put on the acceptability of appointments to the membership as a whole.[39] A balance in representation reflecting "the overall membership of the WTO" should be achieved.[40] In other words, the selection of chairpersons should broadly reflect the share of developed and developing member countries in the WTO membership. For WTO councils, only Geneva-based heads of delegation can be chosen as chairpersons, while both heads or officials of delegations are eligible for chairing committees.[41]

In case of the Ministerial Conference it is the Secretariat, which in consultation with the Chairperson communicates an agenda to the members. Any member may propose items to be included on the agenda up to this point. The Ministerial Conference may also amend the agenda.[42] Meetings of the General Council, other councils and committees are convened by the Director General. The agenda is drawn up in several stages: First, requests for items to be included in the agenda may be directed to the Secretariat until the day on which the notice of the meeting is to be issued. Second, the Secretariat communicates a "list of the items proposed for the agenda of the meeting" together with the convening notice for the meeting. Third, the Secretariat circulates a "proposed agenda" one or two days before the meeting. At the meeting, representatives may suggest amendments to the proposed agenda under other business.[43]

The rules of procedures for meetings of the General Council (and those of other councils and committees) contain some provisions that seek to promote an effective use of time. Thus it is laid down that representatives should keep their oral statements brief, should avoid unduly long debates of other business, and that the repetition of a full debate on issues that has already been debated in the past should be avoided.[44]

Meetings of the Ministerial Conference and the General Council shall ordinarily be held in private. It may be decided that a particular meeting or meetings should be held in public.[45] Records of the discussions of the General Council and other councils and committees shall be in the form of minutes.[46] In case of the Ministerial Conference, summary records shall be kept by the Secretariat.[47]

A 1996 decision on derestriction of WTO documents had placed limits regarding the publication of documents. The Doha Ministerial Declaration of 2001 contained a commitment of members to making the WTO's operation more transparent "including through more effective and prompt dissemination of information", and through a commitment "to improve the dialogue with the public" (*WTO* 2003: 5). In

2002, members made derestriction of documents automatic for almost all documents within sixty days of circulation (*Gallagher* 2005: 27).[48]

While informal meetings are not referred to in the official rules of procedure, some other official WTO documents make a reference to them. Thus the 1995 Guidelines on the Arrangements for Scheduling of Meetings of WTO Bodies seek to avoid overlap of formal and informal meetings of WTO bodies by recommending that no more than two simultaneous formal meetings of WTO bodies should be held, and that the existing schedule of meetings should be taken into consideration when convening informal meetings. Moreover, the guidelines lay down that while "informal meetings may be convened to discuss specific problems as considered necessary by the Chairman, the need to keep the number of such meetings within reasonable limits should be kept in view."[49]

While the rules of procedures are generally applicable in the Doha Round negotiations, some special rules have also been "endorsed." Thus the Doha Ministerial Declaration lies down for a number of issues that so-called modalities have to be agreed upon in a first step before products.[50] Modalities are targets (including numerical targets) for achieving the objectives set out in the Doha Ministerial Declaration (*WTO* 2003).

At the TNC meeting of 1 February 2002, a number of principles and practices for the Doha negotiations was set out by the Chairman of the General Council and "endorsed" by the TNC. Reference is made to "best practices established over the past two years with regard to internal transparency and participation of all members." The Ministerial Declaration is recalled that sets out that "negotiations shall be conducted in a transparent manner among participants, in order to facilitate the effective participation of all." Constraints of smaller delegations should be taken into account when scheduling meetings. Chairpersons should ensure "transparency and inclusiveness in decision making" (*WTO* 2003: 79).

The Secretariat is generally charged under the Doha mandate with the "prompt and efficient dissemination of information relating to negotiations," in particular to non-resident and smaller missions. The Secretariat shall also circulate minutes of meetings of the TNC and other negotiating bodies expeditiously (*WTO* 2003: 79).

2. Implementation of trade agreements

The implementation of the existing Multilateral Trade Agreements has created a number of problems that require renegotiation by members.

Implementation issues therefore have been partially integrated into the Doha negotiations mandate. They are negotiated in special bodies or special sessions of the committees or councils, while other implementation issues are dealt with by the standing bodies (*WTO* 2003: 5). As mentioned under Section II.2 of this chapter, there is no generally applicable implementation procedure. A distinction can be made regarding reporting, assessment of reports, and non-compliance procedures.

(a) Reporting

Surveillance of the implementation of Multilateral Trade Agreements relies heavily on reporting procedures.

As a result, members have a heavy burden of notification duties. In the goods area alone, 175 notification requirements were counted (*Gallagher* 2005: 23). Notification duties scattered across the agreements may concern many different actions taken by member states, e.g. national subsidies, anti-dumping measures, sanitary and phytosanitary measures, trade safeguards, import licenses, etc.

Some WTO agreements require the development of institutionalized structures at the national level, e.g. the designation of national enquiry points (*Quereshi* 1996: 96). For instance, a structure of national notification authorities and national enquiry points is to be established under the WTO Agreement on the Application of Sanitary and Phytosanitary Measures. National notification authorities are single central government authorities responsible for implementing the notification procedures. National enquiry points must provide answers to all questions from other members as well as provide relevant documents regarding any adopted or proposed SPS measures, etc. (*Prévost and Van den Bossche* 2005: 340).

(b) Assessment of reports

The assessment of reported information in international organizations may be delegated to independent expert bodies, to the Secretariat or to a specialized member state committee which may then report to the Conference of the Parties (*Beyerlin et al.* 2006: 364). Under the Multilateral Trade Agreements, assessment of the reported information is left to the standing committees that usually have full membership. Often the committees are to report on the operation of the Agreement in general. For instance, several committees are obliged to "review (annually) the implementation and operation of the agreement"[51] or "to monitor and report annually to the Council for Trade in Goods on the general implementation of this Agreement and make recommendations towards its improvement."[52] Some agreements set out a procedure for the assessment of specific information by requiring implementation committees to "examine" the notified measures, without, however, making an explicit reference to compliance.[53]

Only in a few cases, explicit reference is made to a role of the Secretariat by, for instance, requiring that reports of measures shall be available in the Secretariat for inspection,[54] or by requiring the Secretariat to assist the committee by preparing annually a factual report on the operation of the agreement "based on notifications and other reliable information."[55]

(c) Mechanisms of non-compliance

In international environmental law, there are in some cases formal mechanisms established for the identification and handling of problems of non-compliance (on the Ozone Regime, see Victor 1998: 137; on the Kyoto Protocol and the Aarhus Convention, see *Sands* 2006). By contrast, Multilateral Trade Agreements do not provide for non-compliance procedures on a general basis. In a few cases, implementation committees are explicitly obliged on request of a member to examine reported measures and to assess whether it is consistent with treaty obligations.[56] However, it is not clear what the consequences of the establishment of non-compliance are.

3. Trade policy review

Procedural rules for trade policy review are established in Annex 3 of the Marrakesh Agreement, and in special "Rules of Procedure."[57] The core of the trade policy review consists in a discussion of the TPRB "on the member's trade policies and practices,"[58] based on two pieces of documentation:

- a full report supplied by the member "describing the trade policies and practices pursued by the member," based on an agreed format and
- a report drawn up by the Secretariat on its own responsibility, based on the "information available to it and that provided by the member or members concerned".[59]

The rules of procedure prescribe that the reports by members shall be in the "form of policy statements," the form and length of which shall be determined by the member states. The scope of the Secretariat reports is broadened to a certain extent: Trade policies and practices are the focus, but should be seen "to the extent necessary, in the context of overall macro-economic and structural policies."[60]

In consultation with the member under review, the Chairman of the TPRB may choose discussants, who are to introduce the discussions in the TPRB. Discussants are required not to act as a representative of their country, but in a personal capacity.[61]

Annex 3 C of the Marrakesh Agreement lays down that the TPRB is to establish a "basic plan for the conduct of reviews," and based thereon, an annual program for review. Member states are subject to review of their trade policies in varying frequencies, depending on their "share of world trade." The most important traders are subject to review every two years, while the next 16 shall be reviewed every five years. The rest of the membership shall be reviewed every six years, with the possibility of extension for LDCs.[62] The rules of procedures have relaxed this rule by prescribing that the cycle of reviews shall be applied with a general flexibility of up to six months.[63] The TPRB was to review the operation of the Trade Policy Review Mechanism within five years after the entry into force of the Marrakesh Agreement (so-called appraisal).[64]

4. Dispute settlement

Procedural rules for dispute settlement procedures are set out in the Annex 2 of the Marrakesh Agreement, the Understanding on Rules and Procedures Governing the Settlement of Disputes. There also exists a body of subsidiary rules made up of various working procedures before panels and the Appellate Body (*Footer* 2006: 297). The dispute settlement procedure details of which are shown in Figure 4.2, is a multi-stage procedure.

The Dispute Settlement Procedure can only be initiated by WTO member states. As a first step, consultations are to be carried out between the parties. Only in case that these are unsuccessful for resolving the conflict, panels will be established.[65] So-called good offices, conciliation, or mediation may be entered into before the panels are established. If the parties to a dispute agree, these procedures may also continue while the panel process proceeds.[66] Parties and members are given several opportunities to make their views known before the panel report is adopted. Thus the descriptive sections of the draft report are issued to the parties, which can submit their comments in writing.[67] Also, the panel report is circulated to the members, at least, twenty days before it is considered for adoption by the members in the DSB, and members that have objections to the report shall give written reasons to explain their objections, at least, ten days prior to the meeting of the DSB at which the report will be considered.[68]

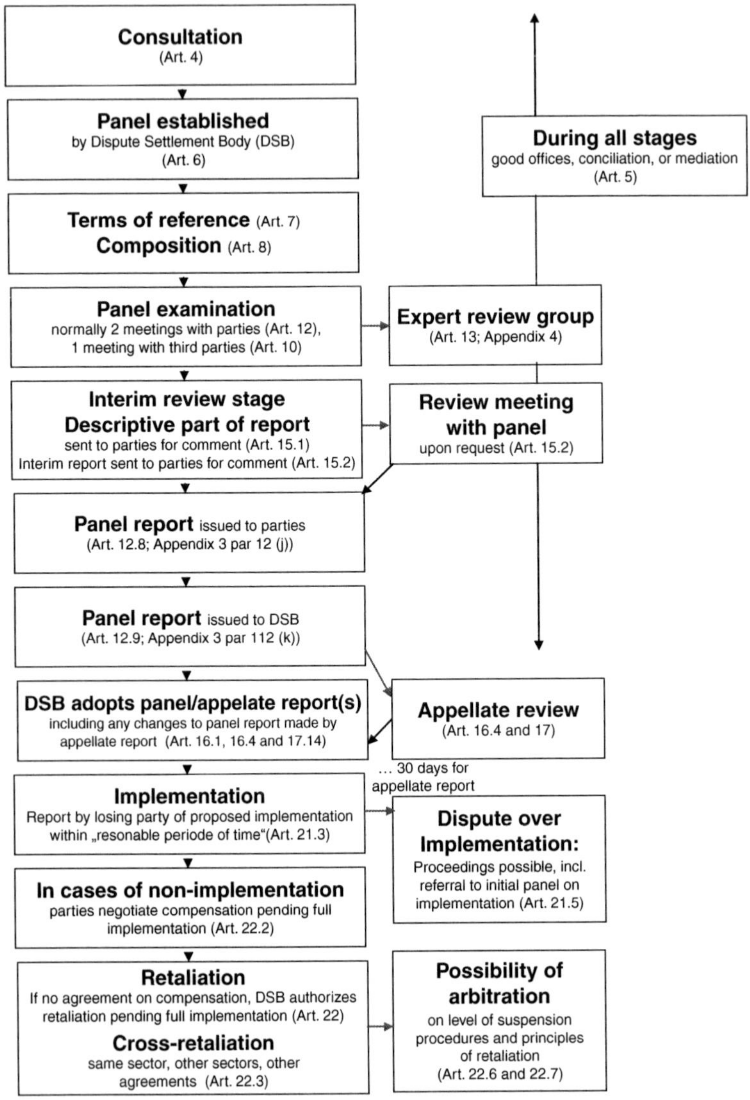

Figure 4.2 WTO dispute settlement procedure
Source: WTO 2008, p.59 rev.

If parties to the dispute fail to file appeal against a panel report, it is referred to the DSB, which can only reject it by unanimous voting.[69] Since this would require the winning party of the DSB to vote against it, panel reports are practically always accepted.

If a member country is dissatisfied with the panel report, it can file an appeal to the Standing Appellate Body concerning issues of law and legal interpretations.[70] Again, the DSB can only reject the appellate report unanimously.[71]

The proceedings of both panels and Appellate Body are confidential.[72] The text of the Understanding on Rules and Procedures Governing the Settlement of Disputes makes no reference to the rights of non-state actors in the procedure.

Special procedures have been laid down for the implementation of the panel/appellate reports. It is the responsibility of the DSB to keep under surveillance the implementation of adopted recommendations and rulings. After a "reasonable period of time" the member concerned shall provide the DSB with a status report that shows the progress in the implementation of the recommendations or rulings.[73] If a member fails to bring measures found to be inconsistent with a covered agreement into compliance within a reasonable period of time, it shall enter into negotiations with the party having invoked the dispute settlement procedure with a view to develop "mutually acceptable compensation."[74] In case that no compensation has been agreed upon within twenty days, the party that has invoked the dispute settlement procedures shall request authorization from the DSB to retaliate. In other words, it may suspend the application (to the member concerned) of concessions or other obligations under the covered agreements.[75]

The WTO Secretariat has a number of special tasks concerning dispute settlement. It has to provide technical and secretarial support, and it shall assist the panels, especially on the legal, historical and procedural aspects of the matters dealt with.[76] On request of a developing country, the Secretariat shall make available a "qualified legal expert" from the WTO technical cooperation service to any developing country member. However, the expert is to assist the developing country member "in a manner ensuring the continued impartiality of the Secretariat."[77]

The Director General – acting in an *ex officio* capacity – is explicitly authorized to offer "good offices, conciliation or mediation" with the view to assisting members to settle a dispute.[78]

It should be noted that the Marrakesh Agreement had already prescribed that the rules governing the dispute settlement procedure be reviewed by the end of 1999. As member states failed to reach an agreement, the matter was integrated into the Doha mandate, without, however, becoming part of the single undertaking. Decisions to accept amendments of the DSU could therefore be taken by consensus and could take effect for all members upon approval by the Ministerial Conference (*Footer* 2006: 212f.).

V. Summary of formal WTO characteristics

It can be concluded that the WTO possesses the characteristics of a public formal organization set out in Chapter 3, I.1. First, the WTO has members which are "actor aggregates" in form of states. Second, the WTO is oriented toward the pursuit of specific goals which serve the public interest. The most important one is trade liberalization. Third, the WTO also exhibits a formalized organizational structure designed to coordinate the activities of members toward goal attainment. Thus the Ministerial Conference, the General Council, and the various committees have been established to ensure that the members can pursue the goal of trade liberalization by making new trade agreements, by administering existing agreements, conducting trade policy reviews and settling disputes. Fourth, execution of these tasks is guided by an elaborate set of procedural rules.

Given that the WTO possesses the characteristics of a public formal organization, it should be analyzed as such. Defining the WTO a priori as a regime and not as an organization, based on characteristics such as the lack of a "separate will" as set out by *Footer* (2006: 78ff.), would be misleading (see Chapter 3, I.1). However, the analysis also has to move beyond formal characteristics, and to take into account actor characteristics and informal decision making which will be explored in Chapter 5.

5
The WTO in Action

The purpose of this chapter is to analyze how the WTO functions in practice. Particular regard is paid to the role of the WTO as a corporate and/or collective actor, the relevance of informal structures and procedures and the role of external actors such as intergovernmental organizations and NGOs. The analysis also includes the areas of technical assistance and research which have a supporting function for negotiations and implementation.

Clearly, the WTO is a conglomerate of formal and informal structures and procedures. Chapter 5 focuses on informal structures and procedures given that formal structures and procedures have already been extensively discussed in Chapter 4. In the literature on international organizations, aspects of informality are frequently mentioned but hardly analyzed in a systematic way. In particular, references to organization theory and other theoretical concepts of informal decision making are missing (see as examples *Karns and Mingst* 2004: 56ff.; *Rittberger and Zangl* 2003: 139). Only recently, scholars have started to describe informal procedures in the European Union (*Christiansen et al.* 2003; *Heisenberg* 2005) and in the WTO (*Steinberg* 2002; *Footer* 2006: 110ff.) in a more systematic way. However, the analyses suffer from the lack of a clear definition of the concept of informality. Furthermore, the different importance of informal procedures in different areas (such as negotiations, implementation, trade policy review, and dispute settlement) is not accounted for. In this respect, Chapter 5 aims at making a contribution by systematically distinguishing between different types of informal structures and procedures within the WTO, and by accounting for the different importance of informal decision making in different areas of activities, based on concepts derived from organization theory.

I. Trade negotiations and related areas of activities

1. Trade negotiations

(a) Informal structure of the WTO

Various informal structures in the WTO can be distinguished. First, there are various groups of member states within the WTO, and, second, so-called friends of the chair who help to establish consensus during negotiations.

Groups in the WTO which have a very limited membership may consist of the major trading powers. Traditionally, this position has been occupied by the "Quad" which consisted of the United States, the European Union, Canada, and Japan (*Footer* 2006: 168). Now the old Quad has been replaced. Efforts to restart the Doha Round after the breakdown in Cancún required negotiations between the Five Interested Parties (the European Union, United States, Brazil, India, and Australia) (*Wolfe* 2005: 639), thereby reflecting the growing powers of Brazil and India. The group is now known under the name G-4 comprising the European Union, United States, Brazil, and India. An NGO has pointed to the fact that the group may also meet with Australia and Japan as G-6, but that G-4 is now considered really as the "inner circle."

There has been a trend in the last two or three years that informal groups have emerged within the WTO, through which developing countries with similar interests work together. Examples for developing country groupings are the G-20,[1] the G-33,[2] and the African Group.[3] It is particularly the G-20 group which is found to be influential in negotiations on agriculture (*Gallagher* 2005: 124): it thwarted European efforts to introduce a series of new issues (investment, procurement, competition policy) into the negotiating agenda of the Doha Round (*Higgott* 2005: 32).

For negotiations in councils and committees delegates are appointed by chairpersons as "friends of the chair." They were used extensively throughout the Uruguay Round "in various consultative procedures in order to bring closure on certain issues in draft text that were taken up in negotiating groups," and they have been a regular feature of the WTO ever since (*Footer* 2006: 172). Their task continues to help building consensus by consulting with delegations individually or collectively or "possibly in so-called closed door confessionals." For Ministerial Conferences, ministers are appointed as friends of the chair and seek to build consensus on specific issues (*Blackhurst and Hartridge* 2004: 712).

The question is whether the various types of informal structures in the WTO described under the preceding section fulfill the criteria for informal structures as described in Chapter 3, I.3.b. Informal structures have the following features: structures are unregulated and legally non-binding. The function of these structures is to enable actions which are based on a "give and take" basis (exchange pattern). The last feature of informal structures is that they complement formal structures or represent alternatives to them.

The various types of informal structures in the WTO described in this section fulfill these criteria. The operation of groups like G-4, G-20, or "friends of the chair" is not regulated through any official rules nor legally binding. In fact, the body of rules governing the operation of the WTO does not even mention their existence. Since the purpose of these groups is to find compromises between conflicting positions, their functioning reflects an exchange pattern. Finally, these groups represent an alternative to setting up new committees or other bodies, and complement the formal organizational structure of the WTO.

(b) Informal procedures within the WTO

Non-regulated meetings or consultations in the WTO come in various forms and formats: first, on a regular basis, there are (a) open-ended meetings, (b) restricted sessions, and (c) the so-called confessionals, all of which are organized under the invitation of the chairman of a committee or council. Second, there are Green Room meetings[4] organized on invitation of the Director General either in Geneva or during Ministerial Conferences. Third, there are restricted meetings between groups of member states which have neither received an official mandate by the chairman of a council or committee nor by the Director General. These meetings are therefore characterized as being "outside the Geneva process." These are for instance meetings of small groups of powerful members and of larger groups representing developing countries.

Table 5.1 summarizes the special features of the different non-regulated procedures related to WTO negotiations.

Open-ended meetings have the broadest range of participants, since the entire membership would be allowed to attend. These meetings are called by the chair of a specific negotiating group to explore to what extent the membership can depart from what their instructions have been. *For restricted meetings,* a chairperson chooses the delegations that could attend. The "*confessionals*" are meetings, in which only one delegation and the chairperson are present. The purpose is the determination of the position of a single country: a delegation would only communicate to the chairperson "what the bottom line" of a delegation is. The member would never communicate it if other persons were in the room.

Table 5.1 Non-regulated procedures within the WTO

Features	Types of procedures					
	Restricted	**Confessional**	**Open-ended**	**Green Room**	**Larger Group Meetings**[a]	**Smaller Group Meetings**[b]
Initiative						
Committee Chairman	x	x	x			
Director General				x		
Members					x	x
Purpose						
Finding compromises	x		x	x		x
Determining position of a single country		x				
Seeking re-insurance on compromises			x		x	
Participation						
Committee Chairman	Partially or Friend of the Chair	x or Friend of the Chair	x			
Secretariat	x		x	x		
Director General				x		
Members	selected	one	All	selected	Group members	Group members

[a]developing countries, e.g. G-20.
[b]powerful countries, e.g. G-4.

Typically, open-ended meetings, restricted sessions and formal meetings are sequenced. A typical negotiation week regarding the negotiations on agriculture in Geneva under the Doha mandate was described by a representative of a G4-Developing Country as follows:

> I mean you start the week with an open-ended meeting, in fact [the chairperson] invites delegations to the meeting, says he is going to leave time for delegations to meet. He hopes that everybody makes the most consultations they can, so that you can help push the process forward. And then he himself has his consultations with groups or with delegations, and then these small meetings during the week, and then by the end of the week, let's say on a Friday, he usually calls up again an open-ended meeting, many times followed by a formal session of the Special Session. The open-ended ... is informal, and then followed by a formal.

The Secretariat used similar terms to describe a back-and-forth process:

> The chairs go through confessionals, they go through small group meetings, they go through big group meetings and then they go back to open-ended meetings followed by formal meetings.

An executive of the Secretariat also confirmed that normally in committees or at the TNC level, one would start with large transparent meetings, where proposals are put forward and debated. If all the material was on the table, then one would try to organize smaller group discussions because negotiations with 150 people in the same room were impossible.

Typically, restricted meetings also dominate the negotiation process of Ministerial Conferences to a large extent. The negotiation process of Ministerial Conferences was described by an NGO as follows:

> I mean there are a lot of rumours, there is a lot of tension in the ministerials, a lot of processes are happening at a parallel time, I think in part it's almost a confusion strategy, you know, like there is an informal here, ... and I think also because different members are trying to kind of group amongst themselves, building their coalitions, so I think it's very hard to see where what decision is precisely being developed. And suddenly then it's like you might have a smaller group, they agree upon something, they then present it to a bigger group, they then present it to an even bigger group, suddenly it's not any more a small group suggesting, but it's something that almost anybody has agreed, and then those that do not agree are seen as those blocking.

A special type of non-regulated procedure is the so-called Green Room meetings, which are organized on invitation of the Director General during Ministerial Conferences. Other Green Room meetings may be organized on WTO premises in Geneva at ambassadorial level upon the initiative of the Director General (*Blackhurst and Hartridge* 2004: 711; *Footer* 2006: 167f.). According to Secretariat staff and a representative of a G-4 Developed Country, 30–40 ministers are invited to find a compromise under the chairmanship of the Director General, which is then presented to the membership. According to a WTO member and the Secretariat, it is the responsibility of the Director General to select members to be invited to the Green Room meetings.

Finally, delegations can also come together on their own initiative in various constellations and in groups, which is qualified as meetings "outside the Geneva process." A representative of the Secretariat stressed that the underlying idea is that they indicate to the rest of the membership that they have met and that they bring the results of these talks back into the "Geneva process." As a representative of the Secretariat explained, some of these meetings outside the "Geneva process" are even organized on ministerial levels. One example is the so-called mini-ministerials, where some member states invite 30 ministers, which talk about important issues. These meetings are held in advance of Ministerial Conferences in order to "take stock of ongoing negotiations" (*Footer* 2006: 169).

Meetings "outside the Geneva process" comprise meetings of the various groups which have been described in the preceding section as informal structures. The purpose of *meetings of small groups* of powerful countries like the G-4 is usually the establishment of compromises, which can then be "sold" to the entire WTO membership. The purpose of *meetings of larger groups of developing countries* is the establishment of a common position and the provision of information on compromises reached in informal "restricted" meetings from which many group members were excluded. A representative of a G-4 Developing Country explained how a group coordinator is given the responsibility to disseminate information to the group regarding smaller meetings or informal meetings from which members of the group had been excluded:

> So when these smaller group meetings take place, it is the G-20 members who are participating in those smaller groups. They will come back immediately to their group, and tell them what is happening, and what the mandate is, whether they can do that, not do that. [...] It's more like a representation.

To summarize the findings, the initiative for the procedures can either lie with the chairman of a committee or council (for restricted, open-ended meetings or confessionals), the Director General (for the Green Room meetings), or with members (larger group meetings or smaller group meetings). The overall purpose is always the establishment of compromises. To this end, confessionals are held for the determination of the position of a single country, while larger group meetings may also be held for the seeking of reinsurance on compromises achieved in restricted informal meetings. Participation in these meetings varies. The Secretariat is present except in group meetings and confessionals. The Director General is only present in Green Room meetings.

The various types of procedures in the WTO described in this section fulfill the criteria of informality as outlined in Chapter 3, I.3.b: unregulated and non-binding, exchange pattern, and alternative or complement to formal procedures. The Green Room procedures may be taken as an example. They are unregulated since WTO rules of procedure do not apply. There are no minutes that account for the course of negotiations and the positions taken by member states. The purpose of a Green Room meeting is to find compromises between conflicting positions and interests of the most relevant actors on a "give and take" basis. At the same time, ministers in a Green Room meeting cannot take a decision that is binding for WTO membership. Binding decisions in Ministerial Conferences can only be reached by the Trade Negotiations Committee. Decisions taken in the Green Room complement formal decision procedures.

Informal meetings play a very important role in the negotiations of the WTO. This has been confirmed in most interviews and also in the survey of member state delegations. Figure 5.1 shows how member state delegates view the frequency of informal meetings in the WTO.

The overwhelming majority of 85% of the member states which responded to the questionnaire view informal procedures as occurring often or very often. Developed countries have a tendency to stress the frequency of informal procedures even more than developing countries, with more than 60% indicating that informal procedures occur "very often."

The dominance of informal meetings is partly explained by the fact that formal meetings have important limitations because everything that one says goes to the minutes. By contrast, informal meetings are never recorded in minutes. Both a G-4 Developing Country and the European Commission argued that the consequence is that in a formal

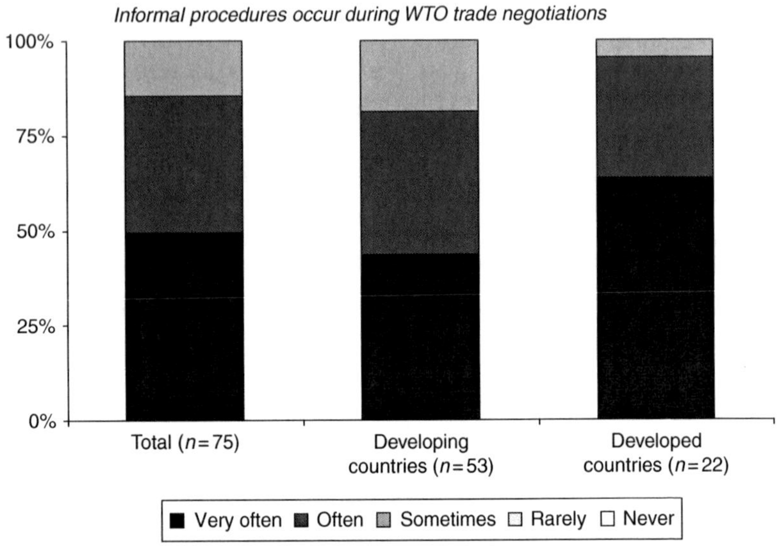

Figure 5.1 Frequency of informal meetings in the WTO

meeting everyone conveys official positions, whereas in informal meetings, according to the interviews, people could talk more freely. A G-4 Developed Country described informal meetings as a laboratory "for exploring possible small progress towards consensus" by avoiding conflicts at the same time:[5]

> Informal meetings are very important. Why? Because the most important criteria for informal meetings is that you don't have records. And this might be a small or minor point, but actually for the heads of the delegates or ambassadors it means that there will not be the opportunity for the capital to check what has been said in the meeting, because there is no record. So you don't have like, the mother-in-law behind you in a position to check, hey, I sent you instructions, and you didn't say that. So the interest of informal meetings is simply that it would allow delegates to take some margin of manoeuvre and to depart a little bit from the instructions that they have from capital. The interest for the chairs of those meetings is to try and see if by departing a little bit from your instructions you can have some room of compromise with others who would also depart a little bit from the instructions.

(c) Role of the Secretariat

The analysis focuses on whether the Secretariat has any influence on the direction of the formal negotiations. Potential ways of exerting influence are by drafting agendas and minutes, by giving advice to the chairpersons of committees and councils and by drafting reports for him or her (which are sent to the General Council and the Ministerial Conference), and by giving information and informal advice to the member states.

In terms of staff, the direct support of negotiations is not the most important task of the Secretariat. An interview partner from the Secretariat estimated that only about 10% of the Secretariat staff service the negotiations. The representative of a developing country pointed out that Secretariat staff is required to attend all formal meetings and to assist the chair. The representative observed that communication during meetings is mainly between the chair and the member states. The Secretariat would only take the floor, if member states explicitly asked it a question. Both Secretariat and a development-oriented NGO confirmed that the Secretariat attends also every informal meeting, as long as it is part of the "Geneva process." By contrast, informal meetings "outside the Geneva process" are not attended by the Secretariat. The Director General may participate, as the Secretariat explained, if he is invited.

Several interview partners denied that the Secretariat can exert influence on the negotiations through the drafting of the agenda or the drafting of the minutes. A developing country explained that the agenda and the calendar of meetings are agreed through the chair and the discussion with the members. The Secretariat only gives some information and some insights if it is called upon.

Also, the influence through drafting the minutes was characterized as "minimal" by representatives of the Secretariat, a G-4 Developing Country and other developing countries. This is because members can challenge them in case they perceive the minutes to be inaccurate. At every meeting the Secretariat tapes the discussion and in the event of a challenge by a member state these tapes can be heard. There were instances in which member states used that possibility, as representatives of member states and the Secretariat explained.

Chairpersons can play an important role in the consensus-building process at all levels (*Footer* 2006: 170). The chairperson usually has the powers to decide whether and in which type of meetings issues shall be discussed separately, and the chairperson can also produce draft texts to the membership (*Footer* 2006: 171). Draft texts are especially important for the preparation of Ministerial Conferences. A representative of the

Secretariat reported that ministers rejected the idea that draft texts sent to ministers before the Ministerial Conference should represent all points of view on the agreement. They made clear to the Director General that if political decisions are to be taken within five to six days, they need "a manageable list of issues and a manageable list of options," which is to be prepared by the General Council and the Trade Negotiations Committee.

To understand the (potential) role of the Secretariat regarding the negotiations, it is important to consider that if a delegate is appointed as chairperson of a committee, he or she is not allowed to receive input in their work from his or her national government or from the Geneva mission. A Secretariat official stressed that he or she has to organize mission work so that he or she is isolated from national positions. The consequence is, according to the Secretariat, that the chairperson really depends on the Secretariat for advice and support.

The same representative was quite frank regarding the influence of the Secretariat on negotiations through the chairperson. Asked whether the WTO Secretariat should be endowed with the formal right to make proposals, the representative of the Secretariat explained:

> We do that anyway informally. We can use our advice to chairpersons and say: This is probably not a good idea, that is a better option to go with and so on. We can influence, not because we want to influence, but because we think we provide our advice and our judgement to chairpersons who then work with the membership to take the work in a certain direction that they are undertaking. So I think we do have that capacity to influence. But it is not overt.

The Secretariat may have opportunities to influence the negotiations by advising the chairperson of committees how to direct negotiations. A G-4 Developing Country and an NGO stressed that the influence of the Secretariat on negotiations must be seen as being contingent on the personality of the chairperson. An NGO representative pointed out:

> So it will depend on the person how much the Secretariat will influence or not. Because it might be a chair that's very savvy and that doesn't want to give everything up to the Secretariat, and there might be others that are really happy.

An intergovernmental development-oriented organization argued that a chairperson coming from a developing country is more likely to rely heavily on the Secretariat than an ambassador from a developed country.

The drafting of the chairperson report (which serves as a basis for negotiations of the Ministerial Conference and the Ministerial Declaration) was seen by the intergovernmental organization as a key opportunity for the Secretariat to influence negotiations:

> The Chair's draft report, for example – that work is for the Secretariat. Whoever writes the first draft, always gets the first crack in shaping whatever will come out in terms of the report.

It usually remains unclear to WTO member countries what the precise influence of the Secretariat on the draft report is, when they enter into discussions with the chairperson. A developing country official observed:

> And that is the time he has to be assisted by the Secretariat. Perhaps, that is where there is a question mark, because sometimes a majority of members would insist on changing the language, and you find the chairman coming up with the same language. [...] You don't have the proof, but at this point you could suspect, because he is assisted by the Secretariat which comes up with a text.

Other interview partners from a G-4 Developing Country and from an NGO emphasized that attempts of the Secretariat to influence negotiations in the WTO by influencing the negotiated text are in any case closely observed and controlled by developing member countries. The representative of a G-4 Developing Country explained:

> I am not saying that there have not been instances where a particular nuance is given [by the Secretariat] to certain things, which would try and influence the discussion. But I think, by and large, nowadays members are more aware, they are more involved in the negotiating process, and hence, this kind of thing is on the decline.

An NGO representative added:

> They also have to be very careful, because especially developing countries really don't want a proactive Secretariat. So if they do one thing, they do what they were not commissioned to do, then that would not be appreciated.

Similarly, an interview partner from a development-oriented NGO emphasized that the "neutrality of the Secretariat is very important to member state delegations." They do not want the Secretariat or the Director General to influence the negotiations or to "take the negotiations on a particular path."

The Secretariat pointed to the fact that it employs another way of informally influencing the member states without working through the chairman or providing formulations for the negotiated text. Informally, the Secretariat meets with delegations which may ask for advice, and "sometimes take account of that advice at an informal level." According to a Secretariat official, the same member country may then say at a formal level, for instance at a General Council, that something is perceived as a problem.

As mentioned above, the role of the Director General in negotiations is not formally defined. In literature (*Gallagher* 2005) and in interviews with a G-4 Developing Country it is described as being one of an "honest broker." The scope of tasks of the Director General is partially based on tradition extending to the GATT times. There is, for instance, a tradition of the Director General chairing the Trade Negotiations Committee of various rounds. An NGO indicated that the role of the Director General in the Uruguay Round was to meet with members, to get members to make concessions in order to reach a consensus. The Secretariat explained that there is also a tradition of the Director General to attend informal meetings that are organized outside the Geneva process on invitation to represent member countries that are not invited and to report back to them.

There is broad agreement among NGOs that the role of the Director General and the scope of his tasks depend mainly on the personality of the person who holds the post, but also on the circumstances.

As outlined above, the Director General lacks the formal right to make negotiation proposals (even in the event of a negotiation impasse). However, a Director General can nevertheless intervene in WTO negotiations with concrete proposals on an informal basis. One example is the so-called *Dunkel* draft produced by Arthur Dunkel who had been Director General of the GATT for many years to move forward the stalled Uruguay Round. The proposal led to the eventual successful conclusion of the round (*Footer* 2006: 171). In the view of an executive of the Secretariat, such a proposal can be made if the Director General is respected as a personality and intervenes at the right point in time:

> At a certain point – admittedly very late in the negotiations – he basically proposed an overall compromised text, encompassing in all of the areas. He basically took all of the work product from these various committees, at whatever stage of completeness they were. Some of them were very much completed, some of them had major gaps in them. Then he proposed a comprehensive text to resolve all the differences. So this was a Director General exercising a certain power of initiative.

Also the Director General *Peter Sutherland* played a very active role. In the view of the Secretariat executive, however, his successor *Ruggiero* faced a "major backlash" both from the members and from the general public when the anti-mobilization movement grew stronger. When *Ruggiero* sought to organize a meeting for the preparation of the Seattle Ministerial Conference, the United States and the European Union basically refused to attend, arguing that the Director General did not have the power to call for these meetings.

In the view of an NGO, the new Director General *Pascal Lamy* is generally regarded as a very active Director General, who "puts steam behind the agenda." He has called meetings of smaller groups or convened ministerials, which would normally take place "outside the Geneva process." *Pascal Lamy* was also the one who presented a draft text for the Hong Kong Ministerial Conference even though this would have normally been the task of the chair of the General Council.

To summarize, the influence of the Secretariat and the Director General on negotiations is highly contingent on persons and situations. In the past, the Secretariat has played, at times, a pivotal role in shaping and facilitating multilateral trade negotiations (*Xu and Weller* 2004: 252). However, the influence of the Secretariat is hidden and informal in nature since many WTO members do not want the Secretariat to exert influence over the negotiations. Secretariat staff has opportunities to influence the negotiations by, for instance, advising the chairperson of committees how to direct negotiations. In other cases, chairpersons may be more reluctant to accept Secretariat advice. Another possibility is that the Secretariat meets members on an informal basis and seeks to influence them.

The Director General can exert some influence on the preferences and policy decisions of WTO members, depending on his personality and the situation. This influence is not necessarily hidden: If the Director General is a respected personality who is seen as being able to overcome a negotiation impasse, he may play openly an active role, by for instance scheduling meetings of small groups. As the Uruguay Round demonstrates, he may even table a proposal on how an overall compromise can be reached. However, with regard to a different person or situation, WTO members may not tolerate this.

(d) Relations between WTO and international organizations

As outlined in Chapter 3, I.2, the analysis of the relationships between the WTO and other intergovernmental organizations is focused here on two intergovernmental development-oriented organizations based in Geneva, the UNCTAD, and the South Centre.

The fact that WTO member countries require resources to participate effectively in WTO trade negotiations which are currently not provided by the WTO Secretariat influences the relationship between WTO and UNCTAD/the South Centre. Both intergovernmental organizations seek to provide expertise and advice to WTO member countries. UNCTAD was established in 1964 with the objective to promote the development-friendly integration of developing countries into the world economy. The first United Nations Conference on Trade and Development (UNCTAD) was held in Geneva in 1964. This conference was then institutionalized to meet every four years, with intergovernmental bodies meeting between sessions and a permanent secretariat providing the necessary support.[6] Hence, UNCTAD has been described as a permanent conference whose aim is to promote economic development. While the organization has 192 member states, including all developed countries, developing countries "have come to regard UNCTAD as their own forum" (*Durán* 2005: 463). The Secretariat has 400 staff and is based in Geneva. The budget of UNCTAD is ca. 45 Mio. US Dollars from the UN budget, and 24 Mio. US Dollars from extra-budgetary sources.[7]

The organization now functions as a forum for intergovernmental deliberations aimed at consensus building, it undertakes research, policy analysis, and data collection, and it provides technical assistance tailored to the specific requirements of developing countries.[8] The UNCTAD Conferences meetings have updated the mandate of the organization every four years. The most recent mandates are set out in the Hong Kong Declaration (2000)[9] and the Sao Paulo Consensus (2004).[10] Following the Hong Kong Declaration, UNCTAD shall provide analytical and technical support to developing countries in possible areas of negotiations and in the area of accession. It shall also support their capacity-building process and provide a forum for the exchange of views and information (136).[11] In the 2004 Sao Paulo Consensus, it is set out that UNCTAD should help develop capacities in developing countries to establish their own negotiating priorities and to negotiate trade agreements including under the Doha Work Programme.[12]

Both UNCTAD and the South Centre have a formal and an informal role in the negotiations at the WTO. Formally, they can be accredited as observers to negotiations depending on the specific WTO body (committee or council). Formally or informally, they can act as consultants or even coalition-builder. UNCTAD is observer in most of the official (formal) bodies, with the exception of some with a very specific negotiating track. According to an interview partner from the organization, the role of UNCTAD in these meetings is a rather passive one:

> Sometimes they would pose a question to us, then we would say, we take note, or yes, we can do that, but we don't really take the floor and say something. Sometimes we are invited for presentations.

The underlying assumption is that observers are not really expected to participate actively in the discussions.

An interview partner from UNCTAD explained that the UNCTAD staff is not invited to the informal meetings within the WTO. Sometimes, if a formal meeting switched to an informal meeting, UNCTAD observers would stay in the same room. However, normally they felt that it was inappropriate for them to attend informal meetings. According to the UNCTAD official, to obtain information and documents on these informal meetings, UNCTAD staff relied much more on member states than on the Secretariat.

Despite the fact that UNCTAD has a formal mandate to help developing countries to negotiate trade agreements, they provide concrete advice usually on an informal basis, thereby acting as a consultant for states that are both members of the WTO and UNCTAD. An UNCTAD official explained:

> The informal advice, we do watch, it's never [UNCTAD] official advice.... And many times we are even careful not to send it by email from A to B. We go and give a document, we go and give a floppy. [...] We have to be that careful.

The same official confirmed that much in this area depends on personal relationships. If delegates of UNCTAD member countries trusted an employee of the UNCTAD Secretariat, they would frequently turn to him or her with specific questions or for a discussion of new ideas.

If a proposal was introduced in WTO negotiations that might harm the interests of member states, the reaction of UNCTAD would be to provide technical analysis. However, the organization could not start a campaign against it.

The second intergovernmental development-oriented organization, the South Centre, was set up in 1994 with the objective of enhancing cooperation among developing countries.[13] Its predecessor was the "South Commission" which was established in Geneva in 1987. The South Commission reported "that the South is not well organized at the global level and has thus not been effective in mobilizing its considerable combined expertise and experience, nor its bargaining power." Hence, the South Centre was set up to assist "in developing points of view of the South on major policy issues," in generating ideas and action-oriented proposals and in responding to ad hoc needs or requests for policy advice and for technical and other support from collective entities of the South such as the Group of 77. To this end, the South Centre shall define and implement programs of analysis and research and give wide distribution to the results of its work.[14]

Any developing country (i.e. a country that is a member of the Group of 77 and China) can become a member of the South Centre by acceding to the Intergovernmental Agreement Establishing the South Centre. Currently, 51 countries are member states. However, the Centre has stressed that it works for the benefit of the South as a whole. Therefore it makes efforts to ensure that all developing countries have access to its publications and the results of its work, irrespective of membership.[15]

The South Centre has a much more limited observer status in the WTO than UNCTAD: It is accredited only to specific sub-bodies, like the Committee on Trade and Development. The organization seeks to provide for more transparency in the WTO trade negotiations by publishing "analytical notes" reflecting the state of play in the negotiations by giving a detailed account of positions of all groups. Other publications are made in form of working papers and occasional papers. However, the organization made it clear that it cannot be seen as "the voice of developing countries, since its publications do not go through any official clearing mechanism by its member states."

The South Centre argued that it seeks to influence negotiations in the WTO by providing "negotiating support" to its member countries. Sometimes its staff even helps "drafting the language of negotiating proposals" for developing countries. Moreover, the organization convenes informal meetings between developing countries to improve coordination between them. According to the South Centre, its objective is to help assist the developing countries "work out their differences, so when they go to the WTO, developing countries can present as a united front in the negotiations."

The South Centre indicated that its contacts with the WTO Secretariat are rather minimal and very informal. Sometimes staff approaches selected personnel to which a relationship had been built to obtain some information. The general approach was, however, to have an "arm's length relationship." A South Centre official explained this distance by the impression that the ethos of the WTO Secretariat is felt to be a different one:

> The South Centre's focus really is on development issues: we believe that trade of course can be an engine for development under certain circumstances, when you sequence it properly, and institutionally the ethos in the WTO Secretariat might not be the same as what we have.

The impression is that developing countries turn to other intergovernmental organizations such as UNCTAD and/or the South Centre for consultancy. This must be seen as an indicator for the need for expertise and advice which developing countries have, and which apparently is not satisfied by the WTO Secretariat.

(e) Relations between WTO and NGOs

NGOs have very few formal rights concerning trade negotiations in the WTO. They have no permanent accreditation to the WTO. They are not allowed to enter the WTO building in Geneva (unless as guest of a delegation), and they are barred from attending formal or informal meetings of trade negotiating bodies. The only exception is the Ministerial Conferences for which NGOs can be accredited (*Davey* 2005: 87), if they fit the description in Art. 5.2 of the Marrakesh Agreement: "NGOs concerned with matters related to those of the WTO." The process of accreditation, however, has met with criticism. In the view of an NGO interview partner, the Secretariat lacks any clear criteria or rules on what an NGO is. As a result, sometimes governmental advisory bodies have obtained accreditation for Ministerial Conferences. Also, there was no clear policy how many representatives of a particular NGO or its sub-divisions could be accredited.

The consequence of accreditation is that NGOs can attend the official meetings and parts of the official statements at the Ministerial Conference, or that they could at least see a video broadcast to another room.

However, they cannot go to informal meetings "where the real negotiations take place." An NGO representative explained that they can seek access to meet delegates in conference breaks, as it happened in Cancún:

> NGOs were kept outside, we could, however, you know, be in the area where the delegations were hanging out for coffee, and you could like there try to chat and figure out what is happening. There is lots of like leaks and information flow going to and from, but you would not go all to the inside.

Much depends, however, on the individual set-up of the building in which the Ministerial Conference is hosted. An NGO pointed out that delegates and NGOs in Hong Kong hardly met in restaurants and cafés. They would rather stay in different parts of the building since member state delegates had their own restaurants, which NGOs were not allowed to enter. As a result, conference delegates would only walk over to those restaurants and cafés which NGOs were allowed to use if they had made specific appointments.

Despite their lack of formal rights, NGOs seek to influence the negotiations in Geneva in various ways. Based on observation of negotiations, NGOs may act as communicator, campaigner, supervisor, or advocate/consultant.

Several NGOs argued that setting up an office in Geneva facilitates the observation of the negotiations, and enables the NGO to understand and communicate what is negotiated and what the positions of the countries are:

> And I would say that most of our work is about finding out what's happening at the WTO, trying to understand what is the situation, what is the balance in terms of different positions, and what are the patterns, the different proposals on the table. So there is a lot of intelligence gathering, information gathering, which is one part.

Information about the negotiations is distributed through the External Relations Division of the Secretariat, which organizes regular informal briefings in which NGOs are informed about what is happening in the negotiations (*Davey* 2005: 87). This is useful for a large number of NGOs. After the new Director General *Pascal Lamy* came into office, he himself started briefing the NGOs. This move is seen as following from the open personal attitude of *Pascal Lamy* toward NGOs.

The Secretariat also increasingly publishes negotiation proposals on the Internet. However, in the view of an NGO this was based on the consent of the member states:

> They increasingly publish negotiation proposals by members, but this is because members let them do that. So it is really the members that have changed their way of looking at these things, and that allows the Secretariat to be more and more transparent.

Even though the Secretariat has made considerable efforts in making information public, member states are generally considered a better source of information for NGOs than the Secretariat. NGOs argued that they often turn to member states to obtain specific documents and information from the negotiations. The reason is that the Secretariat is not allowed to release unofficial documents related to informal meetings to NGOs without the consent of the participating member states. At the same time, NGOs can always find one participating member state which is interested in making a document available to them.

In general, NGOs in Geneva seek to influence the outcome of the negotiations in one way or the other in accordance with the cause for which they are set up. They use both direct and indirect ways. Means employed are

- making information available which is related to negotiations to foster public debates,
- campaigning for NGO objectives,
- complaining to chairpersons on procedural issues, and
- giving advice to developing countries.

One NGO pointed out that a more democratic process could be created by communicating the positions held by WTO member countries back into domestic arenas where they were often unknown. Another NGO representative explained:

> Our main role is to collect information. Because we find that the outside world doesn't have much information on what's going on. Even some of the members don't have enough information. So what we try to do is to find out what is happening. Some information is public, but it's not what you want. I mean if you come and the paper is there, but nobody sort of gives it to the public. We try to do that.

Some NGOs in Geneva are very active in trying to get documents related to informal meetings from member countries and in publishing them on their web page.

This indirect approach, however, is in many cases complemented by a more direct approach. For instance, a development-oriented NGO explained that it campaigns and uses the media to raise awareness in the general public about issues related to the WTO and how they impact on everybody's life, in particular on the life of the population in developing countries.

Attempts of NGOs to influence negotiations at the WTO are not limited to issues of substance; they may also extend to procedure. If a particular NGO with a strong interest in questions of governance finds out that in their view certain decisions at the WTO are taken without proper consultation of developing countries, it will send letters to the respective negotiating committee or to the person in charge, and will criticize the issue. Their experience is that the chairperson would sometimes ignore this, but sometimes he or she invites the NGO to have a discussion on this issue. The NGO explained that while a chairperson would not necessarily admit to be at fault, the fact of being under observation could still have an impact on the organization of the negotiations:

> But they would know that another time they might be watched, there might be more opposition, so they might not do it again, or do it in a different way.

Secretariat staff observed that an increasingly important way of NGOs influencing negotiations is to give advice to smaller developing countries:

> We know for a fact that a lot of delegations have been getting instructions from NGOs for better or for worse. Many of them believe that these NGOs are providing good analytical information, but it may not be to their interest or in the WTO's overall interest.

Figure 5.2 depicts how the usefulness of NGO advice to developing countries is evaluated by developing country and developed countries.

Developing countries are rather reserved regarding NGO advice to them. Forty-three percent believe that NGOs give often or very often useful advice to them. Another 40% of the developing countries believe

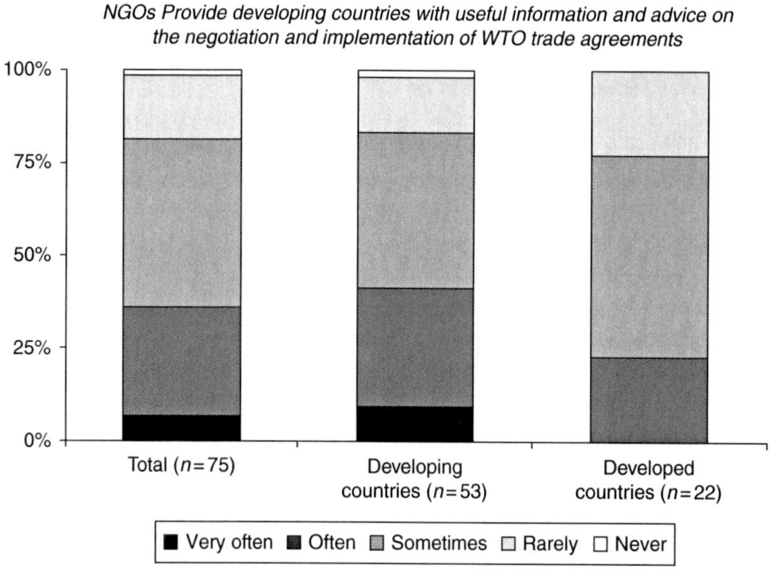

Figure 5.2 Assessment of NGO information and advice to developing countries

that NGOs give at least "sometimes" useful advice to them. Developed countries which themselves do not receive advice are much more skeptical regarding the usefulness of advice by developing countries. Only 20% of the developed countries believe that NGOs give "often" useful advice to developing countries. The vast majority believes that this is only sometimes the case. These findings are confirmed in the interviews. One NGO observed that the European Union and the United States are not satisfied that developing countries receive advice from NGOs. The European Union and the United States argued that it is very dangerous for developing countries to receive advice from NGOs. This reflects probably a certain fear that NGO advice will prevent developing countries from compromising their position.

The Secretariat confirmed that it is rather the smaller developing countries that accept the advice, since they have realized that they lack capacity to deal with the complex trade issues involved in an overloaded negotiations agenda. An NGO explained that while India, Brazil, and China do not need this advice, smaller African countries would often take it. A Secretariat official explained:

> That basically means for a small country delegation with very little support from back home (because the ministry is only a hand full of people), you are going to get analysis from NGOs.

However, the same interview partner from the Secretariat argued that there are also developing countries which have shown themselves to be fundamentally opposed to accepting advice from NGOs:

> A lot of times many developing country ministers have turned up and rejected certain of the NGOs positions because they said, they don't know what's good for us and they shouldn't be telling us what is good for us. So I think, I don't know where the agendas are set, what they are trying to do. It is just creating it seems to me a competing government.

NGOs pointed out that in order to be able to influence and advise developing countries (and to influence the public), many groups conduct their own research and studies. In the view of an NGO, NGOs might even help developing countries in some cases to draft suggestions. Another way of influencing the delegates from developing countries is to inform them on the domestic debates regarding trade policy in industrialized countries. According to an NGO, this is supposed to help developing countries to understand that certain negotiation proposals in industrialized countries are only made for tactical reasons and that they cannot be taken seriously.

An NGO concluded that as a result of the new approach, new issue-specific coalitions between NGOs and developing countries have been built. In the past, developing countries would be very reluctant to engage with NGOs, however, more recently a number of countries has realized that NGOs, as the NGO representative put it, "could be very helpful for them in advancing their own interests." The first issues on which these new coalitions were built were intellectual property rights and their relationship with public health and access to medicine. The NGOs were very supportive of developing countries' position. Another example is, according to the NGO representative, the so-called cotton initiative.[16] The observation that coalitions between NGOs and developing countries have now been built has been confirmed in literature. The trend of building alliances of northern development NGOs with developing country delegations has been noticed since Seattle (*Mason* 2004: 571). It became obvious in Cancún where "most high-profile NGOs, such as Greenpeace, Oxfam, and Public Citizen, explicitly backed the developing countries' stand, and heavily criticized developed countries, in particular the United States and the European Union, for a lack of consideration for their poorer trading partners (*Cho* 2004: 235).

The fact that some developing countries accept advice from NGOs is surprising given their general negative attitude toward the operation of NGOs in the WTO. It must be seen as another indicator for the need for expertise and advice which developing countries have, and which apparently is not satisfied either by the WTO Secretariat and/or the intergovernmental organizations UNCTAD and South Centre.

However, the advice provided by NGOs must indeed be regarded with some skepticism. NGOs are unlikely to act as consultants which are supposed to provide advice 'in the best interest of the client.' NGOs are basically cause groups with a membership which has often very negative views concerning trade liberalization in general. For instance, a common NGO demand is that no new trade liberalization measures should be agreed upon before the social and environmental impact of former trade liberalization rounds have been evaluated carefully under the full consultation of NGOs (*Wallach and Sforza* 1999: 219; *George* 2002: 89; *George and Kirkpatrick* 2004). Advice to developing countries may therefore often be guided by an interest of NGOs to impede further progress in trade liberalization rather than by the wish to act in the best interest of the developing country which receives the advice.

2. Technical assistance

(a) Activities of the Secretariat

The unit with responsibilities for technical assistance in the Secretariat is the Institute for Training and Technical Cooperation. A representative of the Secretariat conceded that the Secretariat has some influence on the preferences and policy decisions of WTO members through its right to propose the Technical Assistance and Training Plan, which is adopted by the Committee on Trade and Development (see Chapter 4, II.2).

Trade Policy courses lasting twelve weeks are both held in Geneva (four) and in the regions (five) on an annual basis. Through the Geneva and field-based courses, a total of around 260 participants is reached annually.[17] The twelve-weeks course in Geneva is provided mainly by Secretariat staff. Visits to the International Trade Centre, to UNCTAD, and to World Intellectual Property Organization (WIPO) are organized, and staff from the World Bank is invited. There are also shorter one-week Geneva-based Specialized Courses,[18] like for instance on dispute settlement or sanitary and phytosanitary issues.

Interview partners from both NGOs and the Secretariat confirmed that the competence of member states delegates negotiating trade matters in Geneva is sometimes very low. Following an NGO, delegates sent to Geneva have usually received only a general diplomat's training, and they lack special trade policy training. A Secretariat official reported that there have been cases in which WTO staff from a unit other than the Training Institute have been asked to provide individual lessons to negotiators "who did not have a very technical background":

> So things that to me are not very technical were extremely complicated for the members, such as linear formula versus non-linear formula, how to calculate a base rate. Things like that, in order to strengthen the negotiations, I needed to spend a lot of time, just doing a lot of basic work like that.

In addition to Geneva-based twelve-weeks Trade Policy Courses, regional courses based on the same model are organized outside Geneva. They are delivered in close partnership with an institution of higher learning in different regions of the world. In 2006, for instance, five courses were organized for the Caribbean, for English-speaking Africa, for French-speaking Africa, for Asia and the Pacific, and for Latin America.[19] Government officials from each specific region participate in the training, and the courses adapt to regional specificities.[20]

In addition to Trade Policy Courses, national and regional seminars and workshops are organized within developing countries on request of member states.[21] The annual Technical Assistance and Training Plan does not lay down in detail which courses are to be provided and where. The response of the WTO Secretariat to a member country request will depend on whether the issue is considered to be relevant, on whether the Secretariat has the capacity to undertake the activity, and whether there is scope for meeting the request through a partner agency.[22]

One criticism of the technical assistance provided by the WTO Secretariat is that there is only a limited quantity of courses available on request, due to a lack of funding. A developing country criticized that his country could only host two national workshops per year:

> So we would like to have some workshop to do some simulation on NAMA,[23] on agriculture. We would like to have some workshop on trade facilitation. We would want to have something on environment

> and so on. But because of the capacity of the WTO, they limit developing countries to two activities, although their activities have been increased. They say two for each country.

However, the Secretariat tries to meet national demand by organizing regional workshops. The representative of a developing country observed:

> Because the demand is too much, they cannot cope. However, they do have some regional workshops. Sometimes when they look at the spectrum of some of the demands, they try to group and see there is more demand on NAMA, so why don't we have a regional workshop on NAMA in East Africa.

An interview partner from the Secretariat emphasized that the technical assistance plan is developed as part of an interactive process with member states. Committees on agriculture, SPS, TRIPS, and services identify needs from their countries by, for instance, issuing questionnaires. By contrast, an NGO has argued that it is sometimes difficult for developing countries to get technical assistance on issues that are of interest to them. The identification of issues is in the view of the NGO very much donor-driven:

> So it is difficult for particular developing countries to get technical assistance on a particular point they would like to be covered. It's more like donor countries saying: I am going to give money, and it's going to be used for this, this, and this. That's not something that we are following at [the NGO], that's something I have heard from various delegations. It was pretty obvious in the year before Cancún.

A development-oriented intergovernmental organization criticized that the technical assistance by the WTO Secretariat fails to help developing countries to decide whether trade liberalization is good or bad for them, and this has led to disappointment by delegates from developing countries. Several NGOs confirmed that the WTO Secretariat does not provide technical assistance in the form of consultancy for developing countries. A developing country suggested that this is the consequence of the WTO principle of impartiality and of the WTO being a "member-driven" organization:

> You have to look at the role the Secretariat is expected to play. And if it has to remain impartial, even in the delivery of its capacity-building, it has to reflect the situation as it is. If it is about the negotiations, they will give you the update: that is how far members have gone; this is where they have differences. But suggesting the way forward, they cannot do that, because it is a member-driven organization.

Hence, two NGOs pointed out that technical assistance for developing countries seems more useful for the implementation of agreements, while its usefulness for negotiations is limited in so far as (a) it does not help countries to identify their interests, and (b) it does not help countries to analyze the impact of existing agreements and of negotiation proposals on their countries. As an NGO representative put it:

> In the technical assistance that they provide, they have very strong limitations. The WTO Secretariat can provide technical assistance to help countries understand and implement existing agreements and make use of their rights and obligations, this is not helping you to identify your interests. This is helping you to understand the system and use the system. So the WTO Secretariat is not going to go to Tchad and tell the Ministry, well you know cotton is important for you and you should do something. They are not going to do that, they cannot do that.

A Secretariat official stressed that its position toward the existing agreements must be a neutral one:

> And clearly, one of the first things we tell them in the beginning is: you're coming here, look we tell you what these agreements are about, and what this organization is about. We're not going to tell you whether it's right or wrong. It's up to you, to then make up your minds, look at the reality of your countries, and see what you can use…

To summarize, the Secretariat has some influence on the preferences and policy decisions of WTO members in the area of technical assistance through its right to propose the Technical Assistance and Training Plan. It also has the right to determine the precise content of the courses since the Technical Assistance and Training Plan does not prescribe the contents of courses in detail. At the same time, the Secretariat is confronted with wishes by some WTO members to receive technical assistance in form of consultancy regarding ongoing negotiations. However, the Secretariat interprets the principle of neutrality in such a way as to prevent it from doing so. Technical assistance as provided by the WTO Secretariat is therefore largely focused on existing agreements and implementation matters. This leaves a gap which is filled by other organizations (see Chapter 5, I.1.d, 2.b).

(b) Activities of international organizations

A development-oriented intergovernmental organization estimated that developing countries receive the bulk of technical assistance and trainings from other organizations than the WTO, e.g. UNCTAD, the World Bank and others. Faced with criticism that the activities of the WTO, UNCTAD, and the South Centre in technical assistance overlap, a developing country expressed the view that the different approaches to technical cooperation by the three organizations WTO, UNCTAD, and International Trade Centre (ITC) complement rather than duplicate each other.

Technical cooperation provided by UNCTAD covers the four areas of its work program: (1) globalization and development, (2) investment, enterprise development, and technology, (3) international trade in goods and services, and (4) services infrastructure for development and trade efficiency. The type of technical assistance provided by UNCTAD is different from technical assistance provided by the WTO Secretariat: Input by UNCTAD has proved valuable for developing countries to decide on most of the trade subjects under negotiation at the WTO (*Durán* 2005: 463). A representative of a developing country confirmed that UNCTAD looks more into the impacts of agreements and negotiating proposals:

> Because on the current agreement, let's take for example agreement on agriculture, [the WTO Secretariat] will come and explain: that's your rights and obligations, that's this and that. They will do that. That is the WTO. But UNCTAD will look at the agreements, and then, this is how it will affect your economy.

The same developing country representative stressed that UNCTAD also strengthens the case of developing countries in ongoing negotiations:

> But UNCTAD will come in, and look at the impact of those measures, which are proposed by other members, for example the impact of

> the Swiss formula. How is it going to affect your preferences? That is where UNCTAD comes in. They do their analysis, their policy analysis, which is quite useful. Because it helps you now to strengthen your case if you are participating in the negotiations. So it's quite useful.

Another organization providing technical assistance is theITC, a daughter organization of the WTO and UNCTAD. Its mission is to support developing and transition economies, and particularly their business sectors, to develop their export potential and improve import operations (*Durán* 2005: 463). A representative from a developing country pointed out that it views things from yet another, third perspective:

> ITC will come and look at it from a different, a businessman approach. Where are the opportunities? This is the agreement. As a businessman, what can you get from there?

Both UNCTAD and the ITC depend to a large extent on United Nations Development Programme (UNDP) and bilateral donors (Canada, Netherlands, Norway, Germany, Switzerland, Japan, and the United Kingdom) to finance their technical assistance activities (*Durán* 2005: 463).

The fact that the WTO and UNCTAD provide different types of technical assistance does not preclude cooperation between the two. As mentioned above, the WTO organizes visits to UNCTAD in the framework of their Geneva-based trade policy courses. An interview partner from the WTO Secretariat pointed out that the approach taken to trade negotiations and trade agreements in UNCTAD is much more critical than in the WTO:

> Our trade policy course is going on Wednesday to spend the day there in UNCTAD, and the speech you are going to hear there is very different from what you hear here. You will hear people being much more critical about some of the WTO agreements, and how they think the negotiations are still being deformated by developed countries, and so on and so forth.

WTO, UNCTAD, and the ITC cooperate under the Joint Integrated Technical Assistance Programme (JITAP) since 1998. It is focused on African countries, aiming at enhancing their capacity to negotiate and implement trade agreements. National networks of trainers and experts in WTO-related issues are established and a single or generic program with activities is implemented. The second phase of JITAP was launched in 2003, covering 16 African countries. The program receives funding from the Common Trust Fund supported by 13 donor countries. In a four-year period (2003–2006) it spent US$ 12.6 million.[24] An interview partner from a developing country described the cooperation between WTO Secretariat, UNCTAD, and ITC as a success:

> Because as I say, the three of them have a role to play, and you have seen it through JITAP. Because JITAP was a practical case where we saw three organizations participate very well, and each giving assistance and we saw really what a country like us [Developing Country] needed.

The analysis shows that the need for consultancy regarding ongoing negotiations is, at least, partially satisfied by technical assistance provided by UNCTAD.

3. Research

(a) Activities of the Secretariat

The Secretariat has a research division which employs approximately 20 staff. The task of the division is both to compile and evaluate research carried out by other organizations, and to carry out own research. In this regard, the WTO Secretariat goes beyond a typical scientific support service of a parliament which is, in general, not allowed to carry out its own research, but is confined to compiling existing research.

However, a developing country and a development-oriented NGO criticized the overall research output of the WTO Secretariat for being a rather limited one if compared to other organizations, such as the World Bank and UNCTAD. A developing country representative argued that the WTO Secretariat does not have the same amount of freedom as these organizations to publish research.

This view was confirmed by an interview partner from the Secretariat. The role of the Secretariat is rather to "audit research" that other organizations have published. The research division collects publications, and it produces internal papers to evaluate them. The Director General may take an interest in specific publications by NGOs and ask for an internal audit by the research division.

The limited output by the research division consists in special studies, WTO discussion papers (meant to stimulate discussion on specific issues) and WTO staff working papers (representing research in progress). A representative of the Secretariat has considered the "World Trade Report" which is published annually to be the main publication of the research division, covering special topics, analysis, and new developments of global trade policy. For Secretariat staff it was amazing that the Secretariat was allowed to publish the report, since member states were thought in general to be "very conscious and nervous" about what the research division was doing:

> Five years ago, one could not imagine the WTO Secretariat doing that. Putting out a publication like that. Literally, it would be impossible. [...] Because it's seen to be too independent. It also creates a problem despite what everyone says being neutral, intellectual, academic work. There is no such thing.

Part of the Secretariat's research work is based on its research program drafted by the Secretariat. In contrast to technical assistance, there is no specific committee that has to approve the program. In this regard, the Secretariat enjoys some autonomy from the preferences of the WTO members. However, Secretariat staff indicated that a substantial part of research follows from specific member states requests. The downside of the lack of responsibility of one particular WTO committee is that member states in all committees and councils have the freedom to direct such requests to the Secretariat to carry out research projects. Requests to other units may be "forwarded" to the research division units because of lack of capacity and personnel.

It is the responsibility of the director of the research division to decide whether research projects "on request" are to be carried out or not. Controversial proposals that have not been acceptable to committees as a whole are rejected. Another limitation for the Secretariat is that it is very difficult to carry out and publicize research that relates to ongoing negotiations. According to a Secretariat official, it is very difficult for Secretariat staff to investigate potential impacts of negotiation proposals on the table, and that it might possibly be incompatible with the principle of neutrality:

> Research can help with trade policy. When it gets to help in the trade negotiations, it gets difficult, because then you encounter the problem of neutrality.

In many cases, the Secretariat staff suspects that the motivation by member states to request research is to show that the impact of trade liberalization on specific countries is negative. However, according to Secretariat officials, the position of the Secretariat toward trade liberalization should be a positive one. At the same time, the Secretariat should avoid presenting themselves as advocates of trade liberalization:

> You know, we could not put something out that says trade is bad. Because we all have the bias that trade is good. So we're putting something out, but at the same time we can't put something out that says, trade is so good and beneficial for everyone that every country should sign an agreement. Right? 'Cause then we cross the boundaries to advocacy. So we have to do research, but not go so far, as being advocates of trade liberalization. But of course, we're advocates of trade liberalization, we're staff of the World Trade Organization.

Hence, in the cases in which the Secretariat has the suspicion that the motivation behind a study is to stop negotiations on further trade liberalization, the research division would find informal ways not to deliver the study. A Secretariat official noted:

> But look at who is making the request, and what they want to get out of the request. Basically, what they are doing is this: the group of countries that are less than enthusiastic about the trade negotiations, has made a formal request in two or three committees for a study to be done. But the objective of the study is to stop the trade negotiations, right, because they want the study to show that trade liberalization is bad. So that is a request. While it is formal, you find ways not to deliver it.

According to a Secretariat official, the Secretariat has usually some latitude in the design of the project, thereby also enjoying some autonomy from the preferences of the WTO members if requests by member states are accepted:

> So, why yes, it is an answer to a member's request, look at what I have done with it. I have taken it, and turned it into my own project. Something that I can do on my own. So you see what I mean? The number [of requests] would be quite high, but it's not that we are so disciplined by members.

Once a study is delivered, member states on the committee that requested it do not always make use of it. Secretariat staff noted that it then remains unclear for them what the impact of their work is:

> But then the study was a big long study. [...] So my colleague who is not here, worked really, really hard for four months. He did an excellent study, and it got discussed once, maybe, in the committee. So it's a very strange kind of set-up.

The research division is also involved in technical assistance activities as part of the official program. Activities include the conduct of workshops for professors in developing countries, the inviting of PhD students from developing countries to the research division of the WTO etc. The objective of this approach is, according to a Secretariat official, to preserve the neutral position of the Secretariat by enabling developing countries to conduct their own studies on trade rather than having the Secretariat conduct studies for them:

> And so that's something that we can do. But we do it in such a way that we don't become their advocates. We do it in such a way so that the stuff that comes out, they can decide whether it's good or bad. Right now, the capacity is so low, they read it and they say, oh yes, this is what we want to say. What we're doing is helping them develop the capacity to evaluate this kind of things, and hopefully write them themselves.

In sum, the provision of research is a very problematic task for the WTO Secretariat given its position as a "neutral" body. It is the view of the Secretariat that it cannot carry out research relating to ongoing negotiations and research that shows negative aspects of trade liberalization. Again, expectations of developing countries regarding consultancy for ongoing negotiations by the WTO Secretariat are disappointed.

(b) Activities of international organizations

As indicated above, many international organizations carry out more research on trade (or on economic matters that are closely related to trade) than the WTO Secretariat. Regarding the relationship between the research division of the Secretariat and other international organizations, Secretariat staff made a difference between the World Bank and several UN organizations (e.g. UNDP, UNCTAD). A Secretariat official characterized the relationship between the World Bank and the Secretariat as a "good working relationship." This is due to the fact that staff in the research division has often attended the same educational facilities, and is in regular contact through conferences.

By contrast, the working relationship with some UN organizations is characterized as more problematic. Sometimes research by UN organizations is not sent to the Secretariat for comments before it is published. The WTO Secretariat has then asked for corrections to be made or for older data to be updated.

(c) Activities of NGOs

Most interviewed NGOs indicated that they are carrying out research on trade matters. One development-oriented NGO indicated that it mainly communicates research carried out by other organizations:

> Or we read from other papers, the FAO has done some studies, and things like that. Sometimes NGOs have done studies, UN agencies have done studies, universities have done studies, but the diplomats don't know. So what we do is summarize the studies, and disseminate them. So we try to bridge the gap between the experts who produce studies, and the diplomats who have no time to do studies.

Depending on the cause for which they are set up, NGO research covers different topics. For instance, an NGO with a "governance focus" researches how trade impact assessments become institutionalized and what their format should be. Other research concerns the relationship between Multilateral Environmental Agreements and trade law. A development-oriented NGO indicated that it investigates the impact of particular trade rules on selected countries and sectors. The NGO observed that since NGO positions receive a lot of attention in the media, developed countries may be forced to react to it, and they may even feel obliged to defend their position in discussions with NGOs:

> Even if we have positions different from theirs, they recognize that what we are publishing and what we are saying is having an impact. So they have to engage with us, and discuss with us, maybe sometimes explain their position.

However, NGOs recognized that research carried out by them has its limitations, and, therefore, they have strong expectations toward the WTO Secretariat delivering more research:

> But in terms of basic statistical work, in terms of I don't know there is a formula item on market access, for example, the Secretariat should run the formula on all the different products of these countries, and being able to come up with a document saying, okay that's what would happen to your economy, to your products. That's something that UNCTAD might be able to do to some extent. We as an NGO would not be able to do that. UNCTAD might be able to do this, might have the capacity or the resources to do this. South Centre to some extent, but [...] more could be done in this respect by the WTO.

Staff of the WTO Secretariat showed a critical attitude toward research published by NGOs. A Secretariat official went as far as denying that certain NGO publications can even be characterized as research:

> It is an advocacy document, it's not research. So they put these things out to give a message, so they know their message, and then they write around it. That's not research.

As a matter of principle, the Secretariat completely abstains from responding publicly to documents published by other organizations. This is even the case if the Secretariat judges an NGO study which clearly seeks to influence the ongoing negotiations to be of extremely poor quality. Secretariat staff, however, regarded a public intervention as compromising the neutrality of the Secretariat:[25]

> There would be no circumstances in which we would react positively to it. You know, I don't think that's our role. Our role is not to mediate and referee the debate. Our role is maybe to help increase the intellectual level of the debate, and at the same time in such a way to help countries negotiate more effectively. So it's a very indirect way. But as soon as we step in, there is an issue of our independence, our neutrality.

However, Secretariat staff is frequently contacted by delegates of member states. The staff does not hesitate to informally give a candid view on the quality of a specific study. A representative of the Secretariat pointed out:

> But I mean I have a good relationship with a lot of them. So this kind of conversation they kind enjoy over a beer. So what do you say? I say it was crap.

In sum, the Secretariat sees itself constrained by the principle of neutrality regarding the type of research provided. Research which evaluates the impact of proposals relating to ongoing negotiations is not carried out, even though developing countries need this information. The analysis shows that this gap cannot be filled by NGOs which have their own interests in the field, and which also lack capacities to perform serious research. Neither does the Secretariat formally comment on research published by other organizations (such as NGOs). On an informal basis, however, the Secretariat gives comments on NGO studies to delegates of developing countries.

II. Implementation of trade agreements

1. The role of the Secretariat

As set out in Chapter 4, IV.2, there is no universally applicable implementation procedure in the WTO. The procedures are established under the various agreements, with some procedures delegated to member state authorities and some procedures delegated to the WTO committee and/or WTO Secretariat. Member states are often put under an obligation to submit certain types of notifications.

At first sight, the role of the Secretariat in implementation matters resembles the role that it has in negotiations: it prepares meetings, drafts the agenda (together with the chairperson), and it drafts minutes of the meetings. However, an interview partner who has been chairperson of both general and special session committees (thereby dealing with both negotiations and implementation) argued that the WTO Secretariat has a stronger role and more leeway in the area of implementation than in trade negotiations. This is because the Secretariat is active in collecting information from member states, and this requires considerable expertise. The Secretariat has, therefore, some influence on the preferences and policy decisions of WTO members through the chairmen, and it has some (limited) autonomy from the preferences of the WTO members by collecting information. However, the Secretariat is unable to pinpoint non-compliance of member states.

2. Formal and informal decision making

Decisions are taken in the regular sessions of committees regarding, for instance, the classification of certain national measures and the format in which information from member states is collected. However, formal meetings in regular sessions of WTO implementation committees are organized less frequently than meetings in special sessions in the framework of the Doha Round negotiations. At most, committees meet once a month. The chairperson may also call for informal meetings if he or she deems it necessary to resolve conflicts by means of open discussion. For instance, in an informal meeting, a member country could tell another member country that it required more time to implement a certain rule. The country would not make the concession that there was an issue to be addressed in a formal meeting.

The issue of implementing WTO agreements often takes a back seat in the view of the member countries and in the view of the public as compared to the negotiations of new agreements. A former representative of a G-4 Developed Country described this as follows:

> The balance has always tipped more in favor of the members being actively interested on the negotiating side. It is more visible to the outside world. I can tell you as a representative here, I spent more time in a negotiating process than I did in the administration and implementation process. Because my government placed higher priority on my being involved in that than they did on my going to regular meetings of the anti-dumping committee or of the committee on import licensing.

However, a Secretariat executive stressed that a fair amount of work is carried out in the standing bodies of the WTO, that does not command a great deal of public attention:

> The work that goes on in just regular sessions in all of those meetings, is very, very extensive. Nobody ever sees it and nobody writes things about it, but we have thousands of notifications per year in those committees. They lead to debates on various measures, and in fact we have quite a few disputes coming out of those issues. If you look at the rules committee, it is very much the same thing going on, and in the committee of subsidies, the safeguards committee. So we have an enormous amount of that work taking place.

Similar to negotiations, influence of the Secretariat on decisions taken by implementation bodies is through the chairperson. This influence is supposed to be stronger than for negotiations due to the greater importance of the technical expertise of the WTO Secretariat in the area of implementation. Informal decision making occurs, but it does not have the same importance as in the area of negotiations.

III. Trade policy review

The purpose of the trade policy review is to enable members to examine and comment on the trade policies and practices of individual WTO members and the effect that those policies and practices have on the functioning of the multilateral trading system (*Davey* 2005: 58f.). The Trade Policy Review Unit of the Secretariat employs some 20 trade and economic policy analysts. The representative of the Secretariat stressed that formally the review as such does not consist in the reports prepared by the member state under review and by the Secretariat, but in the ensuing discussion in the Trade Policy Review Council, including the remarks of the chairperson.

1. The role of the Secretariat

In the area of Trade Policy Review, the Secretariat provides a service that is different from the usual negotiation support. The Secretariat is supposed to have greater flexibility due to a "less tight oversight" by members (*Xu and Weller* 2004: 271). The Secretariat has, for instance, some autonomy in determining the order of review for the least significant group of trading member countries who shall only be reviewed every six years. Secretariat staff indicated that preference would be given to review those member countries that had never been reviewed before. However, the date of review is also a matter of negotiation between Secretariat and country:

> We try to establish a first contact with the country, and then they might tell us look, the next year is not really good, we have elections coming up, politically, or there are many changes to the trade policy regime, so why don't you wait a little bit to review us?

The Secretariat does not see itself restrained by formal rules or by member states in determining the scope of the report it drafts. For instance, Secretariat staff argued that it could very much determine the scope of the trade policy reviews:

> There has never been an explicit agreement saying [...] or a document coming from trade policy review bodies saying these are the areas that trade policy review must cover. This has really developed over time. There had been an initial or basic outline, which we had prepared, again, not formally approved, or anything. But at the very beginning of the mechanism this was developed with the members. But then

> from there, things are added, or things are left aside, by the discretion of the Secretariat.

The prevailing view in the Secretariat is that it can freely cover issues such as competition and investment policy, which are not covered by WTO agreements and the inclusion of which has been highly controversial:

> Well, we keep on talking, we talk a lot about the competition regime of the country under review, we have in every review a description of the investment regime of a country.

Member countries have not really questioned the scope of review as applied by the Secretariat, and hence the Secretariat enjoys clearly some autonomy from the preferences of WTO members. An interview partner from the Secretariat expressed the view that even though some member countries would have preferred not to have their investment and competition policy reviewed by the Secretariat under the trade policy review, they might cave in because it gives them the opportunity to obtain information on the policies of other member countries.

Secretariat staff pointed out that it is not restrained by formal rules or by member countries regarding how information for the report should be collected. It thus enjoys a certain autonomy to research primary sources, such as laws and regulations. Secondary sources are "local press and international press" and publications from other international organizations, for example the World Bank or the IMF, or academic studies. Also, staff of the Secretariat travels to the member countries under review in order to collect information from government officials. It may also talk to non-state actors, such as academic personnel and to socio-economic actors, such as representatives of trade associations and labor unions. The same Secretariat official indicated that NGOs are not included as sources of information, because the Secretariat cannot see what the added value of their integration may be. The official noted that it gives evaluations and recommendations in the report to a limited extent:

> Reports are factual, the nature of it is factual, but we do write a section, which is always a first section in each report. Some area observations, where the Secretariat makes more what some people call value judgements, more of an assessment of the situation in

> trying to keep it to five pages [...]. Well, there could be recommendations. But recommendations are not explicit like a list of bullet points with recommendation, but recommendations could be included in some countries.

As prescribed by the Marrakesh Agreement, the Secretariat should seek clarification from member countries concerned of their trade policies and practices.[26] Accordingly, the draft report is laid before the member country under review and discussed with it. Literature has set out that the drafting of reports is a sensitive issue between member states and Secretariat. Member countries used to "complain loudly when the staff gets too close to hard-hitting analysis." Recent Secretariat reports have shown more bite, but it has taken "the Secretariat about a decade to acquire its own modest voice" (*Hufbauer* 2005: 293).

Secretariat staff confirmed that controversies between member countries and the Secretariat are not uncommon. The Secretariat usually seeks to integrate the view of the member country, but at the same time it would seek to keep its own views within the text. A Secretariat official explained:

> So in that sense, you would certainly find in many of these reports something that "the Secretariat says, and then, however, the authorities noted that x, y and z". So we will take their views into account, but that does not necessarily mean that we get rid of what we want to say.

At the meeting of the Trade Policy Review Council, the Secretariat does not play an active role in the discussion; rather it is again reduced to a "note taker." Secretariat staff outlined the practice as follows:

> We are not allowed to intervene, or we do not intervene, except if the Chairman asks for a clarification by the Secretariat in case that somebody is saying something in the report is wrong. Then we might step in and say, well the source of the data is such and such. But we would not discuss any of the issues on the table, no.

2. Formal and informal decision making

Informal decision making is largely absent from trade policy review. This is because trade policy review does not aim primarily at the resolving of conflicts between members. For the discussion in the Trade Policy

Review Council, the member country also submits its own report. However, even though this used to be a report that equaled the Secretariat report in scope and coverage, this has now been reduced to a "policy statement." In the view of an interview partner from the Secretariat this is because member countries lack the resources to do a full report. Before the discussion in the Trade Policy Review Council, member countries can send questions which the country under review has to answer in written form:

> There is a rule, for example, that they should come in a day before the meeting starts, so that countries have a chance to look at them and may say, well you did not reply to what I wanted, reply to the question I was thinking of.[27]

For the meeting, a member state delegate is nominated as discussant in a personal capacity. This means that he or she should not limit discussions to issues that are of direct relevance to the country in question. A representative of the Secretariat explained that his or her function is more broadly to get a discussion going.

To summarize, trade policy review is an area in which the Secretariat has significant influence on the preferences and policy decisions of WTO members. Other than in negotiations and implementation where the Secretariat mainly acts informally through the chairperson, the influence is an open and formal one since it is based on the right of the Secretariat to draft the Trade Policy Review report. Informal decision making plays no role in trade policy review.

IV. Dispute settlement

1. The role of the Secretariat

Divisions with responsibilities for dispute settlement are the Legal Affairs Division (with responsibilities for the panel) and the Appellate Body Division (with responsibilities for the Appellate Body) that is directly subordinated to the Director General.

Panels and appellate bodies have the decisive role in dispute settlement since they take decisions independently of the preferences of the members. A representative of the Secretariat explained that a Secretariat team is put together when a panel is established. The Legal Affairs Division provides the legal officer. Depending on the subject matter of the dispute, other operational divisions will provide experts from their divisions, also to be part of the Secretariat team. It is then for the panel to request various types of assistance from the Secretariat. Examples are writing issue papers, providing legal advice, setting up the meeting schedule, taking care of the logistics, handling all the documents, etc. The Secretariat provides also drafting assistance to the panel if required. In practice this often means that the Secretariat writes the initial drafts of decisions, but always under the direction of a panel. In this regard, an interview partner from the Secretariat likened the role of the Legal Affairs Division to the one of a law-clerk in the United States.

The same interview partner stressed that the WTO Secretariat has an obligation to be strictly neutral with regard to the parties of the case. This means in practice that the division observes formal rules much more than other units in the WTO. An example is that it must carefully avoid providing any information only to one party while the other remains excluded.

The Secretariat provides technical assistance to developing countries through a different unit, the Technical Cooperation Unit. Secretariat staff, however, stressed that this support is of a general nature:

> Hence, we give general advice on how the dispute settlement system operates. We teach courses on dispute settlement. It's part of our technical capacity building programme. We will answer questions of members on a whole host of legal issues, but when it comes to case-specific matters, we do not give advice, because we don't want to stray from our neutrality position.

The argument is that the prevailing philosophy of neutrality and the text of the Marrakesh Agreement hinder the Secretariat to provide case specific advice to developing countries. For this purpose, two outside legal consultants can be hired by a developing country that is seeking case-specific advice.

The Legal Affairs Division also has a legal publication function. Publications include a handbook on the Dispute Settlement System and a book on the first 10 years of WTO Dispute Settlement. Moreover the division publishes all Dispute Settlement reports. The Secretariat does, however, refrain from critically analyzing the decisions. An interview partner from the Secretariat explained that this would be incompatible with the neutral role of the Secretariat:

> Generally speaking, the Secretariat does not analyse and critique the decisions from a substantive standpoint. We do not do that kind of

legal analysis and publication because the Secretariat performs a neutral role. So whatever we publish is of a descriptive rather than an analytical nature.

2. Formal and informal decision making

The Secretariat has estimated that the phases of the dispute settlement that relate to panel and appellate body proceedings are much more formal in practice than the WTO negotiations procedure. The consultation procedure as established by the DSU has been characterized in literature as "informal, party-controlled and settlement-oriented, rather than a formalized transition stage on the way to panel proceedings" (*Schuchhardt* 2005: 1204). However, consultations in dispute settlement cannot be considered informal decision making as defined in Chapter 3, I.3.b, because their use is formally regulated in Art. 4 of the DSU. The unsuccessful conclusion of the consultation stage is binding since it is a necessary precondition for the establishment of a panel under the DSU.[28]

3. The role of non-state actors

The Dispute Settlement Understanding remains silent on the matter of non-state actors intervening into the dispute settlement procedure by filing so-called amicus curiae submissions. However, both panels and Appellate Body have decided that they are entitled – but not required – to receive and consider amicus curiae submissions even if they are unsolicited. However, they also ruled that they are not obliged in their rulings to rely on such submissions. In practice, in most disputes where NGOs have submitted unsolicited amicus curiae briefs, the panels accepted such submissions, but decided that relying on their content was not necessary for resolving the issues before them (*Zdouc* 2005: 1240). Also, the Appellate Body has never fully considered the contents of an "amicus curiae" brief, although it stated on a number of occasions that it has the authority to do so (*Donaldson* 2005: 1321).

To summarize, dispute settlement is an area in which the Secretariat may exert some influence on decisions of the panel, but it does not have influence over the preferences and policy decisions of WTO members. Consultations preceding the dispute settlement procedure are regulated in Art. 4 of the DSU and, therefore, do not represent informal actions. The interviews revealed no patterns of informal decision making in the context of the dispute settlement system.

V. The informal WTO

Patterns of informal action as analyzed in this chapter differ strongly over the different areas of negotiations, implementation, trade policy review, and dispute settlement. This applies both to the role of the Secretariat and to the degree to which formal decision making is complemented or replaced by patterns of informal decision making. Informal decision making as defined in Chapter 3, I.3.b plays a major role in negotiations and a more limited role in the area of implementation. In trade policy review and in dispute settlement it is largely absent. This uneven distribution of patterns of informal decision making can be explained by the varying importance of settling conflicts on sensitive issues in different areas, and by the inadequacy of formal structures and procedures.

The prevalence of informal decision making in WTO *negotiations* can be only understood against the principle of reaching consensus (see Chapter 4, I). It is a well known principle that international law rests on the consensus of all states bound by it (*Reus-Smit* 2006: 355). In the case of the WTO, however, consensus on new agreements is required to be reached on issues of vital economic interest between 150 diverse member states. Under these circumstances, formal decision making based on meetings of the entire membership with positions officially recorded have proven to be largely inadequate for effectively reaching trade agreements, adapting to changing political circumstances, and solving conflicts between member states. Formal structures and formal procedures in negotiations are therefore complemented with various forms of informal structures and procedures.

Informal decision making helps resolve basic organizational problems (see Chapter 3, I.3.b). It meets the organizational system requirement of conflict resolution among members for two reasons. Since negotiations are not recorded in minutes, delegates can test the ground for new compromises. Hence, the reaching of consensus is facilitated. Moreover, informal decision making is more flexible since it allows for the meeting of smaller groups, and to adapt ongoing negotiations to new problem situations and changing circumstances.

Informal decision making could in theory also fulfill the function of saving scarce resources of poorer member states. Delegations of smaller member states with limited personnel and expertise could save resources if only few informal meetings of selected member states took place (e.g. G-4). More recently, a system of group representation has been built up to ensure that informal meetings of small groups reflect views of larger groups (e.g. through G-20, the African Group, etc.). However, in other instances, informal decision making in the WTO does not have the effect of saving resources due to the proliferation of a multitude of informal meetings of small groups with changeable composition which take place simultaneously. Rather than saving resources, the multitude of informal procedures puts additional strain on delegations with limited personnel and expertise.

Informal decision making in the *implementation* of trade agreements is less relevant for organizational system problems since official sessions of implementation bodies are often mainly concerned with general technical matters, e.g. on how information is to be collected. Conflicts between member states are limited. However, the solving of conflicts becomes important if one WTO member accuses another one of violating a WTO agreement. In this case, informal decision making can facilitate the reaching of a compromise between the member states concerned, if an informal meeting enables member states to have a frank exchange of views on the degree of non-compliance and how to address it. This frank exchange of views would not be possible in a formal implementation committee sitting.

In *trade policy review*, the solving of conflicts between members is not really an issue. Trade policy review as practiced in the WTO does not require that a consensus between WTO members is reached. Rather, the reports by the member state under review and by the Secretariat serve as an input, and the discussion between member states can then bring different opinions and priorities of WTO members to the fore. The lack of necessity to reach a consensus explains the absence of informal decision making.

In *dispute settlement*, the solving of conflicts between disputing members is of major importance. The lengthy and expensive dispute settlement procedures should not be opened before consultations between member states are carried out. However, formal rules prescribe that such a consultation phase takes place. Its decisions are binding in so far as the unsuccessful conclusion of this phase is a precondition for the opening of the dispute settlement procedure. Hence, this consultation phase, cannot be characterized as informal decision making.

To conclude, the dominance of informal decision making in trade negotiations must be seen as following from the limitations of formally prescribed structures and procedures to effectively reach trade agreements to adapt to changing political circumstances, to resolve conflicts between members, and to promote a consensus on sensitive issues. Informal decision making thereby contributes to the resolution of organizational system problems of a functioning WTO. In other areas where the solving of conflicts is less important, informal decision making is less dominant or completely absent.

Finally, in the areas of negotiations, technical assistance and research, external actors such as intergovernmental organizations and NGOs play an important role by informally providing information and advice to developing countries regarding decision making in the WTO. Thus, informal interactions also characterize the external relations of the WTO. All in all, the functioning of the WTO as an "International Organization" can only be understood if its informal organization is taken into account.

VI. The WTO as a hybrid actor

Having considered practices of the WTO in the areas of negotiation, implementation, trade policy review, and dispute settlement, the question is whether the WTO can be qualified as a collective or as a corporate actor. The WTO is frequently qualified by state delegates and member states as a "member-driven organization" (*Xu and Weller* 2004: 261). Characteristics of the WTO in terms of autonomy and influence of the organization and/or the Secretariat have also been a matter of discussion in scholarly literature (*Liese and Weinlich* 2006) even though the concepts of "corporate" and "collective" actors have not been used. Rather, each author has developed his or her own concepts such as the concept of an influential international bureaucracy (*Xu and Weller* 2004), the concept of a "club" (*Keohane and Nye* 2001), and the concept of an international organization endowed with a "will separate from its members" (*Footer* 2006: 78). Views on whether the WTO is an organization which enjoys some autonomy from the preferences of its members, and on whether the organization has some influence on the preferences and policy decisions of its members are strongly divergent. Using the Uruguay Round negotiations as an example, *Xu and Weller* (2004: 6) have argued that the staff of the GATT Secretariat has exerted significant influence over the decisions reached in the Uruguay Round. By contrast, *Keohane and Nye* (2000: 27) have generally characterized the WTO as a 'club,' in which all important decisions are taken by members, and in which the bureaucracy 'is small and weak.' *Footer* (2006: 78) has come to the conclusion that the WTO cannot be characterized as an organization with "a will of its own, separate and distinct from that of its individual Members [which] is able to function separately from its members."

In light of the evidence presented so far, this type of sweeping conclusion is not convincing. The assessment of the WTO must not be confined to trade negotiations as the only relevant area of activity in the WTO. Any discussion of whether the WTO can be characterized as a corporate or as a collective actor requires a separate discussion of each area of activities.

To recall, international organizations are characterized as collective actors if their decisions depend on the preferences of their members. By contrast, they are characterized as corporate actors if they enjoy some autonomy from the preferences of their members, or if they have some influence on the preferences and policy decisions of their members. Since corporate and collective actors are analytical categories, there are likely to be many intermediate forms of corporate and collective actors (see Chapter 3, I.2).

1. Perspectives on the Secretariat

The perception of the WTO as an influential international actor is usually derived from the role of its Secretariat (*Xu and Weller* 2003: 251ff.). Therefore, interview partners were asked to rate the role of the Secretariat with regard to the WTO members on a scale from 1 to 10, with 1 representing the Secretariat to be a perfect tool and 10 representing the Secretariat to be a perfect leader. The concept of leader is supposed to refer to an organization which has autonomy from its members and influence on their preferences and policy decisions. The concept of "tool" is supposed to represent the opposite, i.e. an absence of autonomy and influence.

Figure 5.3 shows how different types of interview partners evaluate the role of the WTO Secretariat as tool or leader.

All representatives of member states and NGOs and also most representatives of the Secretariat have placed the Secretariat on the lower end of the scale between 1 and 3. Hence, most interview partners rate autonomy and influence of the Secretariat with regard to the WTO members as being rather low. One representative of the Secretariat and one development-oriented intergovernmental organization have placed the Secretariat at 5. An outlier is provided by a development-oriented intergovernmental organization, which has placed the Secretariat at 8. The interview partner stressed that he rated the Secretariat influence to be so strong because of its informal role in the negotiations. He explained that

> the Secretariat exercises very strong informal influence in terms of shaping what the agenda is [...]. And from our perspective here at the Centre, it is the Secretariat that writes the reports of the chairs, that sets down basically in writing what's decided. It's the Secretariat

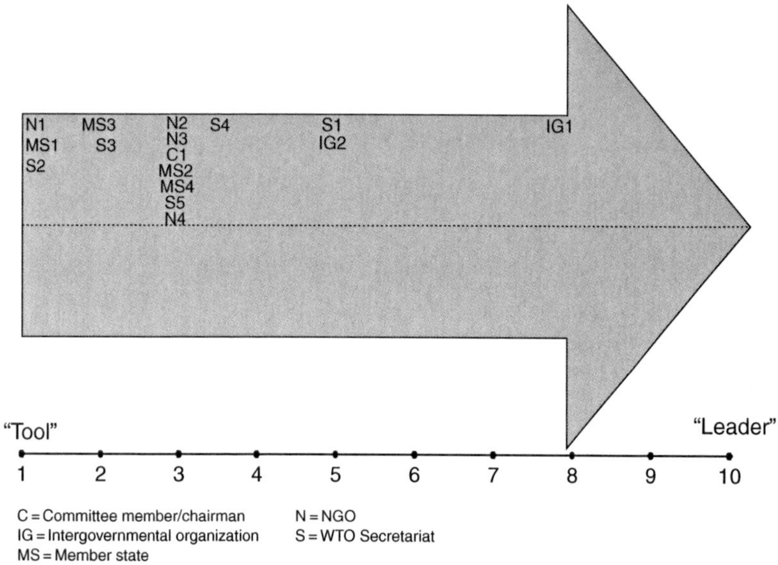

Figure 5.3 Evaluation of the Secretariat as "tool" or "leader" by interview partners

> for example that helps the chairs of the negotiating groups draft the basis for the negotiating discussion.

However, this evaluation seems to exaggerate the role of the Secretariat. As analyzed above, there are chairpersons who will not rely to the same extent on the Secretariat, and moreover, members seek to control the influence of the Secretariat.

Based on the majority of respondents who have placed the Secretariat at the lower end of the scale, it can be concluded that the WTO is perceived as a collective actor with some traits of a corporate actor. A Secretariat official indicated that there are different opportunities for leadership across different areas:

> There are some areas, where the Secretariat can lead, but I would say it is limited in general. It is more that the Secretariat is here as a tool.

2. Negotiations, technical assistance, and research

As shown in Chapter 4, I.1.c, the Secretariat has opportunities to influence the negotiations by, for instance, advising the chairperson of committees how to direct negotiations. In other cases, chairpersons may be more reluctant to accept Secretariat advice. Another possibility is that the Secretariat meets members on an informal basis and seeks to influence them. Influence of the Secretariat is, therefore, highly contingent on persons and situations. The same applies to the influence of a chairperson. An active, skillful, and experienced chairperson may have a stronger influence over the interim result of negotiations of a specific body than a passive and inexperienced one.

The overall influence of the Secretariat and of chairpersons of specific WTO bodies on the end result of the negotiations is, however, weakened through the principle of single undertaking. Following Section 47 of the Doha Declaration, conclusions of the Doha negotiations 'are treated as parts of a single undertaking' (see Chapter 4, I). In other words, interim results in WTO negotiations can be become meaningless since "nothing is agreed until everything is agreed." Any compromises which may be reached in specific special sessions of committees under the influence of the Secretariat or specific chairpersons cannot lead to any changes in WTO agreements unless they are accepted (and possibly amended) by membership as part of a broader package. This package may include some issues that reflect the influence of the Secretariat over the preferences and policy decisions of their members, while the influence of the Secretariat on other choices is absent.

However, at times of crisis, the Secretariat or the Director General may take an initiative to exert influence over the shape of the whole package as adopted by members. One example is the final stages of the Uruguay Round, where the Director General took the initiative to propose an overall compromise to the membership. Since agreement was reached on the basis of this compromise, the Director General has clearly exerted some influence on the preferences and policy decisions of their members (see Chapter 5, I.1.c).

To conclude, the WTO must be mainly seen as a collective actor in the area of negotiations. A characterization of the WTO as a corporate actor in the area of negotiations seems to be highly contingent on times and circumstances.

In the area of technical assistance, the Secretariat has some influence on the preferences and policy decisions of WTO members through its right to propose the Technical Assistance and Training Plan (see Chapter 5, I.2.a). The courses offered are based to a large extent on the Technical Assistance and Training Plan which is subject to approval by member states. Some of the activities are not determined by the plan, but are carried out in response to the wishes of members. The Secretariat has some autonomy from the preferences of WTO members since it cannot grant all wishes by member states for technical assistance activities due to a lack of funding. The Secretariat, therefore, has the right to determine which activities it can offer on the basis of limited resources (like the number and thematic focus of external workshops). Moreover, the precise content of the courses offered is at least in part determined by the Secretariat, since the Technical Assistance and Training Plan does not prescribe the contents of courses in detail. The Secretariat, however, interprets the principle of neutrality in such a way that it cannot offer technical assistance in form of consultancy for developing countries regarding ongoing negotiations. It thereby refrains from exerting influence on the preferences of its members. The effect of this interpretation of the principle of neutrality is that the WTO is prevented from becoming a "fully" corporate actor and that it remains rather a hybrid actor.

In the area of research (see Chapter 5, I.3.a), the Secretariat enjoys clearly some autonomy from the preferences of WTO members. First, it can determine part of the research agenda itself. Second, it can decide to what extent research commissioned by member states is carried out. And third, even if it delivers research in reaction to the wishes of member states, it has some leeway to shape projects according to the preferences of the Secretariat. To conclude, the WTO clearly exhibits traits of a corporate actor in the area of research. However, as in the area of technical assistance, the Secretariat sees itself constrained through the principle of neutrality regarding the type of research provided. It does refrain from carrying out research to evaluate the impact of negotiation proposals, it avoids investigating negative impacts of trade liberalization, and it does not comment on the research published by other organizations. It is important to note that the Marrakesh Agreement nowhere explicitly prescribes which kind of research is to be carried out by the Secretariat. Rather, the Secretariat interprets the principle of neutrality in that way. It thereby refrains from exerting influence on the preferences of its members with regard to ongoing negotiations. Again, the effect of this interpretation of the Secretariat is that the WTO is prevented from becoming a "fully" corporate actor and that it remains rather a hybrid actor.

3. Implementation, trade policy review, and dispute settlement

Similar to the area of negotiations, the Secretariat can exert an informal influence over the decisions taken in implementation via the chairperson of the committees (see Chapter 5, II.1). Influence in this area is supposed to be stronger than for negotiations due to the greater importance of the technical expertise of the WTO Secretariat in the area of implementation. Moreover, decisions by implementation committees are not subject to any "single undertaking" rule in the sense that they will only be adopted as part of an overall package. The WTO can therefore be characterized as exhibiting more traits of a corporate actor in implementation than in negotiations.

In the area of trade policy review (see Chapter 5, III.1), the Secretariat also enjoys some autonomy from the preferences of WTO members. It can (within formal limits) select member states that are reviewed and it can largely determine the scope of review. The Secretariat has then significant influence on the preferences and policy decisions of WTO members through its right to draft the Trade Policy Review report. This report is the most important basis of the concluding member state discussion, which is considered as the official trade policy review. A Secretariat official pointed out that trade policy review is an area where the Secretariat can act as a leader:

> There are some instances, where it's clear that the WTO Secretariat can lead. Trade policy review is a good example. I think there we are very much leading the process, and very much framing the discussion of where it will go, by deciding what goes in and what stays out of our reports.

In the area of dispute settlement (see Section IV.1 of this chapter), WTO most clearly exhibits the traits of a corporate actor. In their decisions, panels and appellate body enjoy complete autonomy from the preferences of WTO members. While a member state body – the Dispute Settlement Body – has to adopt decisions by member states, this is a mere formality. Decisions by panels and the appellate body could only be rejected based on a unanimous decision of the Dispute Settlement Body, which the winning party is certain to block. Decisions by panels and the appellate body therefore do not only influence but determine policy decisions of WTO members.

4. Conclusions

In the prominent area of negotiations, the WTO acts most clearly as a collective actor. Influences of the Secretariat and of chairpersons on the substance of negotiations are hidden, informal, and highly contingent upon times and personalities. Moreover, they do not always lead to decisions due to the principle to conclude only package deals (single undertaking). Hence, the WTO can be characterized mainly as a collective actor in the area of negotiations.

By contrast, the WTO acts as corporate actor in the area of dispute settlement. This is, however, not due to influences of the Secretariat, but it is closely linked to the decision powers of the panel and Appellate Bodies.

The areas of implementation, technical assistance, research, and trade policy review can be characterized as intermediate cases. All of these areas exhibit traits of collective decision making. At the same time, the Secretariat has some autonomy and/or some influence over the decisions and preferences of members.

In the area of implementation, the Secretariat has some informal influences over decisions. In the area of trade policy review, there is a clear and formal influence based on the Secretariat mandate to draft the report. In the areas of technical assistance and trade policy review the Secretariat also enjoys a certain degree of autonomy from WTO members. These findings have been confirmed by *Xu and Weller* (2004: 268) who have pointed to the areas of technical assistance and trade policy review as areas in which the Secretariat "has taken on greater responsibility for it to play a more independent role." The degree of autonomy is probably greatest in the area of research where the Secretariat has the powers to shape its own research agenda.

If all areas of activity are taken into account, the WTO can be described as a hybrid actor which exhibits traits of a collective and a corporate actor. If one focuses on the area of negotiations, it can be characterized as a predominantly collective actor. This analysis places the WTO somewhere between the two extremes in Figure 5.3. It is thus neither simply a "club" of members with a small and weak Secretariat (see *Keohane and Nye* 2000), nor is it necessarily driven everywhere by influences of an "international bureaucracy" on which *Xu and Weller* (2004: 278) focus.

6
Performance Patterns of the WTO

The evaluation of WTO decision patterns against the criteria of effectiveness, equity, and legitimacy is based on the perceptions of interview partners and surveyed member state representations. The views of those actors who are intimately involved in WTO activities serve as one set of indicators for WTO performance (see Chapter 3, I.5.d). Furthermore, factors are identified, as shown in Figure 3.1, which help explain performance patterns by promoting or impeding the attainment of effectiveness, equity, and legitimacy in the areas of trade negotiations, implementation, trade policy review, and dispute settlement.

Effectiveness is understood as the degree of goal attainment focusing on the production of organizational outputs in the areas of negotiations, compliance with trade agreements, trade policy review, and dispute settlement. Indicators of deficiencies of effectiveness are failure and/or delay to conclude implementable trade agreements, to implement and/or comply with trade agreements, and to make and/or comply with trade policy reviews and dispute settlement decisions (Chapter 3, I.5.a).

Equity can be subdivided into equity of members and equity of policy concerns. Equity of members has substantive and procedural aspects, with substantive equity referring to – in a qualitative sense – the ratio of outcome and input of a person's or institution's membership and participation in an organization, and procedural equity referring to equal access to decision-making procedures. Equity of policy concerns denotes the equal treatment of economic, social, and environmental concerns. Indicators of deficiencies of equity are failure and/or shortcomings to balance the trade interests of all WTO members, to participate in WTO decision-making processes, and to balance environmental and/or labor policy concerns with trade policies (Chapter 3, I.5.b).

Legitimacy is analyzed in terms of attitudes of member states and NGOs toward the WTO system. The chapter does not provide a normative discussion on WTO legitimacy. Indicators of deficiencies of legitimacy are perceived lack of due process and transparency in decision-making processes by WTO members, NGOs, and the public (Chapter 3, I.5.c).

I. Effectiveness

1. Task areas

(a) Trade negotiations

Interview partners were reserved in characterizing the WTO as being ineffective in negotiations with regard to its failures to conclude (implementable) trade agreements. A representative of a G4-Developed Country pointed out that one could "make a question mark" regarding the effectiveness of trade negotiations. Several interview partners from the Secretariat conceded reluctantly that negotiations in the WTO may not be considered as very effective:

> If one analyses the WTO, one looks at the negotiations, that's where we may not be effective in the sense that we have not finished the negotiations by the end of last year which we should have. No. So we were not effective there.

Another official differentiated between WTO objectives:

> It's ineffective on negotiations, it's not ineffective as an organization, because the organization has two different objectives. So yes, in that part [negotiations] it would be silly to suggest no.

However, it is also disputed in the Secretariat that the missing of deadlines in the negotiations is an indicator of ineffectiveness. The argument is that ambitious negotiations (the example of the Uruguay Round is given) necessarily require a number of years to be completed.

> Some might well say no, because this round is only four years old, five years old, other rounds were eight years old, it was a very ambitious round, so you need more time. [...] So fine we missed deadlines, and we don't meet them, but then that doesn't mean the institution is ineffective, on that one aspect.

It is clear that those who work for an organization are hesitant to describe their own organization as being ineffective. In this respect, outside observers are more neutral. However, the failures of the Ministerial Conferences in Seattle and Cancún, and, more recently, the complete halt brought to negotiations since summer 2007 are clear indicators of lack of effectiveness as regards trade negotiations in the WTO. This is confirmed in literature. With regard to the Doha Agenda, scholars found it "hard to deny that the Doha agenda was going badly. [...] It is still not certain whether there will be anything more than a face-saving minimalist outcome, or, if, there is, whether it will take several more years." (*Halle* 2006: 115). More generally, it has been claimed that it was now widely accepted that the WTO's "legislative bodies" were working, "if at all, very poorly" (*Blackhurst and Hartridge* 2004: 710). This amounted to the statement that the WTO lost its comparative advantage as a negotiating forum. There were now better places for members to negotiate new trade liberalization measures (*Hufbauer* 2005: 295).

(b) Implementation of trade agreements

There is no general evaluation of the implementation of WTO agreements available. Regarding the implementation of WTO rules in developed countries, there is a noticeable research gap. While the number of cases raised in dispute settlement which involves developed countries suggests that developed countries also have compliance problems, systematic analyses on this point are lacking. Regarding developing countries, however, scholars agree that the implementation of many demanding WTO rules raises particular problems for developing countries (*Shaffer* 2005a: 249ff.; *Sutherland* 2005a: 40).

The evaluation of the effectiveness of implementing trade agreements requires reliable implementation data. The absence of reliable data indicates deficiencies in the implementation of trade agreements. Implementation data are mainly provided by member states through notifications and reports. Figure 6.1 demonstrates how member countries assess the reliability of these implementation data.

Only 50% of the respondents hold the view that member states provide often or very often reliable information on the implementation of trade agreements to WTO committees. The other 50% believe that this is only sometimes or rarely the case. There are no large differences regarding this question between developing and developed countries. However, there is a slight tendency of developing countries to have more diversified views, probably reflecting the different capacities of developing countries to provide information.

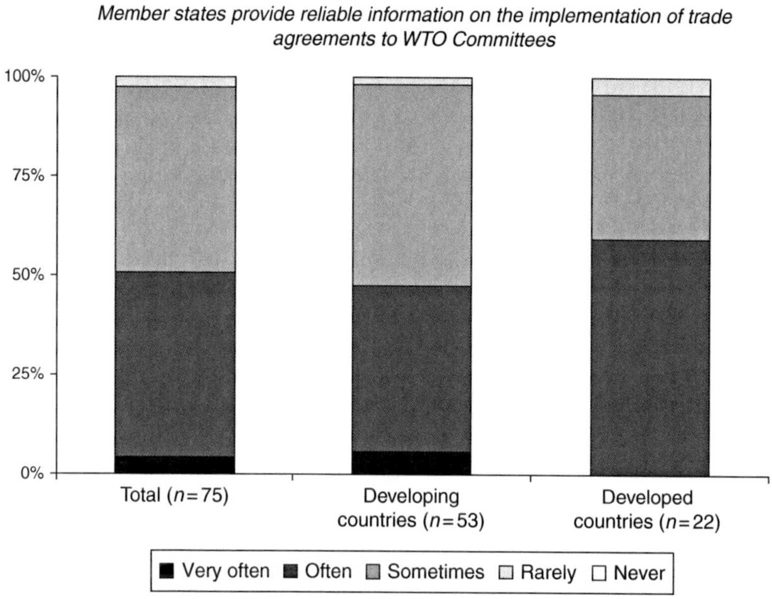

Figure 6.1 Information on the implementation of trade agreements

Moreover, the record of some WTO committees demonstrates that obligations to notify measures are not always respected in practice. For instance, developed country notifications in agriculture were criticized for being too late and lacking in transparency (*Ismail* 2005: 65). Under the Agreement on Subsidies and Countervailing Measures, there have been several discussions with the committee to improve conformity. While most member states comply to some extent with obligations to notify certain subsidies, notifications by member states are rarely complete. The sub-national level represents a particular difficulty in this respect (*Clarke and Horlick* 2005: 729). Another example is the Agreement of Rules of Origin, under which WTO member states are obliged to notify their rules of origin, judicial decisions, etc. to the Secretariat. The committee established under the Agreement shall review annually the implementation and operation of the Agreement. The committee found in several subsequent years that only between 70 and 90 WTO member countries (of more than 140) had made notifications of rules of origin. The Chairperson of the committee expresses each year his or her "concern that a number of members had not yet complied with the notification requirements." Members who have not yet notified to do so are urged to do so as early as possible.[1]

In light of this experience and the survey results the effectiveness of implementing trade agreements does not seem satisfactory.

(c) Trade policy review

As mentioned above, indicators of deficiencies with regard to the effectiveness of the Trade Policy Review Mechanism are failures to make and/or to comply with trade policy reviews.

As regards the making of trade policy reviews, there are no indicators that the effectiveness of the Trade Policy Review Mechanism is deficient. Between 1995 and the end of 2000, 74 WTO members had been reviewed, and 135 reviews had been conducted (*Davey* 2005: 59). In any year there are likely to be at least 14 or 15 reviews (*Xu and Weller* 2004: 268). For instance, the Programme of Reviews of 2007 which was established in consultation with delegations schedules 18 reviews.[2] Information generated through the review is seen as valuable in literature. In most cases, the reports are the only comprehensive description of a country's trade policies (*Davey* 2005: 59). In this sense the Trade Policy Review is certainly effective. To what extent do countries change their policies in line with conclusions made in the Secretariat report?

Figure 6.2 depicts how WTO member countries view the effectiveness of the Trade Policy Review regarding compliance with recommendations.

As regards compliance with recommendations, member countries view the Trade Policy Review Mechanism as weakly effective. The views of developing and developed countries are largely the same. Some 25% of the respondents believe that WTO member states often comply with recommendations made by the Trade Policy Review Committee. The vast majority feel that this is only sometimes the case.

(d) Dispute settlement

Several interview partners from the Secretariat and from member states observed that the dispute settlement is comparatively effective. For instance, a G-4 Developed Country, when asked about the effectiveness of the WTO as a whole, has mentioned that while one could have a question mark with regard to the area of negotiations, the institution was certainly effective regarding dispute settlement. Secretariat staff argued that the WTO dispute settlement mechanism functions perfectly well while deadlines were missed for negotiations:

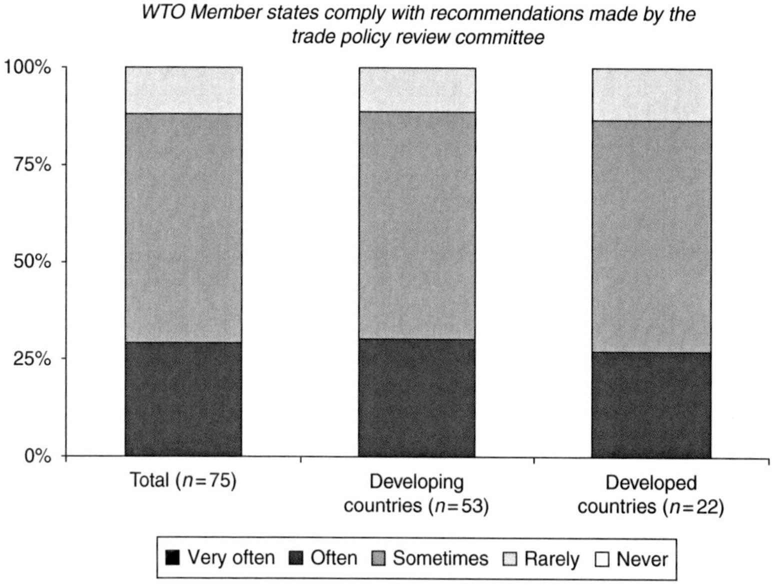

Figure 6.2 Compliance with recommendations in trade policy review

> The point is what we see now is a big imbalance between the treaty side, the legislation side, the text side, and the dispute settlement side. After 1994 when the WTO was created a big imbalance was introduced. It now becomes very difficult to advance the treaty makings. A lot of the gaps are filled by the dispute settlements.

Hence, the interview partners confirmed the view advanced in literature that there is an asymmetry between the effectiveness of the dispute settlement system, and the ineffectiveness of the WTO "legislative process" (*Barfield* 2001: 437). This has resulted in the statement: "To be sure, the WTO dispute settlement mechanism is first class. The same cannot be said of its negotiating capabilities" (*Hufbauer* 2005: 295). The adoption of new interpretations or clarifications to resolve ambiguities in the new WTO rules have not been successful, and hence dispute panels and the Appellate Body are "under increasing pressure to legislate through interpretation and filling in the blanks in WTO disciplines" (*Barfield* 2001: 42).

Indicators of ineffectiveness are the failure to make and/or comply with dispute settlement decisions. Table 6.1 shows how many panel

Table 6.1 Percentage of panel reports appealed between 1996 and 2005

	All Panel Reports		
Year of adoption	**Panel Reports adopted**	**Panel Reports appealed**	**Percentage of Panel Reports appealed (%)**
1996	2	2	100
1997	5	5	100
1998	12	9	75
1999	10	7	70
2000	19	11	58
2001	17	12	71
2002	12	6	50
2003	10	7	70
2004	8	6	75
2005	20	12	60
Total	115	77	67

Source: WTO dispute settlement statistics: Table 2 http://www.wto.org/English/tratop_e/dispu_e/stats_e.htm

reports have been adopted and which percentage of them has been appealed between 1996 and 2005.

Statistics show that an average of 11.5 panel reports per year has been adopted over the last 10 years, with a peak of 20 reached in 2005. Output of the dispute settlement system as regards dispute settlement decisions is thus comparatively high. The making of dispute settlement decisions, however, is one way to resolve the case. Another way is to resolve a case through consultations before or during the panel stage.

Of the 124 cases which have been recorded as resolved between 1995 and 2004, 44 cases were settled during consultations (*Schuchhardt* 2005: 1203). While the consultation stage can be effective in providing for early resolutions of conflicts, in some cases consultations are nothing more than a necessary formality before litigation begins when the responding party has no interest in participating constructively in the consultation process (*Schuchhardt* 2005: 1208).

Figure 6.3 shows how member states assess the compliance of WTO members with binding decisions taken by dispute settlement bodies.

Regarding compliance of WTO members with binding dispute settlement decisions, dispute settlement is deemed very effective, particularly if compared against trade policy review and implementation. Three-quarters of the respondents hold the view that WTO member states

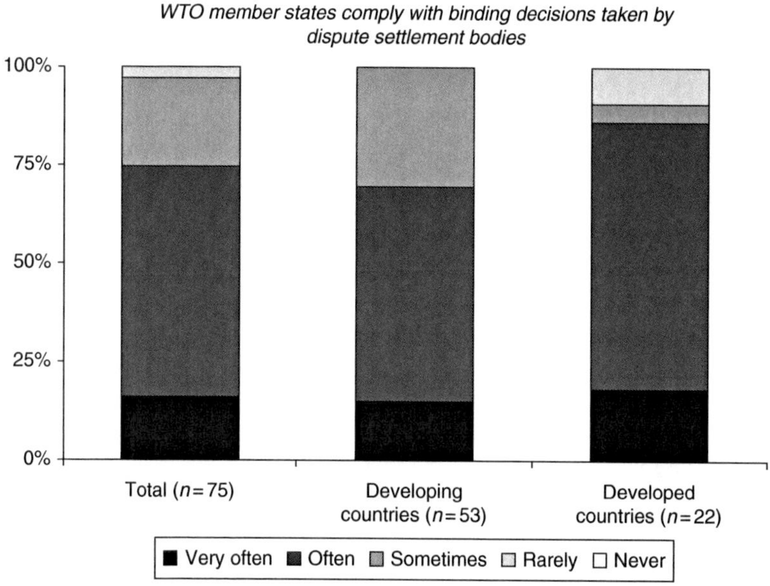

Figure 6.3 Compliance with dispute settlement decisions

comply "very often" or "often" with binding decisions taken by dispute settlement bodies. In this area, developed countries have slightly more diversified views than developing countries.

Literature has sometimes pointed to instances of persistent non-compliance. Although members had expressed their intention to comply with every recommendation and ruling, compliance had not occurred in several cases "and in other cases it has only occurred after lengthy delays" (*Gallagher* 2005: 114; *Shoyer et al.* 2005). Incorrect implementation of measures taken to comply with recommendations and rulings of the DSB can lead to new panels being established under Art. 21(5) of the DSU. Figures show that since 1996, 15 such panel reports have been issued concerning lack of implementation.[3]

2. Explanatory factors

(a) Political conflicts

In literature, the reform of agreements on agriculture is seen as essential for a successful conclusion of the Doha Round (*Walker* 2005: 443). It has been argued that their "economic and political significance is such that the pace of the agricultural negotiations determines the pace of the negotiations overall. The Round as a whole will not be concluded unless and until the agriculture negotiations are ready for conclusions" (*Harbinson* 2005: 121). However, negotiations on agriculture involve highly conflictual items as the reduction of subsidies for agriculture, involving both export and domestic subsidies on agricultural products (for an overview, see *Walker* 2005). In the view of a Secretariat official, negotiations which seem to have worked for the reduction of tariffs in earlier rounds are problematic for solving conflicts in the reduction of subsidies for agriculture:

> The other thing is the sensitivity of the issues. You know, in large part, the GATT was successful in the earlier round in reducing tariff barriers. What remains now is politically hugely sensitive like high tariffs on exports from developing countries into the markets of developed countries.

It is in particular the larger developing countries Brazil and India which now view a phase-out of subsidies for agricultural products as an essential precondition for the conclusion of the Doha Round. At the same time, this phase-out is opposed by the European Union and, also at least partially by the United States. Political conflicts between these four "key actors" (representing the G-4) are clearly difficult, if not impossible to redress through organizational reforms of the WTO. Thus, the ineffectiveness of trade negotiations is, to some extent, explained by profound political conflicts between key members of the WTO.

Political conflicts occupy a less prominent position in implementation and trade policy review. For dispute settlement, the solving of political conflicts is the essential objective. However, as dispute settlement is dominated by a hierarchical mode of governance (see I.2.d in this chapter), the resolution of political conflicts is easier.

(b) Regulatory requirements

In the WTO there are three regulatory requirements, which can impede the *effectiveness of negotiations*. These are the consensus principle, the principle of single undertaking, and the principle that modalities are negotiated before products.

As explained in Chapter 4, I and III, all committees and councils have full membership, and decisions can only be taken by consensus of all members. There is no smaller decision-making body. It has been argued that consensus rule was inadequate for an organization of 150 members.

"Mass membership" impeded efficiency (*Ehlermann and Ehring* 2005: 68; *Moore* 2005: 44). However, so far the principles of full membership and the consensus-making rule have been maintained (*Hufbauer* 2005: 295). Formal decision making has, however, been complemented by various types of informal decisions-making procedures (see Chapter 5, I.1.b).

As outlined in Chapter 4, I the negotiations of the Doha Agenda follow the logic that "nothing is agreed until everything is agreed." Negotiations thus can only be concluded successfully if agreement is reached on all issues on the agenda. In the view of the Secretariat staff the effectiveness of negotiations is negatively affected by the scope of the agenda and the principle of "single undertaking" with developing countries being reluctant to commit themselves. This has been confirmed in literature. Developing countries have realized that the single undertaking increases the "risk of a negotiation that would not produce a balance of obligations and benefits for them, since they do not have the resources to shape a huge agenda during negotiations" (*Gallagher* 2005: 134).

Another regulatory requirement that could impede effectiveness of negotiations is the principle that "modalities" are negotiated before products (see Chapter 4, IV.1). To recall, modalities are targets (including numerical targets) for achieving the objectives set out in the Doha Ministerial Declaration. It has been laid down in the Doha Work Programme for a number of issues that these targets have to be agreed upon in a first step.[4] The WTO has acknowledged that the reaching of an agreement on modalities is an important first step which will determine the shape of the negotiations' final outcome (*WTO* 2004: 9).

An NGO identified specific uncertainties which are caused by the principle that the modalities are applied to different products and an individual scheme of commitments is agreed for each and every single product only in the last stage of negotiations:

> And this negotiating process seems logical, but it might be counterproductive, particularly for poor countries, because you don't really know what you're negotiating. You know that there will be lots of flexibilities, but you don't know whether you are talking about bananas, or beef, or sugar, because you're not looking at specific products.

The consensus principle, the principle of single undertaking, and the principle that modalities are negotiated before products can therefore be considered as regulatory requirements that impede effectiveness.

Concerning *implementation of WTO agreements,* it is questionable to what extent procedures in the regular sessions are really effective in enforcing WTO agreements. As outlined in Chapter 4, IV.1, there are various different procedures employed in different implementation committees for the notification and assessment of information regarding implementation. However, these procedures do not primarily aim at the determination and remedying of non-compliance of member states. As set out in Chapter 5, II.1, the Secretariat is unable to pinpoint non-compliance of member states. An interview partner from the Secretariat acknowledged that

> if somebody violates the anti-dumping agreement, you have a committee, but then you have notification procedures, you have challenges during the committee, but essentially the only real mechanism to get enforcement is to go via disputes.

The fact that there have been recently so many dispute settlement cases in agriculture has led to the recognition that many of the agreed procedures in implementation were too weak, and required, for instance, too little reporting. This confirms the skeptical assessment regarding mechanisms of implementation in literature. Following a careful analysis of the implementation provisions dispersed over various agreements, it is concluded that the WTO itself, without the instigation of a complaint by a member, does not have at its disposal effective enforcement measures (*Quereshi* 1996: 95).

The *effectiveness of dispute settlement* is closely related to the existence of a consensus rule which if compared against the consensus rule in negotiations, is a "reversed consensus rule." In dispute settlement the panels and the Appellate Body are decision-makers rather than member states. Formally, one may doubt whether the dispute settlement mechanism functions as a separate judicial branch given that decisions by panels and Appellate Body can only become effective once they have been adopted by the DSB that represents all the membership. However, a "key procedural rule" demonstrates that despite being formally subordinate to the DSB, panels and the Appellate Body have authority to act in a hierarchical manner. This key rule is that the DSB is directed to adopt panel and Appellate Body reports unless there is a consensus not to do so. In practice this means that any report proposed for adoption by the complaining party will automatically be adopted, because the complaining party would not join a consensus against adoption (see *Charnovitz* 2002b: 227).

(c) Resources

Interview partners from the Secretariat have not only identified lack of resources of many developing countries as a reason for *ineffectiveness in negotiations*, but also enhanced negotiation skills of some developing countries:

> And why is it becoming more and more difficult to negotiate? Because other members than just the rich countries are today important actors. Some things become more and more difficult. Which is not bad news in my opinion.

> They have become a lot more capable in coordinating their positions, in voicing their positions and in making sure that their positions are not overlooked. So they become very, very good at that. In coordinating amongst themselves, in presenting a coordinated position to the membership.

These explanations are confirmed in literature. A greater number of countries now participate actively in negotiations. More generally, new alliances such as the G-20 have increased the bargaining power of smaller countries (*Footer* 2006: 166). In scholarly accounts on why the Ministerial Conference in Cancún failed, it was argued that Brazil and India were enabled to build up the G-21 (now G-20) through the accession of China. The symbolic unity of developing countries maintained in Cancún for the first time was a powerful force against the pressure of developed countries, but ultimately contributed to the failure of the Ministerial Conference (*Cho* 2004: 235).

Even though some countries have better negotiating capacities, a Secretariat official argued that the lack of negotiations skills in many smaller developing countries continues to have a negative impact on the negotiations. While poorer developing countries had few capacities to negotiate and understand trade rules, they had at least understood that they had to implement the rules they had agreed upon. In the view of the Secretariat, they had become reluctant to make concessions:

> This is a large part of the reason why people are so frustrated with the progress of negotiations because we have this huge agenda, and developing countries which have very little capacity at home to follow and analyse these issues are very reluctant to go too fast in one area, without understanding what they are being asked to undertake. As a result, everything runs down to a very slow level of movement,

> because a lot of developing country delegations are trying to grapple with all the issues that are here presented to them.

An NGO argued that lack of resources affects negotiating capacity of smaller developing countries to the extent that they have not been able to define their interests and their negotiating position:

> So, they have nothing to contribute to the discussion in many cases. Because if you don't know what your interests are, you cannot really negotiate.

Finally, interview partners from the Secretariat indicated that member states may not only lack capacities to make progress with the agenda, but they may also simply lack personnel that can attend the various meetings and negotiate the huge agenda:

> Often the membership is not available at the time the chairperson wants to meet with them because they deal with something else in another meeting. [...] It is just impossible to deal with these huge issues.

Literature has also recognized that developing countries have now very divergent negotiation capacities. While the advanced developing countries have the necessary capacity and expertise to guide their delegations in Geneva, the large number of poorer countries is in a completely different situation. While some may not even have an office in Geneva (*Nanz and Steffek* 2004), others may have one or two people to service the vast number of processes in the WTO. An added difficulty can be that these delegates are not supported by guidance or expertise from their capitals (*Sutherland* 2005c: 35).

There were accounts in literature which have blamed the failure of Ministerial Conferences on the failure of the Secretariat to properly prepare negotiations (*Cho* 2004: 223; *Xu and Weller* 2004: 256). However, interview partners from an NGO and from a G-4 Developing Country pointed out that the performance of the WTO Secretariat was not a problem regarding the preparation of conferences and meetings. A committee chairperson observed:

> I think that the WTO is perhaps one of the more efficient organizations you know. Efficiency, when you use it in its narrow sense.

> It should mean that you know the organization of meetings. Procedures, the drawing up of the agenda, preparation of implementation for the agenda. And then the management of the meetings themselves. I would give [the Secretariat] 90%.

The question is, however, whether the Secretariat could not do more, for instance, by providing a different type of technical assistance and/or by carrying out a different type of research. The Secretariat itself has repeatedly referred to the principle of neutrality as a guiding principle. It interprets the principle in such a way as to prevent it from providing specific types of technical assistance or carrying out particular types of research (see Chapter 5, I.2.a).

Regarding *implementation*, it is clearly the lack of resources of developing countries which accounts for many deficiencies. Developing countries often lack capacities to implement WTO rules properly (*Shaffer* 2005a: 249f.). For instance, developing countries encounter systemic and structural problems in the implementation of the Agreement on Customs Valuation (*Forrester and Odarda* 2005: 569). The "long-running implementation debates" of the first 10 years of WTO existence have shown that member countries have only gradually understood the costs involved in the implementation of WTO agreements.

Technical assistance represents an effort of the WTO to enhance resources of developing countries to enable them to better comply with WTO Agreements. However, the impact of technical assistance on the effectiveness of implementation of WTO rules is naturally hard to measure due to its "soft nature."

There are currently no indications that lack of resources of developing countries has negatively affected the *effectiveness of trade policy review*.

Regarding *dispute settlement*, it can be assumed that lack of resources of developing countries also has a negative impact on the number of dispute settlement decisions. Lack of resources of developing countries generally accounts for the low participation rate of developing countries in dispute settlement, thereby causing inequities (II.2.c in this chapter). Another question is whether compliance with rulings of the WTO panels is also negatively affected by lack of resources in developing countries (*Shoyer et al.* 2005). If this was the case, developing countries would probably be overrepresented in the above mentioned cases dealing with a lack of implementation. Currently, there are no figures available which show how often this particular type of disputes involves developing countries.

(d) Organizational systems requirements

Interview partners (both from the Secretariat and member states) often emphasized that there is a positive relationship between informal decision making and the *effectiveness of negotiations* and the implementation of agreements. This can be explained, from an organizational systems perspective, with the need for conflict resolution.

A developing country, for instance, argued that it valued informal meetings because formal meetings do not allow for an open discussion between members due to the fact that minutes are taken:

> Now, you are right, when you say, there are decisions which are made within the informal set-up. And there are no minutes. And this is where the important discussions take place. And I tell you as a country, we value the informals very much, because the formal meetings formalize what has been discussed in the informals. So the informals are very important. That's where you discuss openly, that's where you challenge each other, even academically. You argue your case.

Informal meetings thus enable open discussions because there are no written formal minutes. Hence, a G-4 Developed Country reported that member countries can test the ground in informal negotiations for finding new compromises, without having the delegating country as "mother-in-law" behind them which can check the minutes.

According to member states, informal decision making facilitates the reaching of consensus through limiting participation in informal meetings. This is particularly valued by G-countries. The representative of a G-4 Developing Country experienced that it is impossible to reach decisions with 148 members assembled in one room:

> On the other side they are saying that sometimes decisions cannot be reached with all the 148 members being present, people don't speak up in a bigger room, people cannot come out with their exact concerns in a bigger room. But they can articulate them in a 1 to 1 or in a confined setting.

The Secretariat, however, voted that one specific form of informal decision making, namely meetings by small powerful groups outside the Geneva process, may have a negative impact on the effectiveness of negotiations in the WTO, particularly if media report on the meeting:

> They receive so much press, we will be telling these people: Do it quietly. Why do you have to publicize your meetings? It upsets and annoys the Geneva-based representatives. It's like they have no role here, because the press is all about the G-3 meetings here, the G-6 meetings there. There is currently a G-4 meeting. Where is the real work that is actually going on here? That upsets people because they are reading in the press that these meetings are going to take place. They have no idea of what is going on there.

Worse, the same Secretariat official noted that the Geneva process may go to a halt if major trading powers such as the United States, European Union, India, and Brazil decide to meet. In this case, other delegations in Geneva may say: "We have to wait to see what happens, what are the results from there." Even after the meeting, there may be little transparency, since representatives are unwilling to talk about the meeting, if there was a lack of agreement.

To conclude, it seems that the major share of informal decision-making practices contributes to the effectiveness of WTO negotiations by resolving conflicts. However, meetings of small informal groups of powerful countries may be an exception, in so far as they bring a Geneva process to a temporary halt. If these meetings fail to deliver results, and the Geneva negotiation process is impeded, the overall effect is rather negative. In any case, as the current state of the Doha Round demonstrates, the organization of informal meetings may be a necessary but not a sufficient condition for the successful conclusion of negotiations in the WTO.

As the history of the GATT and WTO has evidenced, the Director General can informally intervene into the negotiation process, even though he has no formal powers to do so. For instance, Arthur Dunkel at one point in the Uruguay Round has made direct and concrete negotiation proposals in particular periods. The problem is, however, that in the absence of a formal right, the effect of any intervention by a Director General is highly contingent on times and circumstances.

Currently, the effectiveness of the Director General seems to be impeded by the growing strength of certain informal groups in the WTO. One interview partner from a development-oriented intergovernmental organization pointed out that the Director General as part of his role as a chairman of the Trade Negotiations Committee would try to bring different countries and groups of countries together to form coalitions. His problem was, however, that groups like the G-20 had become much stronger than in the past, and often thwarted the Director General's efforts.

As in negotiations, the role of informal decision making in *implementation* is seen, according to a committee chairperson, as contributing to effectiveness through a better resolution of conflicts. Since no minutes are taken, informal meetings can be employed as a means for member countries to resolve conflicts through open discussion. For instance, in an informal meeting, a member country could tell another member country that it required more time to implement a certain rule. The concession that there was an issue to be addressed would not be made in a formal meeting.

As outlined in Chapter 5, III.2 and IV.2, informal decision making plays a lesser role in *trade policy review* and *dispute settlement* and can therefore not be considered as relevant factors for explaining lack of effectiveness in these areas.

(e) Governance modes

The comparatively *low effectiveness of negotiations* can be linked to the dominant mode of exchange in this area, while the high effectiveness of dispute settlement can be seen as following from the hierarchy mode of governance. This leads to a trade-off between the two: It seems that some issues cannot be resolved through negotiations because member countries are under strong domestic pressures not to make any concessions, as in the area of subsidies. In this area, progress may be expected rather from dispute settlement than from negotiations, as the decisions in the Cotton Case and the Sugar Case demonstrate. WTO panels found in these cases that subsidies by developed countries (the European Union for sugar and the United States for cotton)[5] had violated existing WTO agreements (*Petersmann* 2005a). However, such progress is only possible in so far as subsidizing practices of developed countries are found to violate existing agreements; the problem of agricultural subsidies in general is not tackled.

However, despite the fact that the hierarchy mode of governance is predominant in WTO dispute settlement, the mechanism is also embedded in an exchange mode of governance. Thus the consultation preceding the establishment of panels constitutes bilateral exchanges. And once panels and appellate bodies have decided, bilateral exchange concerning the mode of implementation follows. Negotiation was therefore found to be an indispensable element of the process (*Shoyer et al.* 2005).

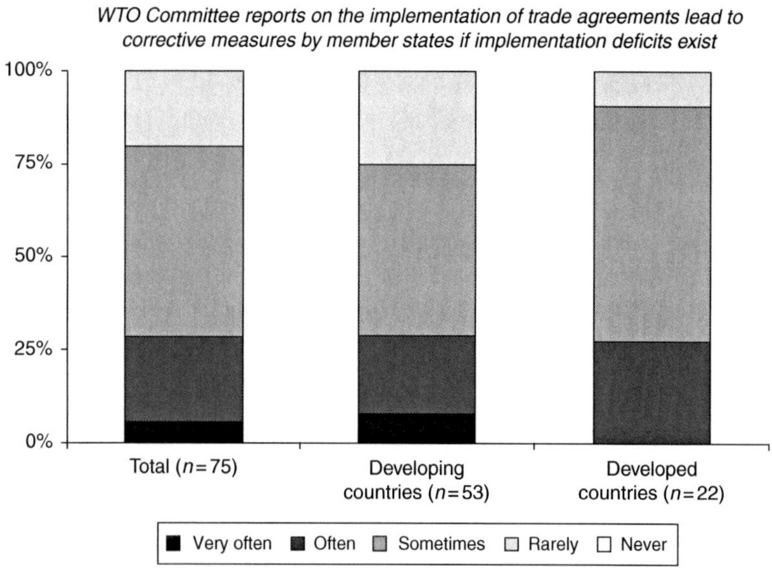

Figure 6.4 Corrective measures in implementation

Implementation as practiced in the WTO must be seen as a mixture of a weakly developed persuasion and exchange mode of governance operating in the WTO. The various notification procedures put information at the disposition of member states. This may be an incentive in itself for member states to implement properly. Moreover, the information can be used by member states to challenge other member states policies through discussion in committees and/or bilateral negotiations. However, implementation procedures employed in the WTO are not always considered helpful in improving compliance of members with WTO agreements. Figure 6.4 depicts how member countries assess the likelihood that corrective measures be taken in implementation after WTO committees have identified implementation deficits, thereby assessing the effectiveness of the persuasion mode of governance.

In total, only slightly more than a quarter of the respondents believe that committee reports on the implementation of trade agreements lead often or very often to corrective measures by member states if implementation deficits exist. The overwhelming majority believes that this is only sometimes or rarely the case. Again, there are no strong differences between developing and developed countries. The figure shows that developing countries have more diversified views on the issue than developed countries. This probably reflects the widely diverging capacities of developing countries in carrying out corrective measures.

Technical assistance to improve implementation of WTO rules can be characterized as a mode of persuasion, too. Developing countries are persuaded to better implement WTO rules: "Technical assistance for implementation, [...] can represent a form of soft persuasion by the Secretariat of what developing countries must do in respect of other Member's demands" (*Shaffer* 2005a: 272). However, there is only an assumption but no clear evidence that technical assistance increases the effectiveness of implementation.

The *trade policy review* mechanism is probably the best example of a persuasion mode of governance operating in the WTO. This applies both to the work of the Secretariat – the drafting of the report – as well as to the discussion of the report. An interview partner from the Secretariat argued:

> The trade policy review on the other hand is not really linked to any particular agreement or committee. It is an overall review of the operation of trade policy in the member government. It examines the whole operation of trade policy. It is not really to censure a government, but to apply peer pressure, to say: here you are doing good and here you are doing less good.

The report devised by the Secretariat and the discussion based thereon by members have thus the function to expose possible deficiencies of their domestic trade and economic policies and, if necessary, to take corrective measures. Moreover, the persuasion mode of governance is linked to an exchange mode of governance. Secretariat staff confirmed that information from the trade policy review is regularly used in trade negotiations. A link to hierarchical elements, however, is missing, since information from the trade policy review cannot be used in dispute settlement (see Chapter 4, II.3).

As regards trade policy review, procedures employed in the WTO are not always considered helpful in improving compliance of members with WTO agreements. As set out in Chapter 5, III.1, the Secretariat report does not always contain a set of explicit recommendations (*Xu and Weller* 2004: 268f.).

Moreover, the approach taken to the implementation of recommendations has not been a systematic one so far. Only recently, it has been decided that the Secretariat should in each of its reviews go back to the previous review and look at the conclusions and eventual corrective measures taken by the country under review.

To conclude, the mode of persuasion employed in WTO implementation and trade policy review is currently a rather weak one, and it may be argued that reforms in this area could contribute to strengthening the two mechanisms.

3. Conclusions

With regard to effectiveness, there are deficits in all four areas: negotiations, implementation, trade policy review, and dispute settlement. However, deficits seem most obvious in the area of negotiations, while dispute settlement can be considered comparatively effective. Implementation and trade policy review can be considered as intermediate cases.

Effectiveness can be linked to the role of the WTO as corporate actor, and ineffectiveness to the role of the WTO as a collective actor (see Chapter 5, IV). In negotiations, where the WTO can be characterized predominantly as a collective actor, it is least effective, while it is most effective in dispute settlement where it functions as a corporate actor (since panels and the Appellate Bodies play the decisive role).

Political conflicts in the Doha Round surrounding the area of agriculture are probably the most important factor for explaining the ineffectiveness of WTO negotiations. Organizational reforms can only make a minor contribution to resolving this difficulty. In other areas, political conflicts are less relevant for explaining ineffectiveness.

Regulatory requirements can partially account for the lack of effectiveness in negotiations and in implementation. In negotiations, the consensus principle, the single undertaking rule, and the principle of negotiating modalities before products are seen as contributing to ineffectiveness. In implementation, procedures under WTO agreements and as agreed by WTO committees can be seen as ineffective for ensuring the correct implementation of WTO rules. In this regard, dispute settlement makes a better contribution to the effective implementation of WTO rules, not at least due to the "reversed" consensus rule.

Resources are important in three of four areas: trade negotiations and implementation are both negatively affected by the lack of resources of developing countries. In trade negotiations some, but not all member countries have enhanced their capacities, and this represents an added difficulty. Regarding dispute settlement, it may be argued that the number of cases could be enhanced if developing countries had more resources.

Informal decision making is mostly seen as increasing effectiveness in negotiations and in implementation since it helps to resolve conflicts. However, it is stressed by the Secretariat that one form of informal decision making (the meetings of small groups outside the Geneva process, such as the G-4) can have a paralyzing effect on negotiations as a whole, if they are unsuccessful.

The informal role of the Director General is likely to be an impediment to effective negotiations. Without a formal mandate for the making of proposals, the Director General's role remains highly contingent on times and circumstances. Any proposal currently made to overcome a negotiating impasse can be ignored by member states.

Regarding modes of governance, all modes are present in the four areas: The hierarchical mode of governance prevailing in dispute settlement is clearly more effective than the exchange mode of governance dominating negotiations. Implementation and trade policy review are dominated by a weakly developed mode of persuasion which, it is argued, could be strengthened through reforms to be discussed in Chapter 7.

II. Equity

Indicators of deficiencies of equity of members are failure and/or shortcomings to balance the trade interests of all WTO members and to participate in WTO decision-making processes. Indicators of deficiencies regarding equity of concerns are failures to balance environmental and/or labor policy concerns with trade policies.

1. Task areas

(a) Trade negotiations

Informal procedures in the WTO have an impact on the protection of trade interests of smaller developing and LDCs in the WTO. Figure 6.5 shows how member countries assess the effects.

Only 40% of the respondents believe that informal procedures make protection and advancing of interests "very often" or "often" difficult for these countries. There is a difference between developing and developed countries: 45% of the developing countries regard smaller

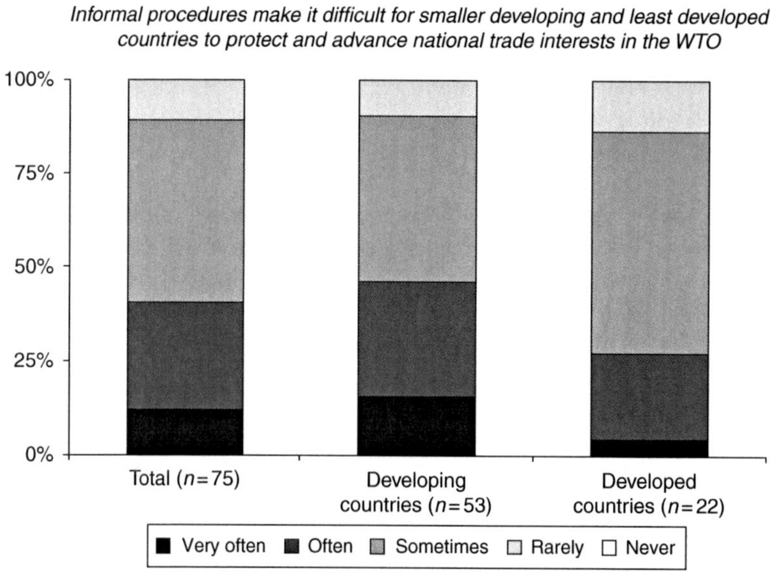

Figure 6.5 Effects of informal procedures on trade interests of smaller developing countries and LDCs

developing and LDCs as being "very often" or "often" disadvantaged. By contrast, with 27% only a smaller share of developed countries supports this view. Since developing countries are the group concerned, their views seem more relevant than the views of developed countries. In sum, the overall attitude of member states toward the WTO is positive in spite of the widespread public criticism that the WTO and its informal practices are disadvantaging developing countries.

The proliferation of informal negotiation patterns within (and outside of) the WTO requires clearly more qualified personnel than a limited number of formal meetings. For a small developing country, participation in the multitude of informal meetings is not possible. In this regard, a Secretariat official pointed out:

> Delegations, especially from developing countries, find it very difficult to attend all the meetings that are going on all the issues and as a result, they cannot defend their positions in all the issues.

Another aspect of informal decision making that detriments equal participation of members is that informal meetings tend to be meetings of smaller groups, which exclude smaller developing countries (see Chapter 5, I.1.b). An executive of the Secretariat, however, argued that efforts have been made to avoid exclusion of smaller members from the decision-making process. Members who still complained about the process often disliked the outcome of negotiations. He observed:

> But very often we knew here, those complaints, these are from members who are fundamentally opposed to some changes that are occurring and who, of course, are going to use process arguments against the outcome because very often that helps strengthen the opposition they might have to it. They might argue that the process to reach that position was unfair to them, it is a lot better than just arguing the substance.

A criticism voiced both by NGOs and by a development-oriented intergovernmental organization is that once a compromise has been reached between a small group of powerful countries in an informal process, developing countries are then put under pressure to accept the result even though they have the formal right not to consent (*Jawara and Kwa* 2003: 148ff.).

A representative of a development-oriented intergovernmental organization identified a reluctance of smaller developing countries to reject what had been negotiated in smaller groups in informal processes:

> But what has often happened is that, when the decisions are ready done in the informal process, if you are a smaller country, and that proposed decision is brought to the formal setting, for a smaller country you would hesitate to speak out, again given the balance of power and the fact that you feel you were not privy to all of the discussions that happened before that proposed decision was brought there.

Figure 6.6 depicts how member countries view the effect of group representation during informal negotiations on the protection and advancement of trade interests of smaller developing and LLDs in the WTO.

The effect of group representation is regarded as overall positive. Approximately one-quarter of respondents express the view that it has positive effects regardless of the specific interests of group representatives. The share of developed countries which are unconditionally positive regarding representation is significantly larger than

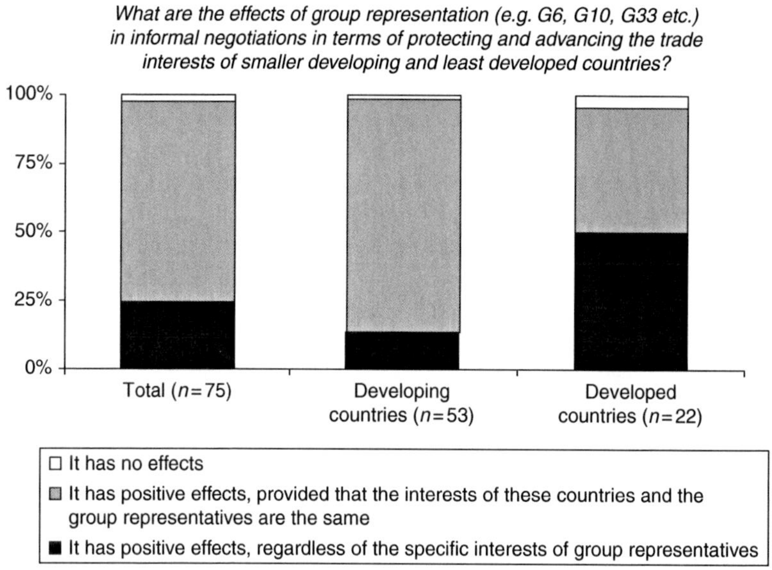

Figure 6.6 Effects of group representation on trade interests of smaller developing countries and LDCs

the share of developing countries with 50%. However, in this regard the views of developing countries as those directly concerned are more important. Only 13% of the developing countries are unconditionally positive regarding group representation. The overwhelming majority of developing countries (83%) argues that group representation has only positive effects, provided that the interests of smaller developing and LDCs and the group representatives are the same.

So far, scholarly literature has not yet noticed the effects of group representation as having a mitigating effect on the negative effects of restricted informal decision making. An interview partner from the Secretariat and an interview partner from a G-4 Developing Country have supported the view that even though informal decision making in general makes the protection of trade interests of smaller developing and LDCs more difficult, one special form of informal decision making, group representation in terms of "re-insurance" meetings of larger groups of small countries (e.g. the G-20) has a mitigating and positive effect. Hence, informal meetings are not having the adverse effect that they would have provided countries were not organized in groups with similar interests. A representative of a G-4 Developing Country argued:

> Countries that are coming together, negotiating together, they are building upon each other's trend, and are not getting isolated in the negotiation process, while a smaller country, a single member, a single vote, can get isolated, merely because it is a marginal player in world trade. But being a part of a grouping like this, with this common interest group, it builds upon its negotiating ability, it strengthens its negotiating ability, being part of a group.

A particular type of informal meeting, the Green Room meeting at the Ministerial Conference, has been subject to extensive criticism for disadvantaging those countries excluded (*Das* 2000: 191; *Blackhurst and Hartridge* 2004: 711; *Footer* 2006: 167f.). However, it has been argued by several interview partners that great care is now taken by the Secretariat to ensure that the member countries invited to the Green Room are representatives for smaller countries and/or for groups:

> I think that enormous efforts have been made to ensure that those smaller groups are not exclusionary to smaller members. If you for example looked at the Green Room composition in Hong Kong, and the same one we use here. Over half of the members participating in that Green Room represented less than 10% of world trade. The continent of Africa which is less than 2% of world trade, had 5 ministers in the Green Room process. So of course, we are very careful to make sure that the African Union representative is there, the African Group, the ACP Group, the LDC Group...

An interview partner from a developing country confirmed this. Moreover, he argued that informal groups have to consult with their members before and after Green Room meetings. Views differ, however, on whether member states present in the Green Room in Hong Kong had enough time and opportunity to consult with the groups they were representing. A representative of a developing country attending the Hong Kong Ministerial Conference gave a positive account of the conference:

> They informed us what went on in the Green Room. And we gave our own advice of what needed to be done. Not everything that we

> suggested was taken into consideration, but of course only some of the issues that we requested and pushed for. They did, they did do that. Because if you look at the Hong Kong Ministerial Declaration, there are few issues that we pushed as ACP or as African Group, and they are captured in the declaration. So they did some good job.

In contrast, an NGO pointed out that countries excluded from the Green Room could not obtain enough information due to time constraints:

> For example, this happened in Cancún or in Hong Kong. They had this Green Room every night until five a.m. And then they say they will tell the group. But they meet again at eight a.m. So where do they have the chance to inform the group? They don't have the chance to... It's all very good in theory, but in practice, those outside the room don't know what's going on.

It can be concluded that certain practices of informal decision making (in particular small group meetings) can hinder smaller developing countries and LDCs from participating in WTO decision making, thereby promoting inequity. However, in recent years efforts by the Secretariat and the practice of member countries to build up larger groups which can be informed by privileged countries able to participate in small group meetings have contributed to mitigating the negative effects of small group meetings.

The participation of developing countries in decision making, however, remains limited through the small number of delegates that small countries can afford to send to Ministerial Conferences. An NGO observed at the Ministerial Conference in Hong Kong that the US delegation comprised 500 delegates:

> And then you have another delegation with five – then which one is more powerful and effective? It's not very hard to guess, okay? So those that are strong, the big trading partners, have such big delegations, that obviously can look at every detail, and everything can be assessed so that it will be in their interest.

A representative of a development-oriented intergovernmental organization argued that developing countries have a tendency to see the Secretariat to be de facto in favor of developed countries as opposed to developing countries, without, however, giving concrete examples

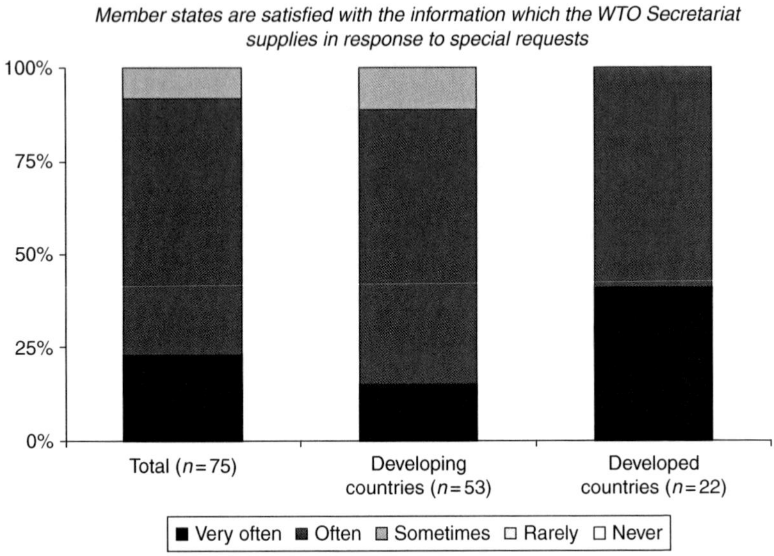

Figure 6.7 Member state satisfaction with information supplied by the WTO Secretariat

of privileges for developed countries. This seems to reflect a view set out by NGOs that the neutrality of the WTO Secretariat is a fiction (*Jawara and Kwa* 2003: 204ff.). There is a controversy over whether or not the Secretariat provides information in a way which disadvantages or privileges developing or developed countries, thereby contributing to the unequal participation in procedures. As mentioned in Chapter 4, IV.1, the Secretariat is generally charged under the Doha mandate with the "prompt and efficient dissemination of information relating to negotiations," in particular to non-resident and smaller missions. Figure 6.7 shows to what extent (different groups of) WTO member states are satisfied with information supplied in response to special requests.

The figure shows a high level of satisfaction among both groups. All developed countries and 90% of the developing countries are very often or often satisfied with the information which the WTO Secretariat supplies. However, developing countries tend to be more critical. A minority of 11% of developing countries believes that member states are only sometimes satisfied, and the percentage of countries that believe that member states are very often satisfied is significantly lower with 15%

than in the group of respondents from developed countries, where 40% believe that member states are very often satisfied.

However, the impression of an overall satisfaction of developing countries with the Secretariat dominates. There is no evidence of the Secretariat disadvantaging developing countries, thereby promoting inequity in terms of unequal participation of developing countries in the WTO.

As outlined in Section I.2.a of this chapter, the reduction of agricultural subsidies in developed countries has become *the* major issue among trading partners. However, while negotiations aim at balancing interests of Brazil and India on the one hand, and the European Union and the United States on the other hand, it is questionable to what extent trade interests of other countries are taken into account. The development-oriented NGO Oxfam has argued that trade interests of African countries play a less important role in WTO trade negotiations: There is, in fact, a risk that some of the main obstacles that limit African exports will not be addressed in a meaningful way during the Doha Round (*Oxfam International* 2005).

Also, there is evidence that environmental and/or labor policy concerns are not properly balanced with trade policies within the Doha Round. Labor concerns are not included in the Doha negotiation mandate. The environmental negotiation mandate in the Doha Agenda has four parts: They comprise the relationship between MEAs and trade rules, procedures for information exchange between MEA secretariats and relevant parts of the WTO, the liberalization of trade in environmental goods and services, and disciplining subsidies in fisheries. Progress in negotiations of these issues has been very slow (*Halle* 2006: 110). In paragraph 51 of the Doha mandate, there is also a broader approach taken to the issue of sustainable development as enshrined in the preamble of the Marrakesh Agreement. It gives authority to the Committee on Trade and Environment and the Committee on Trade and Development to "each act as a forum to identify and debate developmental and environmental aspects of the negotiations, in order to help achieve the objective of having sustainable development appropriately reflected." However, after five years of negotiations, no agreement has been reached on how this challenge will be approached (*Halle* 2006: 114).

(b) Implementation of trade agreements

The question is whether the trade interests of all members are properly balanced considering the implementation of WTO agreements. As indicated in Section I.1.b of this chapter, the implementation of many demanding WTO rules raises particular problems for the capacities of developing countries. One possible result of inequities in negotiations in earlier rounds is that trade agreements are difficult to implement. In this regard, one interview partner from the Secretariat admitted:

> I think that many of the agreements are extraordinarily difficult and unbalanced for developing countries.

Sometimes rules are interpreted by developed countries in a way that make implementation for developing countries even harder. One example is the Agreement on the Application of Sanitary and Phytosanitary Measures. For imported products to comply with certain standards, countries can accept control and inspections systems in place in other countries through recognition of equivalence. However, developing countries have repeatedly raised the concern that developed countries demand "sameness" rather than equivalence of standards and control and inspection systems (*Prévost and Van den Bossche* 2005: 360).

A broad discussion on the implementation of WTO agreements has been going on since the Seattle Ministerial Conference, and in a more concrete fashion, during the preparations for the Doha Ministerial Conference. A number of concerns of developing countries with regard to the implementation of WTO agreements has been the focus of special sessions in the General Council. These have resulted in the adoption of the Decision on Implementation-Related Issues and Concerns (the "Decision on Implementation") at the Ministerial Conference in Doha.[6] For instance, the decision contains recommendations that certain transitional periods granted under specific WTO agreements are extended for LDCs (8.2) or clarifications that "longer time frames for compliance" for developing countries are understood "to be a period of no less than six months" (3.1). Member states are urged not to challenge "measures implemented by developing countries with a view to achieving legitimate development goals" (10.2).

The "Decision on Implementation" has been characterized as a step toward strengthening the provisions of WTO agreements in favor of developing countries (*Prévost and Van den Bossche* 2005: 360ff.). However, other scholars have concluded that the 10-year attempt of developing countries "to trim their obligations to increase the overall net benefit of the agreements" has only produced meager results: "Either developing countries have complied with their obligations or, if they are small economies, their non-compliance has not attracted objection" (*Gallagher* 2005: 136).

(c) Trade policy review

There is no evidence that interests of developing countries are not respected in trade policy review. However, an interview partner from the Secretariat pointed out that participation of developing countries in meetings of the Trade Policy Review Council may be hampered in periods of intense negotiations through a general lack of capacity. Smaller delegations of developing countries often have difficulties to send a representative to meetings in such periods.

In its current set-up the trade policy review as practiced in the WTO cannot adequately balance broader environmental and social concerns with trade liberalization. An interview partner from the WTO Secretariat explained that in its report it does not cover labor issues, arguing that they do not come under the scope of the WTO agreements. By contrast, environmental standards are regarded as being partially covered by WTO agreements. Hence, measures that affect trade which have been taken for environmental purposes are covered in the Secretariat reports. Non-governmental organizations, as outlined in Chapter 5, I.1.e, are usually not consulted by the Secretariat to provide information on trade policies and its impacts in member countries. NGO concerns such as environmental or labor issues are therefore not reflected in the Secretariat reports.

A Secretariat official explained that the Trade Policy Review has been used by some member states (notably the United States and the European Union) to request information on environmental and labor policies from the member countries under review. As he observed, the European Union has shown a tendency to ask questions about sustainable development or to encourage member countries to develop their trade policies in a more coherent fashion with sustainable development in every single meeting of the Trade Policy Review Body. However, such general questions can be answered in a very general way. With regard to labor standards, the United States is particularly active, but reactions of member countries have differed: Some have answered in good faith, while others have argued that labor standards were not a matter under review.

(d) Dispute settlement

There is strong quantitative evidence that participation of developing countries in the dispute settlement system is less than participation of developed countries. Several scholars have systematically compared participation of developing countries and developed countries. Results point to gross asymmetries regarding the two groups of countries. As of February 2003, the United States had participated as a complainant, defendant or third party in every proceeding in 97% of all "fully litigated cases," i.e. cases that resulted in an adopted panel or Appellate Body report. The respective participation rate for the EC is at 81%. By contrast, the vast majority of developing countries had participation rates of 0% or in the single digits with regard to fully litigated cases (*Shaffer* 2004: 471). None of the least developing countries has brought a complaint. There is, however, a fairly limited group of developing countries that participate in proceedings on the complainant side, with the most frequent users being newly industrialized countries such as Argentina, Brazil, and Mexico (*Schuchhardt* 2005: 1230). It may be objected that rare use of the dispute settlement mechanism simply reflects the fact that developing countries' share in world trade volume is comparatively small. However, scholars have calculated that in total the use of the dispute settlement mechanism by developing countries against developed countries is considerably less than their share of developed country trade (*Michalopoulos* 2001: 472). An interesting detail is that developing countries in the role of complainants are less likely to settle during consultations than developed countries. Most often, developing countries request the establishment of a panel (*Schuchhardt* 2005: 1230).

The assessment of whether environmental and/or labor policy concerns are properly balanced with trade policies within WTO dispute settlement is more positive than in negotiations. Some environmental protection decisions by dispute settlement bodies had given early cause for concern amongst environmental NGOs, even though the number of decisions on environmental measures or human health-related measures was limited under GATT.[7] There was the perception of the Tuna–Dolphin Decision taken under GATT that measures protecting the environment were in large parts incompatible with international trade law (*Wallach and Sforza* 1999; *Howse* 2000, 2001; *Hoberg* 2001).

In the WTO, the total number of dispute settlement decisions dealing with environmental issues is also comparatively low with only three proceedings completed since 1995.[8] Evaluation of the Appellate Body work on the balancing of trade concerns on the one hand and environmental and health concerns on the other hand differs. Following *Boisson de Chazournes and Mbengue* (2004: 296ff.), the dispute settlement bodies of the WTO have "shown some reticence regarding the application of precaution." The Appellate Body failed to recognize that the precautionary principle prevails. Rather, precaution in the WTO functions is considered a qualified exemption to trade obligations. The application of which, however, is subject to strict conditions. Moreover, dispute settlement bodies have shown reticence "to have systematic recourse to international treaty and customary law" in the settlement of disputes, insofar as the WTO agreements constitute a *lex specialis* in relation to general international law (*Boisson de Chazournes and Mbengue* 2004). WTO dispute settlement bodies have, however, found that obligations of states enshrined in multilateral environmental agreements "may be considered relevant" (*Halle* 2006). In this regard, work of the dispute settlement bodies in balancing trade concerns on the one hand and environmental and health concerns on the other hand has been recently evaluated more positively. It is argued that WTO dispute settlement bodies have achieved much more for the environment than negotiators (*Halle* 2006: 111).

To conclude, the balancing of trade with environmental and health concerns seems to score slightly better in dispute settlement than in trade negotiations.

2. Explanatory factors

(a) Political conflicts

As argued above, not all political conflicts equally affect WTO *trade negotiations*. Political conflicts between countries which do not have bargaining powers are not negotiated in the WTO (*Oxfam International* 2005). Hence, concerns of countries which lack bargaining power may be marginalized.

Also, the current focus of the negotiations can partially account for the lack of progress regarding the balancing of environmental protection with trade concerns. An interview partner from an NGO predicted that the Director General *Pascal Lamy*, even though he was convinced that environmental issues were important, would not push for the issues to be tackled. This is because the environment is not in the centre of political conflicts, and it is currently not considered by most WTO member countries as a topic of major relevance. An NGO observed:

> Well, he [*Pascal Lamy*] wants the round to be a success, because it would be his success. And if he wants to get something going, then he is not going to obscure the main issue of negotiations with things that most members do not find that relevant.

Scholars have also confirmed the view that member states have other priorities than environmental protection. They have pointed out that the Doha Round is largely about the developing countries seeking access to markets for agricultural goods in developed countries while developed countries need concessions in the area of industrial tariffs, services, and trade facilitation. The most likely use of any environmental agreement, it is argued, would be "for window dressing, to demonstrate that the WTO can deal successfully with the issues that lie at the frontiers of trade policy" (*Halle* 2006: 113).

The focus of political conflicts can thus lead to a marginalization of concerns of smaller developing countries and of social and environmental concerns.

(b) Regulatory requirements

While all decisions in the WTO are formally governed by the consensus principles, there are differences in the weight of members in the *negotiations*, due to an ever-increasing variation in economic development and trade dependence (*De Bièvre* 2006: 36). Nor can the consensus rule ensure a balancing of policy concerns. *Petersmann* (2005b: 653) has pointed out that consensus among WTO governments "in no way proves that agreements result from representative, participatory and regulatory procedures in each WTO member state." Human rights, consumer welfare, and other general citizen interests are not necessarily promoted.

As outlined in Section I.2.b of this chapter, the principle of single undertaking is assumed to have a negative impact on the ability of developing countries to participate in the procedures of the WTO. This is because negotiations organized under the principle of single undertaking have the effect that participation in all negotiating groups is of equal importance for all member states. A Secretariat official confirmed that this puts particular strain on the limited resources of developing countries:

> Meetings take place every day, half a dozen meetings going on, whether informal or formal. Despite our best efforts to reduce overlapping, and because of the single undertaking where everyone has to really be fully aware what they are agreeing to at each step, it's becoming very difficult for a small delegation to function.

One of the factors which deter developing countries from participating in *dispute settlement* is the lack of rights of winning parties to obtain compensation. Developing countries are often unable to profit from retaliatory measures, and compensation can only be agreed on a voluntary basis. In the view of scholars the lack of rights of winning parties to obtain compensation even against the will of the losing party thus acts as a deterrent against developing countries' use of dispute settlement (*Bronckers* 2001: 61).

To conclude, the principle of single undertaking and the lack of right to compensation thus contribute to deficiencies in equity. At the same time, another regulatory requirement, the consensus principle, cannot ensure equal participation of members.

(c) Resources

The continuing need of developing countries to obtain resources to negotiate effectively can be inferred from the detailed analyses in Chapter 5, I and II. Since WTO technical assistance does little to improve capacities of developing countries to participate in *negotiations*, developing countries rely to a great extent on expertise which is provided by actors other than the WTO. Training courses are offered by UNCTAD and the ITC, and concrete advice regarding negotiations is provided by UNCTAD and the South Centre. A new set of actors providing advice to developing countries are non-governmental actors. It can be inferred from the growing importance of NGO advice that the support by intergovernmental organizations is still insufficient for developing countries.

The fact that *implementation* of WTO rules is particularly problematic for many developing countries can be seen as a direct consequence of the unequal distribution of resources and bargaining power in the Uruguay Round negotiations. Many developing countries at the time lacked the capacities to understand what was agreed. Even though some measures have been taken to facilitate the implementation of WTO rules, it may be inferred from the high demand for technical assistance (see Chapter 5, I.2), that developing countries often lack the expertise to implement WTO agreements properly.

Also, inequities in the use of *dispute settlement* can be explained by differences in resources. Most developing countries have developed few in-house legal expertise in trade matters. Shaffer has argued that a developing country that has a limited value and volume of exports is less likely to become a repeat player in WTO litigation. As a result, the developing country is also less likely to benefit from economies of scale in deploying legal resources. Therefore, developing countries have to hire outside experts for bringing a suit, which is quite expensive. Such costs have to be weighed against the uncertain benefits of litigating a WTO case (*Shaffer* 2004: 473).

In contrast to developing countries, the United States and the European Union dispose of abundant in-house legal expertise in trade matters. The EU and US trade authorities employ lawyers, which are assisted by lawyers working for the private sector. Even though trade lawyers often leave the US government to work for the private sector, they often subsequently return to government as part of Washington's "revolving door culture" (*Shaffer* 2004: 473).

To conclude, the unequal distribution of resources is an important explanatory factor for unequal participation of different member countries in decision-making procedures. Historically, this has led to the conclusion of trade agreements from which developing countries can hardly profit.

(d) Organizational systems requirements

The unequal participation of member states in trade negotiations in the WTO can be partially explained by organizational system requirements.

The resolution of conflict (and thereby the attainment of goals in form of new or reformed trade agreements) requires informal decision making, as formal decision-making procedures make the resolution of conflicts very difficult. The price to be paid, however, is inequity among different member states. As outlined in Section II.1.a of this chapter, informal decision making makes it difficult for smaller developing and LDCs to protect and advance trade interests in the WTO. These countries either do not have the resources to participate in the large variety of informal meetings or they are excluded from the important informal meetings, e.g. the Green Room. Group representation, which also solves the purpose of resolving conflicts, has, however, a mitigating effect.

(e) Governance modes

Negotiations are dominated by the exchange mode of governance since agreements are based on a consensus among all members. Member countries are, however, from the start in an unequal position. The question is to what extent a balance of interests can be achieved through an exchange mode of governance among unequals. In this regard, an NGO criticized the attitude of developed countries toward negotiations in the WTO:

> If you really want to achieve more of a balanced world, then you will have the developed world give some concessions. But they don't see

> it that way. They still see it as negotiations where you give and you take, and you give and you take. But if it's already unbalanced from the start, and they do not give more, it will just stay unbalanced. That's how I see it.

An exchange mode of governance is thus likely to foster and promote inequalities rather than resolving them. One may even ask whether negotiations can be described as an exchange if no real concessions are offered from the side of the developed countries. The reduction of agricultural subsidies in developed countries is a case in point.

There is some evidence that at least in principle, a hierarchical mode of governance such as the *adjudication* of panels and the Appellate Body offers greater advantages to developing countries than an exchange mode of governance. This is confirmed in literature. Due to the relative lack of bargaining power of developing countries, they are in a weaker position in a negotiating-type situation such as consultations preceding the panel proceedings. Therefore, they seek adjudicatory decisions rather than settling during consultations while developed countries more often pursue the reverse strategy (*Schuchhardt* 2005: 1230).

The hierarchical mode of governance in terms of rulings by the Appellate Body seems to better promote equity of policy concerns (e.g. taking into account other Multilateral Environmental Agreements and the precautionary principle) than an exchange mode of governance. An indicator is that the Appellate Body has achieved more for environmental protection than negotiations in the WTO (*Halle* 2006: 111).

There is no evidence that the mode of persuasion hampers participation of developing countries in *implementation* or in *trade policy review*.

To conclude, while an exchange mode of governance seems to promote deficiencies in equity, a hierarchical mode of governance tends to contribute to the equity of members.

3. Conclusions

Problems with *equity of members* can be identified in all four areas to different degrees, with trade policy review being affected the least. There are, however, noticeable problems in negotiations, implementation, and dispute settlement. In all cases, these problems can be linked to a lack of resources on the side of developing countries.

One regulatory requirement, the consensus rule, which in principle is designed to promote equity of members, cannot be considered as promoting equal participation of member countries. Furthermore, the principle of single undertaking has a negative effect given that it requires the presence of delegates in all groups and sub-groups of negotiations. Finally, the failure of dispute settlement rules to provide for a right to compensation is also seen as promoting inequity since it fails to offer enough incentives for developing countries to initiate dispute settlement proceedings against another country.

Informal decision making in negotiations is viewed as detrimental to equity, particularly as regards the protection and advancement of trade interests of smaller developing and LDCs in the WTO. However, survey and interview results indicate that the effects of group representation help to mitigate inequity.

It seems that the hierarchical mode of governance (as used in the mid-stage of dispute settlement) is in principle better able to promote equity than an exchange mode of governance (as used in the negotiations and in the first and last stage of dispute settlement).

Equity of policy concerns is affected by political conflicts among member countries. Accordingly, an exchange mode of governance as prevailing in negotiations has done little to help recognize the importance of environmental protection concerns. The persuasion mode of governance has been used in trade policy review, but encounters, at least, partial resistance by member countries. Again, the hierarchical mode of governance can be characterized as most effective in advancing environmental concerns.

III. Legitimacy

1. Task areas

(a) Trade negotiations

In literature the prevailing discussions on legitimacy of the WTO are often normative in nature and focus on an alleged "democracy deficit" of the WTO. As outlined in Chapter 3, I.5.c, the debate tends to obscure normative and empirical aspects of legitimacy. This study is confined to the empirical aspects of legitimacy and analyzes the attitudes of representatives of member states and NGOs concerning the acceptance of the WTO decisions as legitimate (justified). It has been argued in scholarly literature that many countries and people, "in particular the poor and vulnerable," felt left behind or locked outside the WTO (*Pauwelyn* 2005: 336). However, it is beyond the scope of this study to investigate the sweeping statement on the lack of popular support of ordinary citizens for the WTO (*Esty* 2002: 17; *Pauwelyn* 2005: 336). Rather, the investigation of acceptance of the WTO is focused on two groups: (1) member states and (2) NGOs. The choice of member states is an obvious one: If member countries do not accept the authority of the WTO as justified, the negotiation of new agreements and the implementation of existing agreements are severely endangered. The attitudes of NGOs are investigated because NGOs are among the most vocal critics of the organization: "Routine attacks on the WTO's alleged lack of legitimacy" have steadily been undertaken by NGOs (*Cho* 2005: 392), and their criticism has commanded significant media attention. A Secretariat official criticized that NGOs' misinformed views on the WTO are reflected in articles in the serious press.

Interview partners who were asked about acceptance of the WTO as an organization usually made no reference to implementation and/or trade policy review. The discussion therefore focuses on trade negotiations and dispute settlement.

Legitimacy of the WTO is satisfactory with member states. This can be inferred from Figure 6.7. The great majority of member states is satisfied with the information provided by the WTO Secretariat in response to special requests. If the majority of member states did not accept the WTO as an institution, they would probably not be satisfied with the WTO's information services either. Furthermore, informal decision making is often viewed as damaging the legitimacy of the WTO. However, Figure 6.5 suggests that this is not the case among member states. The majority of them believes that informal procedures only sometimes or rarely disadvantage smaller developing or LDCs. If member states did not accept the WTO as an institution, they would probably have supported the notion advanced by NGOs that informal decision making disadvantages developing countries. Moreover, almost all developing countries argue, as shown in Figure 6.6, that group representation has positive effects regarding the representation of interests of smaller developing and LDCs, at least provided that the interests of smaller developing and LDCs and the group representatives are the same. A negative effect on legitimacy would presuppose a more critical attitude of developing countries with regard to informal decision making. This view was confirmed by a development-oriented intergovernmental organization a representative of which pointed out that despite informal decision making the overall member state view is still rather positive due to the "member-driven nature" of the organization:

> I think member states overwhelmingly would say it's a member-driven organization and it works quite well. Maybe they would not

> say so if just some of these, you know, exclusionary meetings happen, but overwhelmingly I would say they say that it's all working well.

This view was disputed by another development-oriented intergovernmental organization which noted that the proliferation of informal decision making diminishes the legitimacy of the WTO among smaller developing countries:

> Many of these countries do care about what is going to come out from that informal process and the fact that they are not able to participate in helping shape the decision that comes out, makes them feel that it is not transparent enough and legitimate.

However, in line with survey results, Secretariat staff and NGOs observed that legitimacy of the WTO with member states is overall rather good. In the view of a Secretariat official, the number of countries seeking to accede the WTO is a proof of the fact that membership of the organization is considered as necessary and useful:

> I think the proof is that members do have the option to leave this organization. I mean that is the option, and there are procedures. Nobody has done so, and many are waiting to get in. So in that sense I think the way they rate it is if anything it is a necessary organization to be a member of.

A representative of an NGO reported that member countries believed that through the WTO interests of developing countries could be better defended than in bilateral agreements:

> And in general what you would hear is that members say, yes it is important because it's a multilateral institution, because developing countries have a better way of defending themselves than with all the bilateral.

As regards legitimacy of the WTO with NGOs, it was recognized by several interview partners that there are very diverse attitudes. An NGO representative made a distinction between different groups such as NGOs, social movements, and trade unions. Social movements which engaged in the debate really rejected the WTO agreements, and "probably in large parts the organization as such." Then there were trade unions, which could be roughly subdivided in Northern and Southern ones. According to the NGO, trade unions from Northern countries had generally positive attitudes toward trade liberalization and the WTO, while trade unions from Southern countries were more skeptical. Within the group of NGOs, there were different factions. Some had a much more "reformist approach" to the organization, while others "were very clearly saying no, we need something different."

NGOs with a reformist approach tend to have the attitude, as the representative of an intergovernmental organization observed, that "having some sort of multilateral regulations to govern trade between countries is better than having none at all and letting the jungle rule." In this vein, an interview partner from a development-oriented NGO mentioned that WTO governance despite being problematic also has aspects that the NGO would appreciate. These were the consensus rule and the dispute settlement which were "still a good basis for an organization." As a result, the WTO was considered by the development-oriented NGO "the best tool we have to negotiate on trade multilaterally."

In contrast, NGOs which fundamentally oppose the WTO point to informal decision making and question the legitimacy of the WTO "because of the lack of due process." Some NGOs consider the WTO, compared to other international organizations, as "one of the least transparent organizations." In sum, the legitimacy of the WTO in trade negotiation is not questioned by the majority of member states. NGOs are divided into two camps: (1) reformist NGOs which accept the WTO as an institution and (2) fundamentalist NGOs which reject the WTO as a legitimate institution in trade negotiations.

(b) Dispute settlement

Dispute settlement decisions of the WTO had mobilized many NGOs in the 1990s (*Wallach and Sforza* 1999; *Hoberg* 2001). The US group "Public Citizen" criticized the adverse impact of decisions on environment and health concerns. A more basic criticism was that the "WTO system gives trade-motivated tribunal members the power to reverse the preferences of national governments" (*Wallach and Sforza* 1999: 196). More recently, however, critical voices against WTO dispute settlement as a force eroding national democracies have been heard less frequently. An interview partner from a development-oriented NGO even characterized dispute settlement provisions as a positive aspect of the WTO. The new NGO attitude is probably motivated by the experience that dispute settlement can be used by developing countries for winning cases against developed countries, as demonstrated by the Cotton and Sugar Case. This was confirmed by an official from a G-4 Developing Country:

> And one of the biggest advantages of the WTO is this dispute settlement system that it has. [...] Now it went lately even better, that even smaller weaker countries can challenge the bigger players in the dispute settlement system, and hope for a fair solution.

In literature, however, it has been pointed out that the imbalance between the ineffective negotiations dominated by the exchange mode and the very effective dispute settlement dominated by a hierarchical mode of governance could weaken the legitimacy of the WTO in the long run. "If legislative response to judicial development is not available or not working, the independent (quasi-judiciary) becomes an uncontrolled decision-maker and is weakened in its legitimacy" (*Ehlermann and Ehring* 2005: 69). This view is an example of a common normative perspective. There is no evidence that a functioning dispute settlement system is going to weaken the acceptance of the WTO by member states in the long run.

2. Explanatory factors

(a) Political conflicts

The inability of the WTO to effectively solve political conflicts as demonstrated by the failure of the *trade negotiations* in the Doha Round may threaten the legitimacy of the WTO. A development-oriented NGO defined the self-interest of the Secretariat to keep "the WTO relevant and legitimate on trade issues" considering failures in trade negotiations:

> I mean Cancún has been a failure, so they need the next ministerial to be a success, at least not a complete failure. They need basically to save the organization in a way. [...] Obviously, if the negotiations are blocked for five, ten years, WTO would become irrelevant. So that's probably their self-interest to keep the WTO relevant, legitimate, and being a major player, a major forum for negotiations on this issue.

By contrast, WTO Secretariat staff disputed that the legitimacy of the WTO depends exclusively on the success of negotiations, pointing to other task areas:

> I mean there are at least two parts to what the WTO does. It is now inching into other areas. But the two core parts that is to service

> the existing agreements, and to negotiate changes to these agreements, or new agreements. That was what the GATT Secretariat did. So if you lose the negotiating side, you are still servicing the existing agreements. There will still be trade disputes, so you still need legal division, you still need rules division, we also have a transparency role, and policy, countries put their trade tariffs into the WTO, so you still need a statistics division, so we are the depository of tariffs, schedules, right.

For many NGOs, the quality of agreement reached in the new Doha Round trade negotiations is more important than the reaching of an agreement as such. A development-oriented NGO pointed out that the existing agreements so far had failed to promote development and that the Doha Round negotiating process was not going into the right direction:

> I mean the end product is not there yet, but if you look at the constant negotiations, it's not looking really good in terms of what should be delivered for developing countries. You are not there yet at all. So that raises questions about relevance and legitimacy of the organization.

If the WTO continues in its failure to reach new trade agreements, acceptance by member states of the organization will be diminished. The WTO may become irrelevant as a forum for negotiating new trade agreements. For NGOs, by contrast, it is less the inability of the WTO to conclude new agreements which accounts for its lack of legitimacy. NGOs are more concerned about the quality of a potential agreement to be reached under the WTO. If new trade agreements fail to balance trade interest of developing and/or developed countries, thereby further aggravating the North–South conflict, acceptance of WTO by NGOs is likely to be further diminished.

In sum, the legitimacy of the WTO among member states and NGOs can partially be explained by its ability to resolve or de-escalate trade conflicts.

(b) Regulatory requirements

A regulatory requirement which is deemed to be of great relevance for the acceptance of the WTO by members is the principle of consensus-based decision making. An executive of the Secretariat expressed the view that WTO member states did not want to depart from decision making by consensus which is considered a "fundamental decision-making model of the WTO." In literature it has also been argued that legislative outcomes generated from a consensus-based system may enjoy more legitimacy than those from a weighted voting system. Historically, developing countries have fiercely opposed weighted voting in international organizations (*Steinberg* 2002: 361).

Another regulatory requirement which is deemed to be of great relevance for the acceptance of the WTO by members is the principle of neutrality of the Secretariat. It was pointed out by NGOs that "neutrality" or "impartiality" of the Secretariat was very important to member states. Member states did not want the Secretariat or the Director General to "take the negotiations on a particular path" (see Chapter 5, I.1.d). The importance of neutrality and impartiality for the legitimacy of international organizations has been confirmed in scholarly literature with respect to bureaucracies in general and to international organizations in particular (see Chapter 4, I.). Neutrality of the WTO Secretariat is thus seen as a factor conferring legitimacy on the organization as a whole. The question is, however, to what extent the interpretation of the principle of neutrality does prevent the WTO from becoming a more effective and equitable organization.

One regulatory requirement that might have an impact on legitimacy is the lack of formal participation opportunities for NGOs. Views differ greatly among different actors to what extent the lack of formal participation opportunities for NGOs in the WTO causes a lack of empirical legitimacy. An executive of the WTO Secretariat linked this issue to legitimacy. He expressed the view that it was very difficult today for an international organization to have legitimacy if it excluded NGOs from formal participation. He argued that more could be done in the WTO in this regard. However, it is also admitted that many developing countries reject formalized participation of NGOs in the WTO:

> Obviously, we have certain members who take very, very strong opinions about whether we should have a more formal advisory structure like, for example, the OECD has it, and several of the UN bodies have a much more formalized structure. But we have a lot of members here who oppose that.

Despite the fact that "coalitions" or "alliances" have been built up between NGOs based in developed countries and developing countries (see Chapter 5, I.1.f), many developing countries have consistently opposed more formalized participation of NGOs in the WTO (*Mason* 2004: 575).

Unsurprisingly, this is an issue which is relevant for NGOs themselves. A representative from a development-oriented NGO recognized that the WTO Secretariat had improved in its dealings with NGOs. However, compared to other UN organizations, the WTO offered too few opportunities for participation. An NGO noted:

> But of course, it's still very bad compared to the United Nations, where NGOs are allowed to go, you know, attend meetings. Here the NGOs are not allowed to be in the building, they cannot attend the meetings.

To conclude, the principles of consensus decision making and the principle of neutrality can account for the satisfactory acceptance of the WTO by member states. The lack of formal participation opportunities of NGOs contributes to a lack of acceptance among NGOs, but is likely to have a positive impact on acceptance of the WTO by member states.

(c) Resources

An unequal distribution of resources and expertise among members is normal within all international organizations which have both developed and developing member countries. However, the question is whether the WTO should take a more proactive approach in addressing the unequal distribution of resources among its members to increase acceptance among member states and NGOs. In this respect a development-oriented NGO pointed out that in their view the efforts of other international organizations and NGOs were insufficient to compensate for the lack of resources in developing countries, and that the WTO Secretariat should increase its efforts:

> More could be done by the Secretariat. It is true that these groups and organizations are independent, and they are providing interesting and useful things. But in terms of basic statistical work, in terms of I don't know there is a formula item on market access, for example, the Secretariat should run the formula on all the different products of these countries, and being able to come up with a document saying, okay that's what would happen on your economy, on your products.

To some extent, a developing country official had the same expectations regarding the Secretariat, which in his view could more act as a "think tank" providing research for developing countries.

(d) Organizational systems requirements

As outlined in Section III.1.a of this chapter, the prevalence of informal decision making does not severely damage acceptance of the WTO by member states while the impact on acceptance by NGOs is apparently more negative. These differences may be explained by the different relevance which organizational system requirements have for member states on the one hand and NGOs on the other. As outlined in Section I.2.d of this chapter, countries have recognized that the solving of conflicts and goal attainment in the WTO requires informal decision making. Hence, member states can still accept the authority of the WTO even if they dislike the promotion of inequities through informal decision making. By contrast, NGOs are less interested in organizational goal attainment in terms of the reaching of new trade agreements as such (see Section III.2.a of this chapter). In fact, NGOs have openly celebrated the failure of the Ministerial Conference in Cancún.[9] They are more concerned about procedural inequities and intransparencies of WTO decision making than about trade liberalization and balancing national trade interests of WTO member states. The relative importance of organizational system requirements can therefore account for the acceptance of the WTO by member states and the lack of acceptance by NGOs.

(e) Governance modes

The importance attached by several interview partners from the Secretariat, from a G-4 Developing Country and a developing country to the principle of "member-driven organization" is also an indicator that the exchange mode of governance can account for acceptance of the WTO by its members. But also the hierarchical mode of governance which prevails in the area of dispute settlement can account for the acceptance of the WTO by its members. Even though the hierarchical mode of governance has at least in the beginning encountered little acceptance among NGOs, this has changed more recently (see Section III.I.b of this chapter).

3. Conclusions

Legitimacy of the WTO is regarded as being closely linked to the areas of trade negotiations and dispute settlement, while implementation and trade policy review are considered less important. Overall, legitimacy of the WTO with its member states is regarded as satisfactory (*Sutherland* 2005b: 341f.). Some hold the view that the recent failures of the WTO to conclude trade negotiations successfully also threaten its legitimacy with members in the long run. There are some indications that informal decision making is criticized by member states for causing inequities, however, there are no signs that this has significantly diminished the legitimacy of the whole organization among member states.

The situation is different with regard to NGOs which have been major and vocal critics of the organization. Points of criticism are the lack of development-orientation regarding the agreements and the negotiation proposals, the failure of the WTO to alleviate the unequal distribution of resources among members, and the failure of the WTO to offer opportunities for participation to NGOs. The prevalence of informal decision making and its contribution to effective conflict resolutions in the WTO account for the acceptance of the WTO by members and for the lack of acceptance by NGOs. This is because the functioning of the WTO is a priority for its members but not for NGOs. Moderate NGOs, however, also recognize some regulatory requirements as enhancing legitimacy, and perceive the organization as a good tool.

IV. Interdependencies between effectiveness, equity, and legitimacy

From the analysis carried out in Section III of this chapter, it is clear that legitimacy, effectiveness, and equity are closely interrelated and interdependent. In this regard, it is useful to turn to the distinction between input and output legitimacy, which is frequently made in literature (see Chapter 3, I.5.c). Broadly speaking, effectiveness and equity of policy concerns can be considered as preconditions for output legitimacy, while equity of members represents a precondition for input legitimacy. At the same time, effectiveness of the WTO also requires a certain amount of equity and legitimacy. The WTO would not be able to conclude new agreements, administer implementation and trade policy and dispute settlement, if the organization systematically obstructed participation of developing countries in its decision-making procedures, resulting in a lack of acceptance by its members. Finally, creating a more balanced trade order presupposes that new trade agreements can be concluded. Equity of member states and policy concerns therefore also requires effectiveness.

A reform discussion of the WTO should take into account that effectiveness, equity, and input and output legitimacy should be optimized.

Reforms that can be expected to boost one issue should not be implemented at the expense of the other. For instance, reforms that aim at promoting equal participation of members in WTO decision-making procedures (and thereby equity and input legitimacy) should not make it impossible for the WTO to conclude trade negotiations or to reach decisions in dispute settlement procedures (and thereby effectiveness and output legitimacy). Conversely, it is not useful to suggest reforms such as the abolishment of the consensus rule to promote effectiveness and output legitimacy, if input legitimacy is reduced.

7
Reform Perspectives and Proposals

I. Overview of reform proposals

1. Strengthening the Secretariat and Director General

The Sutherland Report was rather circumspect in recommending a stronger position of the Secretariat. In taking stock of the current situation, the report argued that the role of the Secretariat was not intended as merely servicing the WTO's committees and councils, but that its role was to promote the overall effectiveness of the institution. The Secretariat had a duty "to help ensure that the WTO system functions efficiently, is properly understood and delivers on its mandate." (*Sutherland et al.* 2004: 73). In this regard, the Sutherland Report bemoaned that the Secretariat was lacking "voice" and left a vacuum, which was filled by other international institutions, "not always in a manner that serves the system well." The Sutherland Report renewed the commitment to neutrality by stressing that the Secretariat had a "duty of absolute neutrality, care, and respect in dealing with the rights and obligations of members." At the same time, however, the report stressed that the Secretariat had a "parallel responsibility as guardian of the system [...] to act in the common interests of Members." Hence, the report even used the expression "Guardian of the Treaties" (*Sutherland et al.* 2004: 73), a clear reference to the role of the European Commission. However, it did not explicitly suggest that the Secretariat (or the Director General) be endowed with a *right of proposal*. Instead the report somehow vaguely suggested that "a clearer – though always careful – lead on policy issues should emerge from the Secretariat" (*Sutherland et al.* 2004: 77). The report also shied away from explicitly supporting to assign to the Secretariat the *power to take legal action against a member state* (*von Bogdandy and Wagner* 2005: 446).

The report noted that the Secretariat lacked resources in some areas, and it concluded that in general "there will certainly need to be more meaningful increases, and annual growth rates in excess of other better-funded institutions." The Sutherland Report reminded member states that the WTO delivered significant benefits which were "far out of proportion" with the means invested by member states (*Sutherland et al.* 2004: 78).

The report supported spelling out the powers and duties of the Director General clearly by the General Council as required by the Marrakesh Agreement, to make trade negotiations more effective. The role of the Director General had to be strengthened to become less dependent "on the prevailing and often very transient political mood of members rather than on the long-term interest of the institution." The report argued that the Director General should chair the General Council and, as appropriate, other committees and councils. Further, his independent right to manage the Secretariat in the limits of the budget was to be strengthened (*Sutherland et al.* 2004: 74).

2. Developing the WTO structure

There is a variety of different proposals relating to a reform of WTO task structures and organizational structures. Regarding task structures, it has been proposed by NGOs to widen the scope of trade policy reviews at the WTO to include social and environmental issues. The Sutherland Report proposed to move all technical assistance activities out of the WTO and out of other international organizations and to transfer it to an "independent agency" (*Sutherland et al.* 2004: 78). This proposal, which aimed at delivering technical assistance in a more cost effective way than through the current "proliferation of largely uncoordinated and sometimes inconsistent policy advice" (*Sutherland et al.* 2004: 78) went unnoticed in literature.

The Sutherland Report has taken up two proposals for WTO structural reforms from literature and discussed them: the creation of a WTO interparliamentarian body and the creation of a small formal group of member states providing input into trade negotiations. While the report has rejected the creation of an interparliamentarian body (*Sutherland et al.* 2004: 46), it supported the creation of a consultative body to be chaired and convened by the Director General "to meet on a quarterly or six-monthly basis without executive powers and with a broad agenda." (*Sutherland et al.* 2004: 82). The proposal in literature as introduced by *Guzman* (2004; see Chapter 2, II.2) regarding the creation of new departmental structures at the WTO with responsibilities for environmental and social issues, negotiation rounds and new mega-rounds, however, was not taken up by the Sutherland Report.

The Consultative Council as proposed in the Sutherland Report is "to meet on a quarterly or six-monthly basis without executive powers and with a broad agenda." Membership of the body should be limited and composed on a partly rotating basis (*Sutherland et al.* 2004: 82). In literature, the Consultative Council is viewed as a resurrection of the senior officials group, known as the Consultative Group of Eighteen established in 1975. The group was characterized as a "fertile source of new trade policy ideas" in the Tokyo Round and an early stage of preparing for the Uruguay Round. However, in the 1980s, it gradually fell into disuse (*Wolfe* 2005: 642).

The impact of an interparliamentarian body on effectiveness, equity, and legitimacy of the WTO has been discussed in several contributions in an edited volume by Petersmann (see *Shaffer* 2005b; *Skaggs* 2005; *Hilf* 2005; *Mann* 2005). The Sutherland Report also discussed the establishment of a WTO interparliamentarian body. The report recognized that a link existed between the operation of national parliamentary bodies and legitimacy. The creation of an interparliamentarian WTO assembly, however, was dismissed by the report as not practicable given that it met with massive resistance of developing countries. Hence, the report argued that the most which could be done in that area was the promotion of transparency by WTO governments toward their own parliamentary institutions, and advocacy of domestic parliamentary involvement (*Sutherland et al.* 2004: 46).

3. Improving WTO relations with NGOs

The Sutherland Report has shown some skepticism toward an improvement of WTO relations with NGOs, and has therefore been qualified as an attempt to "disillusion NGOs" (*Cho* 2005: 391). The report discussed both a system of accreditation and participation of non-governmental groups in decision making of the WTO. Regarding accreditation, the Sutherland Report pointed out that such a move would "impose a continuing bureaucratic burden to receive, sieve and make judgments about candidate organizations." Given that accreditation would probably not imply the right to observe WTO meetings at first hand, it is not clear what the purpose of accreditation would be. The practical benefits of formal accreditation could be obtained with a simple system of ad hoc registration for conferences and other events (*Sutherland et al.* 2004: 46).

Hence, the current practice with regard to accreditation was confirmed in the Sutherland Report.

In discussing the advantages and disadvantages of NGO participation in WTO decision making, the Sutherland Report acknowledged that within the United Nations, non-governmental participation in intergovernmental debates on global issues was recognized as valuable. At the same time, it pointed to skepticism among governments who hold the view that direct non-governmental participation was incompatible with the character of the WTO as an intergovernmental organization (*Sutherland et al.* 2004: 46). Also, NGO participation is thought to affect the effectiveness of negotiations negatively, given that trade negotiations, as the Sutherland Report claimed, "require some level of confidentiality" (*Sutherland et al.* 2004: 45).

The Sutherland Report recognized that the WTO has made "significant progress" regarding communications and the strengthening of relations with civil society over the past few years, thereby lauding it for the steps already taken (*von Bogdandy and Wagner* 2005: 441). A further strengthening of dialogue is supposed to be controversial given the North–South divide among WTO members on this issue. Administrative and financial implications of a more active program of civil society engagement had to be carefully assessed (*Sutherland et al.* 2004: 42ff.).

Reception of the Sutherland Report's proposals on NGOs in literature was mixed. *Cho* (2005: 397) focused on the engagement and dialogue of the WTO with NGOs. Even though, in his view, this dialogue enhanced the WTO legitimacy to some extent, WTO legitimacy was linked more closely to ordinary people than to NGOs. WTO was to be "fully appreciated and accepted by everyday people," and hence, people were to be informed and educated about WTO norms (similarly *Pauwelyn* 2005: 342).

Literature has also discussed some more institutionalized approaches to NGO participation in WTO operations. Modeled on the European Union, Petersmann (2001: 109) proposed the establishment of an Advisory Social and Economic Committee "with the right to submit recommendations to all WTO bodies subject to procedures which ensure more accountability and representativeness of NGOs." This was supposed to enhance legitimacy of the WTO more than "sporadic and selective meetings" with NGOs. Under the former Director General, Panitchpakdi, the Secretariat had considered to establish an advisory NGO committee (*Mason* 2004: 580). Finally, two concepts which are not discussed in literature is to give NGOs generally the *right to comment* on the results of negotiations without necessarily limiting this to a committee and the right of NGOs to participate in trade policy reviews. The participation of NGOs is known to be a characteristic of other reviews, e.g. labor policy reviews of member states in the European Union (see *Casey and Gold* 2005: 25).

4. Formalizing structures and procedures in the area of trade negotiations

The Sutherland Report sought to maintain the consensus principle, i.e. the principle that all WTO member countries have to agree with decisions reached in trade negotiations. However, it sought to increase the effectiveness of negotiations by making the sabotaging of consensus more difficult. Its proposal was that members which block a measure, "which otherwise have a very broad consensus support shall only block such consensus if it declares in writing, with reasons included that the matter is one of vital interest to them." (*Sutherland et al.* 2004: 64). An alternative, which so far has been discussed, neither in the Sutherland Report nor in literature, is that WTO members could block consensus on trade measure which otherwise have a very broad support, if member states were excluded from informal negotiations on said measures.

Non-governmental organizations have made more radical proposals for formalizing structures and procedures by regulating access to negotiations. These proposals, however, tend to be ignored in literature. Thus a group of NGOs have examined problems with informal processes in the WTO in the run-up to the Ministerial Conference of Cancún (*IATP* 2003), calling for a number of changes that amount to a prohibition of informal decision making in terms of restricted informal meetings. The principle is that all meetings must be inclusive and transparent, and no member may be excluded from meetings. Further, informal "green room meetings", including "mini-ministerials" in the preparatory process of Cancún have to be stopped, and all negotiating texts must be produced by the membership while all members should have the opportunity to effectively participate in the drafting and approval of texts (*IATP* 2003: 12f.).

Another proposal advanced by Khor from the developing-oriented NGO "Third World Network" also aims at formalization but pays due attention to effectiveness (*Khor* 2002: 20). He was inspired by experience with negotiating the UN Cartagena Protocol on Biosafety. His principle idea is that negotiations are conducted by representatives of groupings, but that all members are to be present in the room. All members closely observe how representatives negotiate, and they may interrupt the negotiations and ask for time to consult with the group representatives if they felt that their interests were not adequately represented.

5. Developing the dispute settlement system

The Sutherland Report's dealing with the WTO dispute settlement has been qualified as an "unabated defense of the current [...] system" (*Pauwelyn* 2005: 344). The question of private access to litigation has not been discussed in the Sutherland Report, even though it has been advocated in literature (*Shell* 1996).

The Sutherland Report, did, however, discuss the matters of compensation and public observation of dispute settlement proceedings (*Sutherland et al.* 2004: 53–59). The report remained skeptical with regard to monetary compensation based on the argument that while equity of members might be enhanced, effectiveness could be damaged. Although it was acknowledged that many poorer countries could not use the weapon of retaliation, monetary compensation was portrayed as potentially damaging to the whole rules-based system. If monetary compensation was used, rich and powerful members could adopt a "buy-out" attitude while "retaining trade distorting measures" (*Sutherland et al.* 2004: 54).

Finally, the Sutherland Report viewed the current level of confidentiality as damaging to the credibility of the WTO, and it urged that panels and Appellate Body hearings should be generally open to the public (*Meagher* 2005: 416, see *Sutherland et al.* 2004: 58).

II. Assessment of reform proposals

As outlined in Chapter 3, III, the effects of the aforementioned reform proposals, listed in Annex 1, on WTO performance in terms of effectiveness of goal attainment, equity of members,[1] and legitimacy were estimated by the interview partners on an ordinal scale ranging from −2 (very negative effects) to 0 (no effects) and +2 (very positive effects). The means of estimated effects are reported here if their values are, at least, ±.5.

1. Strengthening the Secretariat and Director General

Reform proposals to improve the effectiveness of WTO goal attainment often attribute a stronger role to the Secretariat in WTO activities. Interview partners were asked which role they wanted the Secretariat to play in future with regard to WTO members, and to place the Secretariat

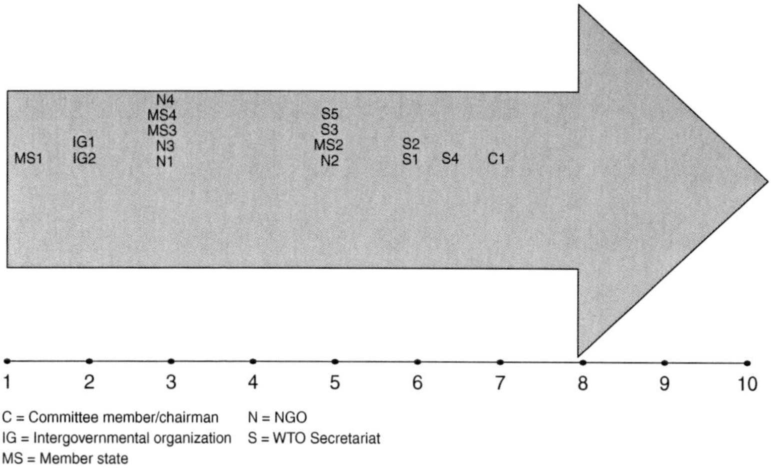

Figure 7.1 Future role of the WTO Secretariat as preferred by interview partners

accordingly on a ten-point scale representing the Secretariat as a mere tool of member states (1) and as a strong leader (10).

Figure 7.1 displays the preferences of interview partners concerning the future role of the Secretariat.

A comparison of Figure 7.1 to Figure 5.3 suggests that most interview partners do not want to change the current role of the Secretariat in the future.

Figure 7.1 confirms that most member states and externals are skeptical with regard to strengthening the role of the Secretariat. Most member states, NGOs and other intergovernmental organizations want the Secretariat to remain closer to the role of a "tool." It is only one member state and all of the Secretariat staff that would like to move the role of the Secretariat more to the role of a leader. Interestingly, however, a committee chairman would also like to increase the role of the Secretariat.

Table 7.1 shows how interview partners evaluated the potential impact of different proposals for reforming the WTO Secretariat and the Director General on the effectiveness of the WTO, equity of members and acceptance by members and externals.

(a) Increasing resources

The Sutherland Report argued in favor of increasing resources for the WTO. The interviewees in Table 7.1 estimate that an increase of

Table 7.1 Estimated average effects of proposed reform measures concerning the Secretariat on WTO performance (means)[a]

	Performance			
Reform proposals[b]	**Effectiveness of goal attainment**	**Equity of members**	**Acceptance by members**	**Acceptance by externals**
Increase resources (1)	1.0	.5($n=12$)		
Define role of DG (2)	.9		.6($n=11$)	.7($n=12$)
Secretariat right of initiative (3)	.9		−1.2	−.6
Secretariat watchdog procedural rules(9)			−.5	
Secretariat complaints mechanism for violation of trade rules (4)	1.0($n=11$)	.6($n=11$)	−.7($n=11$)	

[a] $N=13$, except where otherwise indicated
[b] See Annex 1

resources would produce a small increase of effectiveness, and an even smaller increase of equity. There is no perceptible effect of an increase of resources on acceptance of the WTO by members and externals. This probably reflects the longstanding experience of the Secretariat with discussions on the WTO budget in the Budget Committee. As an interview partner from the WTO Secretariat put it:

> Like I said that would require beefing up the Secretariat in terms of resources or persons. I am not sure members are willing to do that because I have been here now long enough to know that budget battles are pretty intense. For many, many years delegations have been very keen not to have any increase in real terms of the WTO budget. Even though physically it is a much smaller Secretariat than the OECD or the IMF, the World Bank and so on. So this is a point. It is

> a tough sell for trade ministers to tell their finance ministries to give more money for the WTO Secretariat.

Given this general aversion against increasing the funds for the WTO, it is no surprise that an increase of resources will not enhance the perception of the WTO's legitimacy.

Another question is for what purpose the additional resources should be used. The Sutherland Report called for the WTO to carry out research that enabled it to make a "pre-eminent intellectual input into public and political debate on trade policy matters, globalization, development and other pressing issues." It qualified the current publicly available WTO research as "unadventurous" (*Sutherland et al.* 2004: 77). Other areas in which resources were limited were the dispute settlement area, media relations, public information initiatives, and outreach to NGOs (*Sutherland et al.* 2004: 78).

Interview partners from a member state and from NGOs stressed the need for more research to be carried out by the WTO Secretariat. A representative of a developing country pointed out:

> But it would be good for the WTO to have more resources. In fact, I would like to see WTO doing more research work than anything else. Because to me that research informs you, and it should be ahead of negotiations.

Secretariat staff conceded that economic research capacity in the Secretariat could be strengthened. The same interview partner, however, saw an increased role in research as endangering neutrality of the organization:

> I am not sure we can change the Secretariat to provide those functions because we might not be an impartial Secretariat any more, or may not be perceived as an impartial Secretariat any more. I think there are other organizations that can provide that research role and an advice role. There is UNCTAD, the World Bank, the International Trade Centre here.

Also in literature, a stronger role of the Secretariat in research and policy analysis is seen as compromising its neutrality. The *Sutherland Report* (2004: 77) had emphasized that this was not the case. However, in literature this assumption was qualified as being too casual and simple, based on the experience that member countries' reaction to a Secretariat report taking a clear position on a contested issue was a very negative one (*Blackhurst* 2005: 385f.). More fundamentally, it was also doubted that strengthening of the analytical capacity of the Secretariat could promote the effectiveness of negotiations. Rather, analytical capacity of domestic member state institutions was to be strengthened (*Messerlin* 2005: 302).

Increased resources might also be used for strengthening the role of the WTO Secretariat regarding external relations. One Secretariat official indicated that more personnel in this area were needed together with an increase of the travel budget. Another Secretariat official would have liked to see a more active participation of the WTO Secretariat in the public debate including "full-page advertisements in newspapers" to correct misinformation from irresponsible NGOs.

(b) Defining the role of the Director General

The Sutherland Report also supported a clearer definition of the role of the Director General. Interview partners believe, as Table 7.1 indicates, that the definition of the role of the Director General will produce a small increase in effectiveness, acceptance by members, and acceptance by externals.

In literature, the revaluation of the role of the DG was welcomed (*von Bogdandy and Wagner* 2005: 446). The General Council could increase the standing of the DG through the adoption of guidelines. *Petersmann* (2005b: 651) clearly supported a stronger role of the Director General, including the right to "initiate independent reform proposals." The focus of the Sutherland Report on a strengthened role of the Secretariat was viewed more critical, given that international bureaucracies lacked "direct democratic legitimacy."

(c) Right of initiative

As explained above, the Sutherland Report has not directly proposed that the WTO Secretariat or the Director General be given the right to make proposals on what should be negotiated, for instance, in case of a negotiation impasse. The Sutherland Report only pointed into that direction by using the term "Guardian of the Treaty."

The evaluation of the reform proposals by the interview partners shows that the right of the Secretariat to make proposals for negotiations could lead to a small increase in effectiveness. However, the effects of such a reform measure on the WTO's legitimacy are estimated to be negative. This view reflects the prevailing distrust of a strong Secretariat, as outlined by a developing country:

> And the Secretariat [...] should not be seen to be siding with any particular delegation. Because anything that the Secretariat may come up with may please one delegation or a number of delegations, and not others. And then there is going to be a conflict. So it's better when it comes from members, than when it comes from the Secretariat.

However, the results of the survey seem to indicate that the negative effects of a Secretariat's right to make proposals on the legitimacy of the WTO with its members may be absent if this right is confined to the Director General and to *overcoming a negotiation impasse*. Figure 7.2 depicts to what extent respondents of the survey agree with the proposal to endow the Director General of the WTO with the formal right of making policy proposals for overcoming a negotiation impasse in the interest of effective trade negotiations.

Figure 7.2 indicates that a tight majority of member states supports this reform measure. There is, however, a strong divide between developed and developing countries. While more than 70% of developed

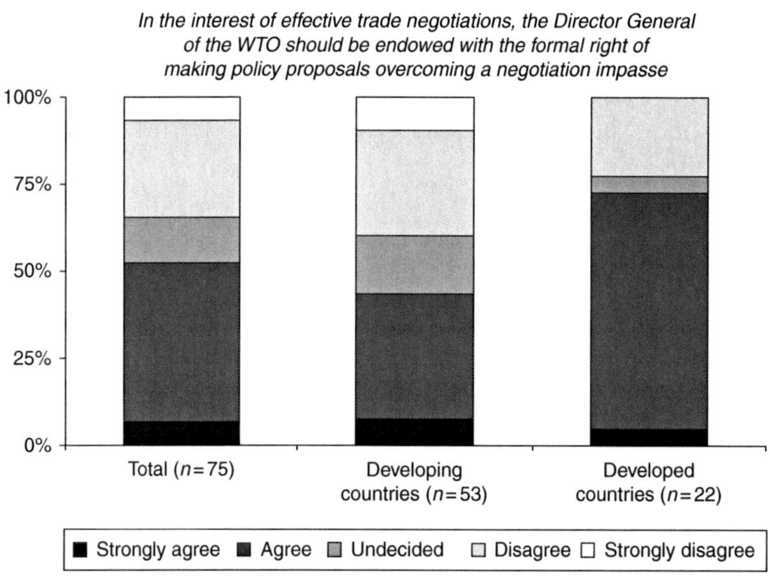

Figure 7.2 Formal right of Director General of making policy proposals for overcoming negotiation impasse

countries agree or strongly agree with the reform proposal, there is only a minority of 43% of developing countries which is supportive.

(d) Supervision of procedural rules

The establishment of the Secretariat as a supervisor of procedural rules was not discussed in the Sutherland Report. A developing country described the current situation as follows: if a member raises the issue of violation of procedural rules by another member, the chair may give the floor to the Secretariat, and the Secretariat can then explain whether a member had violated a rule or not. However, the WTO Secretariat could not intervene on its own initiative. As Table 7.1 indicates, interview partners see no positive effects on WTO performance when the Secretariat supervises compliance of member states with procedural rules. Not surprisingly, slight negative effects on the legitimacy of the WTO are expected from this measure.

(e) Complaints of the violation of substantive trade rules

The characterization of the WTO as "Guardian of the Treaties" in the Sutherland Report may also suggest to endow the Secretariat with the right to investigate complaints of the violation of trade rules (*von Bogdandy and Wagner* 2005: 446). In this regard, the total number of respondents predicts a small increase of effectiveness and equity, but a small decrease in acceptance by members. Representatives of the Secretariat did not endorse this reform proposal. This may be an indicator that the Secretariat is not eager to take up this new task.

(f) Conclusions

The realization of four out of five proposals is generally seen as having a positive impact on effectiveness of the WTO. Of these four proposals, only the definition of the DG role is seen as leading also to increases in WTO legitimacy. The realization of this proposal should, therefore, be recommended. Increasing resources of the Secretariat is also seen as having a positive impact on equity of members. This proposal is recommended provided that the specific use of resources does not compromise the neutrality of the Secretariat.

By contrast, the Secretariat's right of initiative, its supervisory role concerning procedural rules, and its right to investigate complaints of the violation of trade rules are estimated to lead to decreases in WTO legitimacy. This demonstrates that even if effectiveness is increased member state acceptance is reduced. Member states and also externals may be afraid of too strong a Secretariat. The picture is more nuanced, however, if results of the survey are taken into account. Slightly more than 50% of the respondents which are member state delegations agree or strongly agree with endowing the Director General with the right to make policy proposals to overcome a negotiation impasse. The realization of this proposal is, therefore, recommended.

In sum, recommended reform measures are proposals no. 1, 2 of Annex 1, and the right of the Director General to make policy proposals for overcoming a negotiation impasse.

2. Developing the WTO structure

Table 7.2 depicts how interview partners evaluate the potential impact of different proposals for reforming WTO structures on the effectiveness of the WTO, equity of members, and acceptance by members and externals.

Table 7.2 Estimated average effects of proposed reform measures concerning the organizational structure on WTO performance (means)[a]

	Performance			
Reform proposals[b]	**Effectiveness of goal attainment**	**Equity of members**	**Acceptance by members**	**Acceptance by externals**
Independent agency for technical assistance (15)	.6($n=12$)	.9($n=12$)	.8($n=12$)	1.1($n=12$)
TPR for social and environmental issues (14)	−.9($n=9$)	−.6	−.9($n=11$)	1.0($n=11$)
Departmental structure (6)	−.8($n=12$)	−.8($n=12$)	−1.3($n=12$)	
Consultative council (5)	.8			
Advisory Parliamentary Assembly (7)	−.8			1.2

[a] $N=13$, except where otherwise indicated
[b] See Annex 1

(a) Task structure

(aa) Independent agency for technical assistance

The *Sutherland Report* (2004: 78) had proposed that all technical assistance activities be moved out of the WTO and out of other international organizations and be transferred to a semi-independent agency, so that technical assistance could be delivered in a more cost-efficient way.

Of all proposals rated by interview partners, this proposal receives the broadest approval as Table 7.2 indicates. Small increases in effectiveness, equity of members, acceptance by members, and acceptance by externals are predicted.

However, this generally supportive view was differentiated in the interviews. Secretariat staff observed that funding would have to be supplied through the WTO members who would also continue to decide on the output. Further, according to the Secretariat, it was probably unrealistic to move technical assistance activities out of other international organizations such as UNCTAD and the ITC:

> If it is too independent, the members don't have a word to say anymore, I'm not sure that you would find two members that accept that idea. Members are those who are paying, we cannot forget that. The technical cooperation we provide is provided by the members, you know. So, it's going to be difficult. On the other hand, it's completely unrealistic. How could you bring the other technical cooperation agencies in one single agency?

A representative of a developing country expressed doubts that there was a need for an agency centralizing the technical assistance activities of the WTO, UNCTAD, and the ITC:

> To me, having a central agency to do that, I think we will need to evaluate the effectiveness of the current approach. And see whether it is delivering, or not. And see whether by centralizing, and putting it outside the WTO or UNCTAD or whatever, would be the right thing. Because as I say, the three of them have a role to play.

To sum up, the, on average, positive assessment of creating a central agency for technical assistance is met with some skepticism both from the Secretariat and from developing countries.

(bb) Trade policy reviews extended to social and environmental issues

The effects of extending the trade policy review to social and environmental issues are seen as predominantly negative by interview partners in Table 7.2. Small decreases were expected concerning effectiveness, equity, and acceptance by members. In interviews, Secretariat staff confirmed that the proposal would decrease effectiveness of the trade policy review by making trade policy review reports less focused and thereby less useful:

> Our clients are trade negotiators, trade policy makers, members of this organization. By incorporating issues, social issues, labor standards, what would be our value-added in that area? I am not sure that we would have something to say that would be valuable to the debate. That's basically what I say. We would lose focus on the sense of the trade policy, and we would be adding lots and lots of topics, plus what would be the value-added for this organization to that kind of issue.

Acceptance of the WTO by externals, by contrast, is thought to increase. The positive attitude of NGOs was confirmed in an interview with a development-oriented NGO. While the NGO rejected the extension of the dispute settlement to cover labor standards as too political, it viewed an extension of trade policy review as being an alternative way of integrating labor standards into the work of the WTO:

> At this point I couldn't see the WTO much more than a consultative type of role on this issue, maybe looking at labour standards as part of trade policy review [...], but not being able to challenge anything before the dispute settlement. It's too political.

(b) Departmental structure

Guzman (2004) had proposed to create a new departmental structure of the WTO with responsibilities for environmental and social issues, negotiation rounds and new mega-rounds (see Chapter 2, II.2). The evaluation of this proposal is, on average, negative in Table 7.2.

The proposal was not discussed in the Sutherland Report. In the interviews it provoked strong reactions. A developing country completely rejected the proposal, based on the argument that the WTO was not qualified to deal with issues other than trade, and that while the interface between trade and environment had to be discussed within the

WTO, environmental regimes like the climate change regime had to be kept out:

> Let us not try to create a monster, because I think it's better when you have different organizations qualified in their own field. Let's handle trade because that is what we are good at in the WTO.

(c) Consultative Council

The *Sutherland Report* (2004: 70f.) proposed to set up a Consultative Council with a maximum of 30 members on a partly rotating and partly permanent basis, which was to provide input into trade negotiations at the WTO. Table 7.2 shows a small increase in effectiveness but no effects on WTO performance in terms of equity and legitimacy.

The interviews revealed a more critical view of this reform measure. A representative of a G-4 Developed Country stressed that he had no objections to the Consultative Council, since his country was sure to be represented there. However, in his view it was not acceptable to other member states. Smaller member states would not consent to being represented by a larger member state (for example, if Paraguay was represented by Brazil). Moreover, even if two countries had similar interests in one area, interests were totally different in other areas ("variable geometry") so that it became impossible to provide for a composition of the Council reflecting the divergent interests in all areas.

A similar view was taken in literature. *Wolfe* (2005: 642) doubted that the establishment of a Consultative Council could make negotiations in the WTO more effective. Informal coalitions in the WTO following different issues and reflecting the diversity of members were considered a great strength of the organization.

However, there are also positive views on the Consultative Council in literature, with *Blackhurst and Hartridge* (2004: 710) stressing that the new Consultative Council could promote equity of members and legitimacy. Given the partly rotating basis of membership, countries which were currently excluded from Green Room meetings could be better integrated into decision making. The establishment of predictable and transparent participation rights compared favorably to the operation of informal groups and would strengthen the legitimacy of the process.

This seems, however, to be a normative view on the positive effects of the Consultative Council which is not supported by the interviews. Furthermore, the hope that a Consultative Council would replace Green Room negotiations (*Jones* 2004: 162f.) is unfounded. As the theory of informal organization suggests (Chapter 3, I.3.b), new informal meetings of member states are likely to precede or run parallel to the formal meetings of the Consultative Council. Thus, the immediate effects of officially privileging some members through the establishment of a Consultative Council are likely to be protests by all members excluded.

(d) Advisory parliamentary assembly

According to Table 7.2, the establishment of an advisory parliamentary assembly is expected to lead to a decrease in the effectiveness of the WTO.

At the same time, responses point toward an increase in acceptance of the WTO by externals. Interviews showed indeed that the assessment of external actors (intergovernmental organizations/NGOs) was a positive one.

These views are reflected in literature where opponents of an interparliamentarian body also expected a decrease of effectiveness given that the body would "add further institutional complication to an already extraordinarily difficult negotiating process" (*Shaffer* 2005b: 400). Regarding equity, some scholars expected an increase. According to Shaffer, it is difficult for many parliamentarians from developing countries to obtain information about WTO developments. Thus, parliamentarian attendance at WTO Ministerial Meetings could help them. Also, it was argued that an interparliamentarian assembly could help developing countries to advance their perspectives and agendas in global forums such as the WTO. However, *Petersmann* (2005b: 654) conceded that special help from developed countries would be required to ensure that parliamentarians from less developed countries could actually participate in parliamentary meetings "in no less an effective manner than members of parliaments from developed countries."

(e) Conclusions

In this area, no reform proposals can be recommended. The extension of the trade policy review to cover social and environmental issues, the creation of a departmental structure, and the creation of an advisory Parliamentary Assembly are all supposed to lead to decreases in the effectiveness of the WTO. Given the current problems with WTO effectiveness, these proposals could only be supported if there were strong increases on other dimensions of WTO performance. This is not the case. By contrast, the creation of an independent agency for technical assistance is, in Table 7.2, considered to have positive effects on WTO performance in terms of effectiveness, equity, and legitimacy.

However, the interviews revealed considerable doubts as to the practical desirability and political feasibility of this proposal.

Finally, the creation of a Consultative Council shows a positive impact on the effectiveness of the WTO in Table 7.2. While this effect is partly supported in literature, the reform proposal does not seem to be politically feasible in an organization which is dominated by developing countries with a wide range of divergent interests.

3. WTO relations with NGOs

Table 7.3 shows how interview partners assess the potential impact of different proposals which aim at improving WTO relations with NGOs on WTO performance in terms of effectiveness, equity of members, and legitimacy.

(a) Accreditation system

The *Sutherland Report* (2004: 46) was critical of introducing a permanent accreditation system for NGOs because it would generate continuing bureaucratic burden on the Secretariat, while it had no practical benefits as it had to be clearly distinguished from allowing NGOs to attend negotiations as observers. Table 7.3 shows that a small increase of equity

Table 7.3 Estimated average effects of proposed reform measures concerning WTO relations with NGOs and the public on WTO performance (means)[a]

	Performance			
Reform proposals[b]	**Effectiveness of goal attainment**	**Equity of members**	**Acceptance by members**	**Acceptance by externals**
Permanent accreditation system for NGOs (10)		.6		1.4
NGO observer status in negotiations (11)	−.9	.6	−.9	1.2
Advisory NGO Committee (12)		.7($n=9$)	−.6($n=9$)	1.1($n=9$)
TPR in cooperation with NGOs (13)			−.7($n=12$)	.9($n=12$)

[a] $N=13$, except where otherwise indicated
[b] See Annex 1

of members and acceptance by externals is expected. The Secretariat indicated that, by and large, the accreditation system would have no effects on WTO performance, but that it would decrease acceptance by members and increase acceptance by externals.

Several NGOs stressed during the interviews that they would see some merit in receiving a batch from the WTO and being granted the right to freely enter the WTO building to meet delegations. Currently, NGOs were only allowed to enter the building as guests of member state delegations. This compared poorly to the situation at the United Nations. An NGO observed:

> In the UN building. I mean we are accredited to the ECOSOC, and that gives us yearly badges, yearly accreditation to the UN. We can enter the building without any problem. Meetings and workshops we can access. So it's much more open and formalized. That does not exist at the WTO.

Another NGO commented:

> I think I would to like to see that those based in Geneva have a more easy access to the WTO. You know, just walk in and out by having a batch. Like I mean I have an official UN batch. Because we are officially registered with the UN, so whenever I want to go to the UN buildings, I have a batch, and I can enter.

NGOs stressed that the WTO Secretariat should devote more time to a permanent accreditation policy compared to the current ad hoc approach to accreditation for Ministerial Conferences. More attention had to be paid to details, such as the developing of a stricter definition of an NGO which excluded governmental advisory bodies or which provided a basis for dealing with national and international offices of the same umbrella NGO. In sum, the establishment of a permanent accreditation system for NGOs can be recommended as a reform measure which would improve, at least, atmospheric relations between the WTO and NGOs without generating any negative effects, in particular on the WTO's effectiveness in negotiations.

(b) NGO observer status in trade negotiations

Table 7.3 shows that the effectiveness of the WTO and its acceptance by members would be slightly decreased, if NGOs were granted observer status in WTO negotiations. The Sutherland Report dismissed this idea given that confidentiality for trade negotiations was required and that effectiveness of negotiations could be infringed. However, in literature the negative impact on effectiveness was contested. *Von Bogdandy and Wagner* (2005: 441) criticized the WTO for its emphasis on confidentiality of trade negotiations. In their view, negotiations could be set up "with considerably more transparency than is the case today" without reducing effectiveness.

The lack of acceptance by member states was also regarded in the Sutherland Report and in literature as a reason for not further pursuing this proposal. A developing country delegate showed a more nuanced view of this issue in an interview. He had no objection to NGOs participating as quiet observers in general debates, provided that they understood that sometimes sensitive issues required confidentiality:

> When the matter is sensitive then one would say sorry this time we are not allowing anybody. What we are discussing is very sensitive. But if it is a general debate, I see no reason why they should not be allowed to come and listen.

Table 7.3 shows that acceptance of the WTO by externals is viewed to slightly increase if NGOs were granted observer status. However, far from being enthusiastic supporters of an observer status, interview partners from NGOs showed themselves divided regarding the desirability of this reform measure. The opposition was based on the argument that NGO observership would further increase informal decision making within the WTO, thereby decreasing equity of members. A development-oriented NGO stressed that the member state position was that the negotiation process was closed to civil society and that it would require a major reform to change that. Therefore a permanent accreditation system for NGOs was seen as a more realistic goal.

Finally, another NGO pointed out to the experience of NGOs participating frequently in meetings in the United Nations to become co-opted. NGOs feared that the same might happen in the WTO. To add to this, the establishment of an NGO right to attend meetings would create many problems of representation and selection.

(c) Right to comment

A concept which is not discussed in literature is to give NGOs generally the *right to comment* on the results of negotiations without necessarily limiting this to a committee.

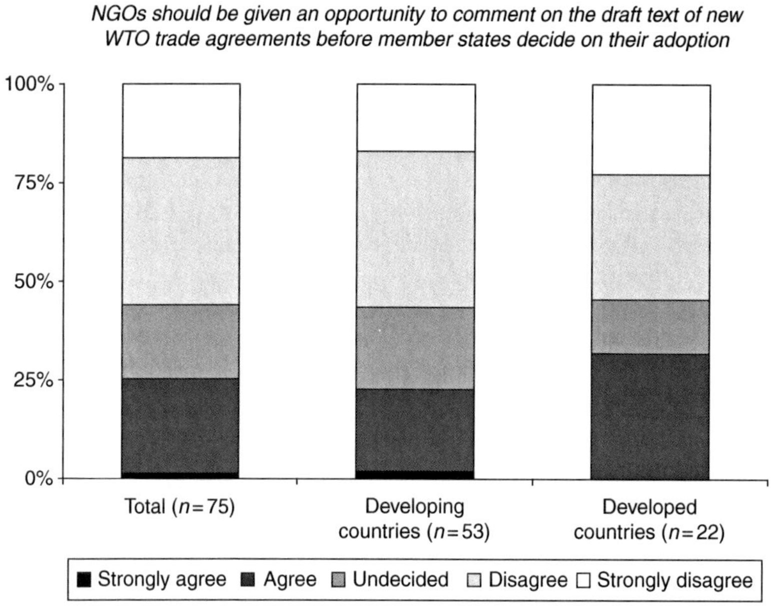

Figure 7.3 NGO right to comment on WTO draft agreements

Figure 7.3 depicts how surveyed member states assess the desirability of the introduction of a right of NGOs to comment on draft texts of new agreements before member states decide on their adoption.

Only slightly more than 20% of the developing countries agree or strongly agree with this measure. Developed countries have a slightly more positive view on this proposal. The majority of member states, however, rejects this reform proposal. This rejection reflects the general reservation of member states toward NGOs and their concerns not to be patronized by NGOs (see Chapter 5, I.1.e and Figure 5.2).

(d) Advisory NGO committee

Under former Director General Panitchpakdi the Secretariat had once considered to establish an advisory NGO committee (*Mason* 2004: 580). A similar proposal was made by *Petersmann* (2001: 109) suggesting that the creation of an "Advisory Social and Economic Committee" with the right to submit recommendations to all WTO bodies would ensure more accountability and representativeness of NGOs. Table 7.3 indicates that weak positive effects are expected from this measure, not surprisingly, on the acceptance of the WTO by external actors like NGOs, and on equity of WTO members, while no or negative effects are predicted with respect to the effectiveness of the WTO and its acceptance by members. The interviews revealed an even more negative attitude of the interview partners from the Secretariat toward this reform measure. This may reflect internal controversies over this measure once considered by the Secretariat but later abandoned.

Clearly, the realization of the proposal would create even more problems of representation and selection than the granting of observer status to NGOs. *Lacarte* (2005: 449f.) argued that there was naturally a problem of selection involved, since probably as many as 100 or 200 NGOs might wish to express their views on given WTO subjects. NGOs would have to work out differences among themselves to be able to agree on recommendations. Even though the work of the committee would be exclusively advisory in nature, its establishment would already constitute a significant departure from current practice. Given the problems with selection and representation, it is questionable whether the reform would really lead to greater acceptance of the organization among NGOs, if many of them felt that their ideas were not represented in the views of the committee.

(e) Trade policy reviews in cooperation with NGOs

Table 7.3 shows that the cooperation of the Secretariat with NGOs in the drafting of trade policy review reports is viewed as having no impact on the effectiveness of the WTO but a negative impact on acceptance by members and a positive impact on acceptance by externals. The view of the Secretariat is, as in the case of an advisory NGO committee, in each case more negative. The Secretariat predicts decreases in effectiveness, equity, and legitimacy of the WTO.

(f) Conclusions

For all proposals, increases in acceptance of the WTO by externals are expected. This is no surprise since these measures are aimed at strengthening the role of NGOs. At the same time, three out of four proposals are expected to decrease member state acceptance. This pattern reflects the complexity of legitimacy from an empirical perspective. Legitimacy of an institution in terms of its acceptance by other actors is contingent upon specific actor interests. Therefore, the frequent claim that the WTO lacks legitimacy as well as the numerous proposals to remedy this deficiency are too simplistic and often unfounded.

The proposal to establish a permanent accreditation system for NGOs is expected to have positive effects on WTO performance in terms of equity of members and WTO acceptance by externals without negative effects on the other dimensions of WTO performance. Therefore, this reform measure is recommended.

4. Formal elements in informal trade negotiations

(a) Partial reformalization of informal negotiations

Informal decision making is pervasive in the WTO, and constitutes an extensive "informal organization" which complements the formal WTO (see Chapter 5, V). There is an inherent conflict between informality on the one hand, and equity and legitimacy of decision making on the other hand. Informal decision making is intransparent, and tends to disadvantage actors with little bargaining power. Therefore, several reform proposals aim to (re)formalize decision-making procedures. Figure 7.4 depicts how member states assess a partial reformalization of informal procedures in general.

Almost half of all member states support the notion of partially reformalizing informal procedures of trade negotiations. Particularly

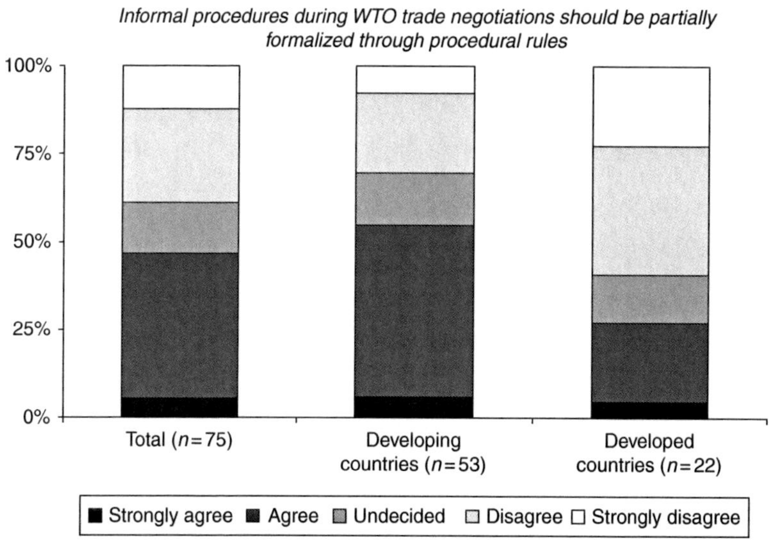

Figure 7.4 Partial formalization of informal procedures

developing countries favor new formal rules while developed countries reject them. These attitudes are no surprise because developing countries seek protection of their interests from formal rules. In contrast, developed countries favor the greater flexibility of informal procedures which makes it easier for them to achieve their negotiation objectives.

Two concrete proposals for reformalizing informal trade negotiations were subject to the assessment by surveyed member states. The first one was developed by the author and the second one was taken from the Sutherland Report.

(b) Restrictions on blocking consensus

The conflict of effectiveness versus equity and legitimacy in informal decision making creates two problems for the adoption of formal decisions after informal negotiations. Informal negotiations are often used, on the one hand, by powerful member states to build a consensus among themselves and to impose this consensus on smaller member states – usually developing countries – which were excluded from informal negotiations. Informal negotiations often lead, on the other hand, to frustration among smaller member states and trigger their vetoes to translating the informal negotiation results into formal decisions. Consequently, trade negotiations fail, or the adoption of formal agreements is delayed indefinitely.

These problems are addressed by the following proposal to partially reformalize informal negotiations which was included in the written survey and subject to the assessment of member states: Procedural rules provide "that WTO members could only block consensus on trade measures which otherwise have a very broad consensus support, if these member states were excluded from informal negotiations on said measures."

In other words, a member state could not veto the formal adoption of trade measures based on a very broad consensus if the member state was included in the preceding informal negotiations, and had not objected to the consensus.[2]

This proposal is based on the assumption that powerful member states have an interest to minimize the negative effects of the veto powers of other members, while countries with little bargaining power have an interest to gain access to informal trade negotiations. Consequently, powerful member states are expected to minimize the risks of vetoes by inviting all member states to participate in informal trade negotiations which have specific interests in the subject of the negotiations.

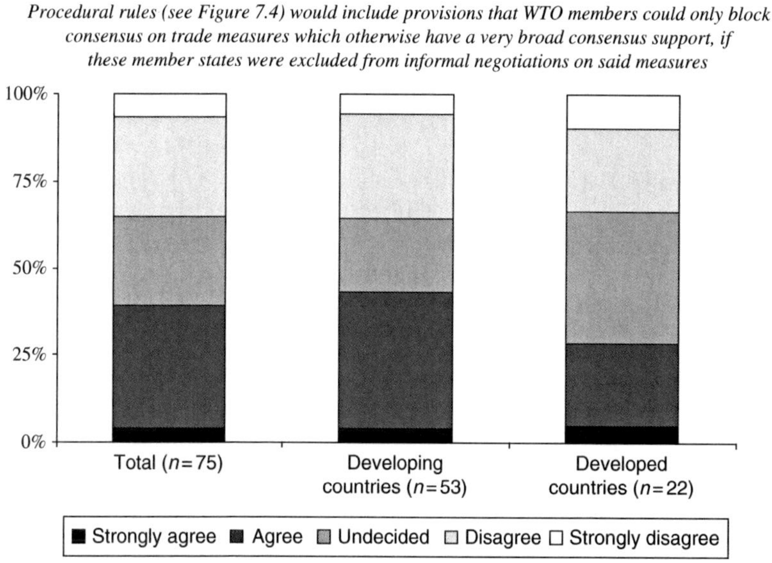

Figure 7.5 Restrictions on blocking consensus after informal negotiations

Furthermore, member states with little bargaining power are expected to participate in informal negotiations thereby accepting restrictions on their veto powers.

Figure 7.5 shows how member states assess this proposal.

Over 40% of developing countries support the proposal, while only little over 25% of developed countries are in favor of it. However, the largest group (38%) of developed countries is undecided. About one-third of developing and developed countries explicitly reject the proposal. The reservation of the responding countries can be, to some extent, explained by the fact that the proposal was unknown, and introduced, for the first time, by the author. The interviews indicate that support for the proposal increases the more an interview partner becomes familiar with the functioning and possible effects of the reform measure.

While stressing that this proposal was new and had not yet been discussed, an interview partner from a development-oriented intergovernmental organization nevertheless expressed his support:

> I think this would be a very useful recommendation to have. We have not thought about it in that light. We have always tried to go for more

> formal rules and tried to use the formal route, I suppose, as opposed to going the informal route. But trying to link informality to formal outcomes, in the way that you are suggesting, is what we haven't thought about yet.

The proposed "link" between informality and formality – in the words of the interview partners – aims to optimize the requirements of effectiveness, equity, and legitimacy on WTO decision making.

Effectiveness is served by restrictions on the veto power of member states. These restrictions will make it difficult to participate in informal negotiations merely for tactical reasons, and to exercise vetoes simply as part of a political power game. Equity is served by facilitating access of member states with little bargaining power to informal negotiations.

Legitimacy is served by partially reformalizing informal negotiations in line with the idea of estoppel. This idea is part of the fundamental principles of good faith and equity (*Shaw* 2008: 515) which are essential for the general acceptance of WTO activities by member states and external actors. Estoppel is a principle of international law[3] which prohibits a state to alter its position if it had previously made a statement or consented to a state of affairs upon which another state in good faith relied in subsequent activity (*Shaw* 2008: 102f., 517f.). It is certainly not a violation of the principle of estoppel in a legal sense, when a member state vetoes a trade measure supported by a very broad consensus although the member had explicitly or tacitly consented to the measure in preceding informal negotiations. However, the veto represents contradictory behavior which, in a political sense, is contrary to the idea of estoppel. A procedural rule prohibiting vetoes under these circumstances would, therefore, be in line with the principle of estoppel, and contribute to the legitimacy of the WTO.

The Sutherland Report also addresses the issue of how to restrict the veto power of member states against trade measures with a very broad consensus support. The Report recommends a declaration by the General Council that such a consensus can only be blocked if the member state declares "in writing, with reasons included, that the matter is one of vital national interest to it" (*Sutherland et al.* 2004: 64). Figure 7.6 shows the assessment of this proposal by member states. The assessment of this proposal is very similar to the one of the previous proposal in Figure 7.5 with the difference that no country expresses strong support in Figure 7.6.

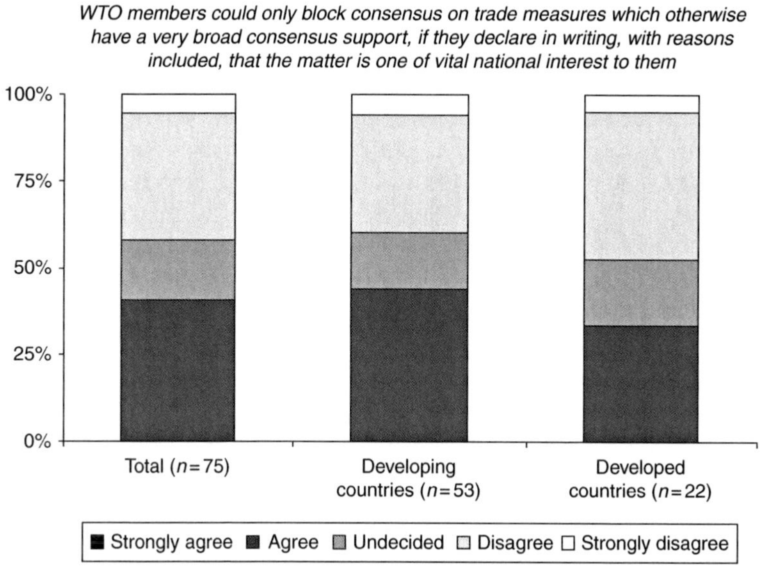

Figure 7.6 Consensus blocking based on written reasons

Some 40% of all member states support the proposal while about the same number rejects it. Developing countries are more in favor of it than developed countries.

The literature is rather skeptical about this proposal. One scholar regarded it as being too "timid"; a more radical review of the consensus principle was required in order to make negotiations in the WTO more effective (*Hufbauer* 2005: 296). Another one qualified this as a "non-starter" (*Wolfe* 2005: 635), given that it would be pointless to force countries to dissimulate about their tactical and substantive reasons for withholding consensus, which other members knew about anyway.

The practability of this proposal is doubtful because member states will, in most cases, find reasons to invoke national interests. While the effectiveness of the proposal is, therefore, questionable, it is likely to have negative effects on WTO performance in terms of equity and legitimacy. The proposal applies to formal and informal trade negotiations. With respect to informal negotiations the tendency to exclude member states with little bargaining power will increase, because they cannot veto the outcome of informal negotiations from which they were excluded unless they invoke national interests in writing.

In sum, the proposal to restrict the veto power of member states to cases of vital national interests should not be pursued.

However, it is recommended to partially reformalize informal negotiations by a procedural rule which restricts the veto power of member states against measures with a very broad consensus support to cases where the member state has been excluded from informal negotiations or consensus.

(c) Formalizing access to informal negotiations

A radical solution to the problems of informal negotiations is to prohibit informal meetings like the so-called Green Room negotiations. This proposal is made by NGOs (*IATP* 2003: 12; *The Third World Network et al.* 2003: no. 52, 69).

Table 7.4 depicts how interview partners assess the potential impact of this proposal on WTO performance.

Not surprisingly the proposal is expected to have positive effects on the acceptance of the WTO by external actors like NGOs. However, negative effects are predicted on the effectiveness of the WTO, while no effects are expected on WTO performance in terms of equity and acceptance by members. Interview partners from the Secretariat emphasized that the prohibition of informal negotiations would have

Table 7.4 Estimated average effects of proposed reform measures concerning access to trade negotiations on WTO performance (means)[a]

	Performance			
Reform proposals[b]	**Effectiveness of goal attainment**	**Equity of members**	**Acceptance by members**	**Acceptance by externals**
Prohibition of restricted sessions (8)	$-1.6 (n=12)$			$1.3 (n=12)$
Some member states negotiate, while others are observing (19)		$.5 (n=7)$	$.8 (n=7)$	

[a] $N=13$, except where otherwise indicated
[b] See Annex 1

detrimental effects on the WTO to achieve its tasks. Besides that, it seems unlikely that the prohibition of informal negotiations can be successfully implemented. Organization theory suggests that organizations cannot function without patterns of informal behavior (see Chapter 3, I.3.b). Therefore, the proposed prohibition would be circumvented by new forms of informal meetings.

A more subtle way to abolish the current practice of informal negotiations than a prohibition of these negotiations is to formalize access to, participation in, and conduct of informal negotiations. *Khor* (2002: 20) of the NGO "The Third World Network" suggested that negotiations are conducted by representatives of member state groupings but that all members have the right to be present in the room. All members closely observe how representatives negotiate, and they may interrupt the negotiations and ask for time to consult with the group representatives if they felt that their interests were not adequately represented. Table 7.4 shows how interview partners assess the potential effects of this proposal on WTO performance.

Small positive effects on equity of members and acceptance by members are expected with no impact on effectiveness of the WTO and its acceptance by external actors. However, interview partners from the Secretariat stressed that this proposal would have negative consequences for the effectiveness of the WTO. A developing country representative expressed apprehension of his country being properly represented in such a negotiation scheme. In any event, the realization of this proposal requires comprehensive procedural rules, for instance, on establishing country groups, the selection of the group leader who does the negotiations, the procedure by which the negotiation mandate of the group leader is determined, the form conditions and effects of interventions into ongoing negotiations by member states which are attending but not conducting negotiations. Ultimately, informal negotiations may be transformed into some kind of formal negotiations. Again organization theory suggests that such a comprehensive formalization process would trigger new patterns of informal negotiations.

(d) Conclusions

Informality is an inevitable characteristic of formal organizations. Formal prohibitions of informal negotiations will generate new forms of informal interactions. This is why it is futile to try to eradicate informal negotiations in the WTO. A reform strategy with the chance of being successful must accept informal negotiations as an inevitable part of organizational life. This is not a way of saying that every specific pattern of informal behavior is acceptable. On the contrary, the organizational, procedural, and informational framework conditions of decision making are to be altered in a way that specific illegal or abusive informal practices are eliminated, and a balance is struck between the requirements of effectiveness, equity, and legitimacy. Partial reformalization of informal negotiations is a reform strategy which almost 50% of member states support (Figure 7.4). Tactical and political gaming in informal negotiations could be decreased if the inclusion of member states in informal negotiations and consensus triggered the loss of veto power against trade measures with a very great consensus support (Figure 7.5).

5. Developing the dispute settlement system

Table 7.5 depicts how interview partners assess the potential impact of different reform proposals for the dispute settlement system on WTO performance.

Table 7.5 Estimated average effects of proposed reform measures concerning the dispute settlement system on WTO performance (means)[a]

	Performance			
Reform proposals[b]	**Effectiveness of goal attainment**	**Equity of members**	**Acceptance by members**	**Acceptance by externals**
Access of private parties to DS (16)		−1.5	−1.7	−1.1
Compensation right for winning party (17)	1.2($n=10$)	.5($n=11$)		.6($n=11$)
Public observation of DS proceedings (18)	.6($n=11$)		.6($n=11$)	1.6($n=9$)

[a] $N=13$, except where otherwise indicated
[b] See Annex 1

(a) Access of private parties

In literature, some scholars have advocated an "Efficient Market Model" which gives private commercial parties access to the WTO trade resolution machinery to resolve disputes which involve private interests more effectively. *Shell* (1998: 370f.) advocated a Trade Stakeholder Model, which emphasized direct participation in trade disputes not only by states and businesses but also by non-governmental organizations. Thereby more equity of policy concerns could be achieved (see Chapter 2, II.2). However, these scholars have remained isolated (*Charnovitz* 2002a: 392). The Sutherland Report even failed to discuss the proposal.

The assessment of the proposal in Table 7.5 is negative. In the interviews a developing country expressed the concern that the introduction of this new right would only benefit big business.

(b) Compensation right for winning party

The effects of introducing a right of financial compensation for winning parties are evaluated positively in Table 7.5 on almost all dimensions of WTO performance.

While the *Sutherland Report* (2004: 54) failed to support the proposal to establish the right to compensation, literature has been more supportive. *Bronckers and van den Broek* (2005) provided many arguments in favor of the introduction of monetary compensation. Also, Matsushita (2005: 624f.) and *Meagher* (2005: 416) have been supportive. *Bronckers and van den Broek* disputed that the introduction of monetary compensation damaged the effectiveness of dispute settlement. It would "in no way obviate the priority and legal necessity of compliance with WTO law" (2005: 118). *Matsushita* (2005: 625) even argued that compensation was preferable to trade retaliation in form of a suspension of concessions which represented a "second blow to the trade system." The reform proposal is recommended.

(c) Public observation

A frequently made proposal is to open dispute settlement proceedings to public observation. Its assessment in Table 7.5 is positive.

The *Sutherland Report* (2004: 58) also supported to open panel and Appellate Body hearings to the public. In literature the recommendation of the Sutherland Report has been welcomed given that the WTO required for its operation the support of civil society (*Matsushita* 2005: 628). Another scholar, however, cautioned that the opening up of proceedings could reduce equity of members. He noted that developing countries opposed this reform measure out of fear that the increased transparency "may exacerbate their resource constraints by providing private and non-governmental organizations in developed countries greater opportunities to influence their litigation strategies" (*Meagher* 2005: 416). This view was not supported in the interviews. Rather they suggest that more transparency of the dispute settlement system would alleviate the legitimacy problems of the WTO with the public.

The proposal is, therefore, recommended.

(d) Conclusions

The reform proposals to open panel and Appellate Body hearings to the public, and to provide the winning party with a right to financial compensation are likely to contribute to the effectiveness of the dispute settlement system, and to alleviate the legitimacy problems of the WTO with the public and external actors. The realization of these reform measures is, therefore, recommended.

III. Time to act

1. Need for reform

Structures and procedures of the WTO are basically a continuation and modification of the GATT system. It is "based upon consensus diplomacy: multilateralizing bilateral tariff reductions within defined trade rounds, ... and expanding memberships on the basis of negotiated and agreed terms in protocols of accession" (*Cottier* 2007: 497, 499). The analysis in Chapter 5 (see I.3, II.3, and III.3) revealed shortcomings with respect to the effectiveness and equity of WTO performance, particularly in the area of trade negotiations, as well as deficits of acceptance of the WTO among NGOs and the public.

In literature (*Cottier* 2007: 499–501), structural and procedural deficiencies of the WTO are primarily attributed to the shift of the WTO from traditional GATT-type negotiations on multilateral tariff reductions to more complex and politically controversial negotiations on non-tariff barriers. They include issues like technical barriers to trade, sanitary and phytosanitary measures, subsidies, service, intellectual property, anti-trust, and government procurement. Existing GATT-based structures and procedures of the WTO are said to be inadequate for resolving "the current and future issues of complex non-tariff regulation" (*Cottier* 2007: 501).

Furthermore, the organizational structures and procedures of the WTO have traditionally received little attention. This is best illustrated by the fact that the Secretariat is not displayed in the official WTO organigram (see Figure 1.1). The general indifference toward WTO organizational structures and procedures followed from the prevailing notion that international organizations are merely tools, arenas, or clubs of nation states and, therefore, do not matter (see Chapter 2, I.1). Consequently, organizational and procedural inadequacies were not remedied.

Finally, recurring administrative modernization is a necessity for any public formal organization in order to adapt to the requirements of a changing environment. Unlike companies which are compelled by the market forces to adapt to changing market conditions if they are to survive, public formal organizations are not subject to market forces, and can survive without adaptations even if their performance is poor. After almost 15 years of operation on the basis of GATT, concepts and principles which were developed when many of today's problems did not exist, it is time for the WTO to modernize its organizational structures and procedures.[4]

2. Strategy of reform

Starting point for a strategy of reform is the notion of optimization. Reform measures must be designed in a way that they find a reasonable balance between the requirements of effectiveness, equity, and legitimacy rather than maximizing one of these principles at the expense of others. This is because the three principles coexist in a state of interdependence (Chapter 6, IV). One consequence of this interdependent relationship is the need to retain the consensus principle as the base of a member-driven organization. At first glance, the consensus principle seems to be an impediment to effective decision making. However, this principle is a necessary though not sufficient condition for the acceptance of the WTO by member states and for equitable relations among them. Without the acceptance of the WTO by its members the organization could not function. Hence, effective decision making would be impossible.

From the analysis of WTO performance in Chapter 6 and of possible effects of various reform measures in this chapter the following elements of a reform strategy can be derived:

- strengthen the executive functions of the WTO,
- create more equitable framework conditions for informal negotiations,

- increase transparency,
- improve sanctions against non-compliance with dispute settlement reports.

The effectiveness of WTO activities is different in different task areas. Activities are most deficient in trade negotiations and reasonably efficient in dispute settlement, while there is a mixed performance with respect to the implementation of trade agreements and trade policy review (Chapter 6, I.3). Many factors are responsible for these performance patterns some of which are of a political nature and cannot be influenced by institutional reforms. To the extent that institutional shortcomings impede the effectiveness of WTO activities, the analysis of reform measures in this chapter suggests a reform strategy of strengthening the executive functions of the WTO.

The second element of a reform strategy is derived from the knowledge that informal decision making is an inevitable part of organizational life. This means that informal trade negotiations cannot be abolished. Rather the framework conditions of informal negotiations should be changed and made more equitable for countries with little bargaining power, for instance, by providing them with more resources, by partially reformalizing informal procedures, or by other measures which would enable these members to represent their national interests more effectively in informal trade negotiations.

Given the globalization of information, communication, and numerous economic, technological, ecological, security, and other problems, international organizations addressing these issues cannot effectively function without some basic acceptance by NGOs and the public, at least, in key member states (empirical legitimacy). Therefore, the prevailing view among students of International Relations holds that existing international institutions need to be reformed by incorporating actors of civil society in one way or the other into the system of global governance (*Karns and Mingst* 2004: 25; *Clark* 2006: 738f.).

Transparency of organizational structure and procedures is a prerequisite for the acceptance of an international organization by NGOs and the public. It has, therefore, become a core concept of governance reforms of international organizations in general and the WTO in particular (*Deese* 2008: 175).

The effectiveness of any legal order depends on its acceptance by the addressees of legal norms. This general acceptance requires that the addressees perceive the legal norms as just and their application as based on equity (*Friedrich* 1963: 192f, 202). The notion of the equal application of law implies that non-compliance is corrected and, if necessary, punished. The system of sanctions to be imposed under Art. 22 of the DSU when panel rulings are not complied with is relatively weak. Trade agreements cannot be enforced by the WTO or national courts. The only sanctions against non-compliance with panel rulings encompass negotiations over compensations between the parties of the dispute, and an authorization of the winning party by the DSB to suspend the application to the non-complying member state of concessions or other obligations under the relevant agreement. In other words, the winning party may retaliate. However, this is no practical option for small countries because they have no economic means to really punish bigger countries but would only hurt their own economies (*Shoyer, Solovy, and Koff* 2005: 1362, 1366). Therefore, a reform strategy should include improvements of the system of sanctions against non-compliance with panel rulings.

3. Recommended reform measures

Table 7.6 summarizes the reform measures which are recommended on the basis of the preceding analyses.

Strengthening the executive functions of the WTO primarily encompasses a redefinition of the functions and rights of the Director General. Art. VI. (2) of the Marrakesh Agreement provides for the Ministerial Conference to "adopt regulations setting out the powers, duties, conditions of service and term of office of the Director General." This authorization has never been fully used. Instead, a role of the Director General has emerged in practice which is characterized in the *Sutherland Report* (2004: 74) as "a form of international spokesperson and marketing executive" for trade affairs which has undermined the leadership functions of the Director General in the WTO. Therefore, the executive function of the Director General should be redefined including, for instance, his management powers and duties, and an extension of his role as chairman of committees and councils (*Sutherland et al.* 2004: 74).

Of paramount importance for the leadership role of the Director General is to vest him with the right of making policy proposals for overcoming an impasse in trade negotiations. After all, 50% of the member states responding to the questionnaire support this proposal (see Figure 7.2).

Last but not least, the strengthening of the executive functions of the WTO requires to increase the comparatively modest resources of the Secretariat.

Table 7.6 Recommended reform measures

Strategy	Reform measures
Strengthen executive functions	1. Define the role of the Director General more precisely (2)[a] 2. Authorize the Director General to make policy proposals for overcoming negotiation impasse[b] 3. Increase resources of Secretariat (1)[a]
Create more equitable framework conditions for informal negotiations	4. Partially formalize informal procedures[c] 5. Restrict the right to block consensus to member states which were excluded from informal negotiations and consensus[d]
Increase transparency	6. Establish a permanent accreditation system for NGOs (10)[e] 7. Open panel and Appellate Body hearings to the public (18)[f]
Improve sanctions against non-compliance with dispute settlement reports	8. Establish the right of winning party to monetary compensations (17)[f]

(a) Table 7.1; (b) Figure 7.2; (c) Figure 7.4; (d) Figure 7.5; (e) Table 7.3; and (f) Table 7.5.

Creating more equitable framework conditions for informal negotiations can be achieved through partial reformalization of informal procedures which increases their transparency and reduces unequal treatment of member states. The contents of concrete rules depend on the characteristics of given task and problem areas. One problem area is the blocking of trade measures after informal negotiations even if they have a very broad consensus support. Transparency and equal treatment of member states as well as the effectiveness of informal negotiations could be improved if member states which were included in the informal negotiations and consensus could later not veto formal conclusions and decisions based on the consensus. Such a rule would formalize a trade-off between access to informal negotiations and the veto power of member states. Although this proposal has not been part of the general reform debate and was, therefore, unknown to surveyed member states, about 40% of responding members support the proposal (see Figure 7.5).

Increasing the transparency of WTO structures and procedures is politically a very sensitive reform issue. This is because member states are afraid of NGOs and the public to impair their national sovereignty once they are granted more informational and participatory rights. However, establishing a permanent accreditation system for NGOs is a reform measure which has primarily symbolic value of recognition for NGOs without negatively affecting the national interests of member states. The bureaucratic burden for the Secretariat used by the *Sutherland Report* (2004: 46) as an argument against this reform measure seems manageable as, for instance, the UN Economic and Social Council has demonstrated.

Since formal accreditation of NGOs does not include the right to observe WTO meetings, the public should be given the right to attend panel and Appellate Body hearings. Public observation is a fundamental principle of the due process of law (*Zippelius* 2007: § 36 II 3).

Improving sanctions against non-compliance with dispute settlement reports should focus on sanctions which small countries can afford. The right to claim monetary compensation from the losing party is more economic welfare-enhancing for small countries than retaliation. The latter remains the last though often only theoretical option when the losing party refuses to pay monetary compensation (*Matsushita* 2005: 625).

The recommended reform measures do not represent an institutional reform of the WTO which will heal all ills. Rather they entail incremental improvements for a public formal organization which is a hybrid international actor with characteristics of a corporate and collective actor. These contradictory characteristics defy the postulates of normative democratic or rationalistic reform models. But if the impossible is not feasible, the feasible should not become impossible.

Annex 1

Proposals for WTO reform which were evaluated by interview partners

1. Increase of resources to the WTO Secretariat and the Director General
2. Defining the role of the Director General more precisely
3. Creation of Right of Initiative for the WTO Secretariat
4. Establishment of a complaints mechanism in the WTO Secretariat for investigating violation of trade rules
5. Creation of a Consultative Council chaired by the Director General as proposed in the Sutherland Report
6. Creation of WTO departments with responsibilities for existing and new agreements (Labor, Environment), organization of departmental negotiation rounds and periodic "Mega Rounds"
7. Creation of an Advisory Parliamentary Assembly
8. Prohibition of restricted sessions between and during Ministerial Conferences (Exception: only with consent of all member states)
9. Supervision of these and other formal negotiation rules by the Secretariat
10. Creation of a permanent accreditation system for non-governmental organizations
11. Opening up of trade negotiations (including Ministerial Conference) to accredited non-governmental organizations with observer status
12. Creation of an Advisory NGO Committee
13. Carrying out Trade Policy Reviews through the Secretariat in cooperation with NGOs
14. Extending the Trade Policy Review to cover social and environmental issues
15. Creation of an independent agency for capacity-building that replaces member states' and WTO Secretariat capacity building
16. Enabling Private Parties to bring cases to the Dispute Settlement
17. Creation of an obligation to compensate the winning party of a Dispute Settlement case
18. Enabling observation of the Dispute Settlement proceedings by the public
19. Trade Negotiations through a limited Number of Representatives of Groups, but with all WTO Members having the right to be in the room and to intervene if they do not feel represented

Annex 2

Survey Questionnaire

"Institutional Development and Reform of the WTO"

WTO negotiations of agreements

According to organization theory, informal procedures are indispensable for the functioning of an organization, but may entail unequal treatment of powerful and less powerful organization members.

1. **Informal procedures occur during WTO trade negotiations.**

   ☐ Never ☐ Rarely ☐ Sometimes ☐ Often ☐ Very often

2. **Informal procedures make it difficult for smaller developing and least developed countries to protect and advance national trade interests in the WTO.**

   ☐ Never ☐ Rarely ☐ Sometimes ☐ Often ☐ Very often

3. **Informal Procedures during WTO trade negotiations should be partially formalized through procedural rules.**

   ☐ Strongly disagree ☐ Disagree ☐ Undecided ☐ Agree ☐ Strongly agree

4. **The procedural rules referred to in question 3 should stipulate that WTO members could only block consensus on trade measures which otherwise have a very broad consensus support, if these members states were excluded from informal negotiations on said measures.**

   ☐ Strongly disagree ☐ Disagree ☐ Undecided ☐ Agree ☐ Strongly Agree

5. **Or WTO members could only block consensus on trade measures which otherwise have a very broad consensus support, if they declare in writing with reasons included that the matter is one of vital national interest to them.**

   ☐ Strongly disagree ☐ Disagree ☐ Undecided ☐ Agree ☐ Strongly Agree

Implementation of existing WTO agreements

Trade agreements remain dead letters unless they are properly implemented by members.

6. **Member states provide reliable information on the implementation of trade agreements to WTO Committees.**

☐ Never ☐ Rarely ☐ Sometimes ☐ Often ☐ Very Often

7. **WTO committee reports on the implementation of trade agreements lead to corrective measures by member states if implementation deficits exist.**

☐ Never ☐ Rarely ☐ Sometimes ☐ Often ☐ Very often

Trade Policy Review

Trade Policy Review is intended to help member states to design sound economic and trade policies.

8. **WTO member states comply with recommendations made by the Trade Policy Review Committee.**

☐ Never ☐ Rarely ☐ Sometimes ☐ Often ☐ Very Often

Dispute Settlement System

The dispute settlement system distinguishes the WTO from other international organizations.

9. **WTO member states comply with binding decisions taken by dispute settlement bodies.**

☐ Never ☐ Rarely ☐ Sometimes ☐ Often ☐ Very often

Relations between member states and Secretariat

The WTO is said to be a member-driven organization.

10. **Member states are satisfied with the information which the WTO Secretariat supplies in response to special requests.**

☐ Never ☐ Rarely ☐ Sometimes ☐ Often ☐ Very Often

11. **In the interest of effective trade negotiations, the Director General of the WTO should be endowed with the formal right of making policy proposals overcoming a negotiation impasse.**

☐ Strongly disagree ☐ Disagree ☐ undecided ☐ Agree ☐ Strongly Agree

Role of NGOs in the WTO
The relationship between NGOs and the WTO is highly controversial among member states and in the public.

12. **NGOs provide developing countries with useful information and advice on the negotiation and implementation of WTO trade agreements.**

☐	☐	☐	☐	☐
Never	Rarely	Sometimes	Often	Very often

The consultation of NGOs is a frequently used method by national governments and the EU before they adopt public policies.

13. **NGOs should be given an opportunity to comment on the draft text of new WTO trade agreements before member states decide on their adoption.**

☐	☐	☐	☐	☐
Strongly disagree	Disagree	Undecided	Agree	Strongly Agree

Information on the Respondent

For a better evaluation of the survey we need some information on the country you are representing and on your own focus concerning WTO-related responsibilities.

14. **To which category of countries does the country you are representing belong?**

- ☐ Least-developed country (based on UN list)
- ☐ EU member state, US, Canada, Japan, Australia
- ☐ Other Developing Country
- ☐ Other Developed Country

15. **What has been the focus of your responsibilities in WTO activities?** *Multiple answers are possible.*

- ☐ Negotiations of new trade agreements in the WTO
- ☐ Trade Policy Review
- ☐ Implementation/ Administration of existing agreements in the WTO
- ☐ Dispute Settlement

Notes

1 The WTO as an International Organization

1. See below Chapter 4, I.
2. Figures are taken from "World trade in 2005 – selected long term trends", Table II.2 and II.3, http://www.wto.org/english/res_e/statis_e/its2006_e/its06_overview_e. Pdf
3. See ibid.

2 Approaches to the Analysis of International Organizations and the WTO

1. Realism has been the dominant theory of world politics since the beginning of academic International Relations. The unifying theme of realists is that states act in the shadow of anarchy, with the result that their security cannot be taken for granted. Therefore states compete for power and security *(Karns aud Mingst 2004*: 45ff.; *Dunne and Schmidt* 2006: 165).
2. See *Gordenker and Saunders* 1978, *Liese and Weinlich* 2006: 512 on the lack of research into the interactions between different sub-units of international organizations.
3. See the comments by *Pauwelyn* (2005: 330) on the Sutherland Report.

3 Conceptual Framework, Variables, and Method

1. See for similar perspectives on public administration: *Henry* 2007: 3, 40ff.; *Milakovich and Gordon* 2007: 39ff. These authors only implicitly include legal aspects in their definitions of public administration.
2. There is a certain degree of convergence between US public administration with its managerial tradition and German administrative science with its legalistic tradition, see *Rosenbloom et al.* 2009: 14ff., on the one hand, and *Schuppert* 2000: 44ff., *Bogumil and Jann* 2009: 53ff., on the other hand.
3. Some authors seem to exclude all private organizations, regardless of their functions, from public administration (*Rosenbloom et al.* 2009: 13). However, governments often prefer the legal form of private organizations for their activities (e.g. municipal utilities) over organizational forms under public law in order to avoid restrictions of public law. Therefore, it is justified to treat private organizations as public administration provided they meet the two criteria of publicness mentioned in the text. Other authors (*Milakovich and Gordon* 2007: 10) seem to include all private and public "stakeholders" with an interest in public administrative actions in the concept of public administration. This makes public administration undistinguishable from private actors without public functions and courts or legislatures.

4. The indices of leading US and German text books on public administration do not even mention international organizations, see for the United States: *Gortner, Nichols, and Ball* 2007; *Henry* 2007; *Rosenbloom et al.* 2009, and for Germany see: *Schuppert* 2000, *König* 2008, *Bogumil and Jann* 2009 (glossary). An exception is *Püttner* (2007: 52f.) who mentions international organizations as part of public administration but deplores the fact that they are ignored by public administration literature. German text books, though, cover the European Union which is an international organization but a special case due to its supranational decision powers.
5. Examples are public water and waste management cooperatives in Germany which are part of public administration and whose members are municipalities and private actors.
6. See the contributions in *Schuppert* (2005).
7. For a different typology of governance modes see *Benz* (2006) who proposes hierarchy, networks, negotiation, and competition as basic governance modes. The usefulness of this typology is doubtful, because it mixes categories of actors (network) with categories of actions (hierarchy, negotiation competition). Besides that, negotiation and competition seem to be subcategories of the exchange mode while governance by persuasion is not taken into account.
8. For an example see *Porter* (2001: 5ff.) who suggests the concept of efficiency for the analysis of the WTO but actually talks about the effectiveness of the free trade system in generating economic prosperity around the world.

4 WTO as a Public Formal Organization

1. Marrakesh Agreement, Art. VIII (1)
2. Ibid., Art. XII (1).
3. Ibid., Art. XII (2).
4. See: WTO Secretariat budget for 2008, http://www.wto.org/english/thewto_e/secre_e/budget08_e.htm
5. Contribution of the United States in 2008 was app. 25 Mio. CHF and for Germany app. 16 Mio. CHF. See: WTO, Members' contributions to the WTO budget and the budget of the Appellate Body for the year 2008, http://www.wto.org/english/thewto_e/secre_e/contrib08_e.htm
6. Marrakesh Agreement, Art. II (2).
7. Ibid., Art. IX, X, XII.
8. GATT, Art. 1; GATS, Art. 2; TRIPS, Art. 4.
9. GATT, Art. 24.
10. Marrakesh Agreement, Art. III (2).
11. Guidelines for WTO Technical Cooperation of 15 October 1996, WT/COMTD/8.
12. The International Trade Centre was established by GATT in 1964 at the request of the developing countries to help them promote their exports (WTO 2008: 109).
13. Guidelines for WTO Technical Cooperation WT/COMTD/8, Section II.3.
14. Memorandum of Understanding between the World Trade Organization and the United Nations Conference on Trade and Development (2003), Art. II.

15. Guidelines for WTO Technical Cooperation WT/COMTD/8, Section II.4.b).
16. See: WTO, Factsheet on trade-related technical assistance, http://www.wto.org/english/tratop_e/devel_e/teccop_e/ta_factsheet_e.htm
17. Art. III (4) of the Marrakesh Agreement.
18. Annex 3 to the Marrakesh Agreement, Section A. (i).
19. Annex 2 to the Marrakesh Agreement, Art. 3.
20. Ibid., Art. 3 (3).
21. Ibid., Art. VI (1).
22. Ibid., Art. 16 (4).
23. Ibid., Art. 17 (1) and (6).
24. Marrakesh Agreement, Art. VII (1) and (3).
25. Guidelines for WTO Technical Cooperation, WT/COMTD/8, Section I Objectives and Principles.
26. Ibid., Section II.4.
27. Ibid., Section II.4.(a) and (c).
28. Staff Regulations, Pension Plan Regulations, Staff Rules, and Administrative Rules of the Pension Plan and Compensation Philosophy as laid down in Annex 2 to Conditions of Service Applicable to the Staff of the WTO Secretariat, 16 October 1998, WT/L/282.
29. Marrakesh Agreement, Art. V (1).
30. Marrakesh Agreement, Art. V (2).
31. Guidelines for Arrangements on Relations with Non-Governmental Organizations, WT/L/162.
32. Rules of Procedures for Sessions of the Trade Policy Review Body 2005, WT/TPR/6/Rev.1.
33. Rules of Procedure for Sessions of the Ministerial Conference (WT/L/161), Rule 7 and 8, and Rules of Procedure for Meetings of the General Council (WT/L/161), Rule 8 and 9.
34. Rules of Procedure for Sessions of the Ministerial Conference and Rules of Procedure for Meetings of the General Council, WT/L/161, Annex 3 Observer Status for International Intergovernmental Organizations in the WTO.
35. Ibid.
36. Rules of Procedure for Sessions of the Ministerial Conference (WT/L/161), Rule 17, and Rules of Procedure for Meetings of the General Council (WT/L/161), Rule 17.
37. Guidelines for Appointment of Officers to WTO Bodies, WT/L/510.
38. Ibid., Section 6.1.
39. Ibid., Section 2.4.
40. Ibid., Section 3.
41. Ibid., Section 5.1.
42. Rules of Procedure for Sessions of the Ministerial Conference, WT/L/161, Rule 4.
43. Rules of Procedure for Meetings of the General Council, WT/L/161, Rule 3–6.
44. Ibid., Rule 23, 25, 27.
45. Rules of Procedure for Sessions of the Ministerial Conference (WT/L/161), Rule 32, and Rules of Procedure for Meetings of the General Council, WT/L/161, Rule 37.
46. Rules of Procedure for Meetings of the General Council, WT/L/161, Rule 36.

47. Rules of Procedure for Sessions of the Ministerial Conference, WT/L/161, Rule 31.
48. Procedures for the Circulation and Derestriction of WTO documents, WT/L/452.
49. Guidelines on the Arrangements for Scheduling of Meetings of WTO Bodies, WT/L/106.
50. For instance, the Ministerial Declaration in Section 16 lays down regarding market-access for non-agricultural products: "We agree to negotiations which shall aim, by modalities to be agreed, to reduce or as appropriate eliminate tariffs." On agriculture the Ministerial Declaration lays down that modalities for further commitment shall be established in a first step (Section 14).
51. Agreement on Technical Barriers to Trade, Art. 15 (2), Agreement on Rules of Origin, Art. 6, Agreement on Sanitary and Phytosanitary Measures, Art. 12 (7).
52. Agreement on Safeguards, Art. 13 (1) (a).
53. Agreement on Subsidies and Countervailing Measures, Art. 26.1 and 2; Agreement on Safeguards, Art. 13 (1) (d).
54. Agreement on Subsidies and Countervailing Measures, Art. 25.11.
55. Agreement on Safeguards, Art. 13 (2); Agreement on Import Licensing Procedures, Art. 7 (2).
56. Agreement on Subsidies and Countervailing Measures, Art. 27.14 and 15; Agreement on Safeguards, Art. 13 (1) (b) with regard to procedural requirements.
57. Rules of Procedures for Sessions of the Trade Policy Review Body 2005, WT/TPR/6/Rev.1.
58. Annex 3 to Marrakesh Agreement, Trade Policy Review Mechanism, Art. C. (iii).
59. Ibid., Art. C. (v) (b).
60. Chapter 4, Rules of Procedures for Sessions of the Trade Policy Review Body 2005, WT/TPR/6/Rev.1.
61. Annex 3 to Marrakesh Agreement, Trade Policy Review Mechanism, Art. C. (iv).
62. Ibid., Art. C. (ii)
63. Rules of Procedures for Sessions of the Trade Policy Review Body 2005 (WT/TPR/6/Rev.1), Chapter I, 3
64. Annex 3 to Marrakesh Agreement, Trade Policy Review Mechanism, Art. F.
65. Annex 2 to Marrakesh Agreement, Understanding on Rules and Procedures governing the Settlement of Disputes, Art. 4.
66. Annex 2 to Marrakesh Agreement, Art. 5 (5).
67. Ibid., Art. 15 (1).
68. Ibid., Art. 16 (1).
69. Ibid., Art. 16 (4).
70. Ibid., Art. 17 (6).
71. Ibid., Art. 17 (14).
72. Ibid., Art. 14 (1) and Art. 17 (10).
73. Ibid., Art. 21 (6).
74. Ibid., Art. 22 (2).
75. Ibid., Art. 22 (2).

76. Ibid., Art. 27 (1).
77. Ibid., Art. 27 (2).
78. Ibid., Art. 5 (6).

5 The WTO in Action

1. The G-20 is a group of developing countries established on 20 August 2003, in the final stages of the preparations for the V Ministerial Conference of the WTO, held in Cancún, from 10 to 14 September 2003. Its focus is on agriculture, the central issue of the Doha Development Agenda. Five members are from Africa (Egypt, Nigeria, South Africa, Tanzania, and Zimbabwe), six from Asia (China, India, Indonesia, Pakistan, Philippines, and Thailand) and 10 from Latin America (Argentina, Bolivia, Brazil, Chile, Cuba, Guatemala, Mexico, Paraguay, Uruguay, and Venezuela).
2. The G-33 is a group of developing countries established in 2006 to better represent the interests of developing countries. Membership partially overlaps with the G-20 group.
3. All African members of the WTO, currently 41 countries, belong to the African Group.
4. According to a Secretariat official the "Green Room" is the conference office of the Director General which used to be a green-colored room. The name "Green Room" came into use in the mid-1970s when Arthur Dunkel was Director General of GATT, and called in small group meetings in his conference office. The name has stuck since then.
5. A Deputy Director General described in very similar terms the whole idea of informal meetings as being to explore in a kind of no-risk situation what possible options there are before going to a larger group.
6. See: A brief history of UNCTAD, http://www.unctadxi.org/templates/Page____470.aspx
7. See: Goals and functions of UNCTAD, http://www.unctadxi.org/templates/Page____473.aspx
8. See ibid.
9. See: UNCTAD (2000), Plan of Action, Tenth Session Bangkok, 12–19 February 2000, TD/386, 18 February 2000, http://www.unctad.org/en/docs/ux_td386.en.pdf
10. See: UNCTAD (2004), Sao Paulo Consensus, UNCTAD Eleventh Session Sao Paulo 13–18 June 2004, TD/410. http://www.unctad.org/en/docs/td410_en.pdf
11. See note 9, no. 136.
12. See note 10, no. 95.
13. See: Agreement to establish the South Centre (1994), Preamble, and A South IGO, http://www.southcentre.org/
14. Agreement to establish the South Centre (1994), Art. III.
15. See: A South IGO, http://www.southcentre.org/
16. The governments of Benin, Burkina Faso, Chad, and Mali claimed in June 2003 at the General Council that domestic production subsidies for cotton in the European Community, United States, and China were depressing prices of cotton, which was an essential export from West and Central Africa.

The governments called for the subsidies to be eliminated, and for compensation to be paid for while the subsidies are being phased out to cover economic losses. While no decision was reached in Cancún, the "Framework Decision" of August 2004 stipulated that cotton would be addressed "ambitiously, expeditiously and specifically" within the agricultural negotiations (Gallagher 2005: 125).

17. World Trade Organization, Technical Assistance and Training Plan 2006, Section 20.
18. Ibid., Section 54.
19. Ibid., Section 31.
20. Ibid., Section 28.
21. Ibid., Section 56.
22. Ibid., Section 57.
23. Non-Agricultural Market Access.
24. World Trade Organization, Technical Assistance and Training Plan 2006, Section 118ff.
25. According to a representative of the Secretariat, exceptions are made in rare cases, for instance, when a study that sought to demonstrate that the WTO had no impact on trade received a lot of publicity. In this case, the director of the Research Division responded through a letter published in a newspaper.
26. Marrakesh Agreement, Annex 3 Trade Policy Review Mechanism, C.(v) (b).
27. Section 15, Rules of Procedure for Meetings of the Trade Policy Review Body WT/TPR/6/Rev.1.
28. Art. 4 (7), Understanding of Rules and Procedures governing the Settlement of Disputes.

6 Performance Patterns of the WTO

1. See, for example, reports (2003, G/L/656) (2004, G/L/704) and (2005, G/L/747) of the Committee of Rules of Origin to the Council for Trade in Goods.
2. See Trade Policy Review Mechanism, Programme of Reviews for 2007, WT/TPR/193/Rev.1.
3. See WTO dispute settlement statistics: Table 2 (reports of panels established pursuant to DSU Art. 215), www.wto.org/English/tratop_e/dispu_e/stats_e.htm.
4. For instance, the Ministerial Declaration in Section 16 lays down regarding market-access for non-agricultural products: "We agree to negotiations which shall aim, by modalities to be agreed, to reduce or as appropriate eliminate tariffs." On agriculture the Ministerial Declaration lays down that modalities for further commitment shall be established in a first step (Section 14).
5. WT/DS266/R: European Communities – Export Subsidies on Sugar – Complaint by Brazil – Report of the Panel; WT/DS267/R: United States – Subsidies on upland cotton – Report of the Panel.
6. See WTO (2001), Implementation-Related Issues and Concerns, Ministerial Conference Fourth Session, Doha, WT/MIN(01)/17, 20. November 2001.
7. Under the GATT, six panel proceedings involving an examination of environmental measures or human health-related measures under GATT Art. XX

were completed. Of the six reports, three were not adopted. Since 1995 under the WTO regime, three such proceedings have been completed. See WTO, Environmental Disputes in GATT/WTO, http://www.wto.org/english/tratop_e/envir_e/edis00_e.htm
8. Ibid.
9. See "WTO entgleist – NGOs feiern", http://de.indymedia.org/2003/09/61707.shtml

7 Reform Perspectives and Proposals

1. The estimates of reform effects on equity of policy concerns are not reported here, because they are generally below the cutting point of $\pm.5$.
2. The exclusion of a member state from the informal consensus was not specifically mentioned as a condition for exercising the right to veto as formulated in the questionnaire. However, it is implied in the formulation of the questionnaire that member states do not lose their veto power if they participate in informal negotiations but object to the negotiation results. In this case, they are excluded from the informal consensus.
3. The principle of estoppel expresses the same idea as the continental law principle of prohibiting "venire contra factum proprium" (Herdegen 2007: 137).
4. This judgment is based on the author's opinion that the WTO trading system is, in principle, worth to be conserved. Contrary to the view of some radical NGOs which call for a derailment of the system (Focus on the Global South 2005), it must be emphasized that international institutions and rules-based global governance are the best safeguards for protecting the economic interests of small and developing countries (Stone 2004: 6, 14). The absence of strong international institutions which contributed to the global financial crises in 2008/2009 is a case in point. Therefore, it is time to modernize the WTO as a public formal organization.

Bibliography

Abbott, K. W. and D. Snidal 1998. "Why States Act through Formal International Organizations", *The Journal of Conflict Resolution*, 42, 1, 3–32.
Alston, P. 1997. "The Myopia of the Handmaidens: International Lawyers and Globalisation", *European Journal of International Law*, 8, 435–48.
Aman, A. 2004. *The Democracy Deficit*. New York: New York University Press.
Applbaum, A. I. 2000. "Culture, Identity and Legitimacy", in J. S. Nye and J. D. Donahue (eds), *Governance in a Globalizing World*. Washington: Brookings Institution Press, pp. 319–329.
Archer, C. 2001. *International Organizations*, 3rd edn. London: Rontledge.
Arts, B. 1998. *The Political Influence of Global NGOs: Case Studies on the Climate Change and Biodiversity Conventions*. Utrecht: International Books.
Barfield, C. E. 2001. *Free Trade, Sovereignty, Democracy: The Future of the World Trade Organization*. Washington: The AEI Press.
Barkin, J. S. 2006. *International Organization: Theories and Institutions*. New York: Palgrave Macmillan.
Barnard, C. I. 1938. *The Functions of the Executive*, 27th printing, 1976. Cambridge, MA: Harvard University Press.
Barnett, M. and M. Finnemore 1999. "The Politics, Power and Pathologies of International Organizations", *International Organization*, 53, 4, 699–732.
Barnett, M. and M. Finnemore 2004. *Rules for the World: International Organizations in Global Politics*. Ithaca: Cornell University Press.
Barnett, M. and M. Finnemore 2005. "The Power of Liberal International Organizations", in M. Barnett and R. Duvall (eds), *Power in Global Governance*. Cambridge: Cambridge University Press, pp. 161–184.
Bauer, S. 2006. "Does Bureaucracy Really Matter? The Authority of Intergovernmental Treaty Secretariats in Global Environmental Politics", *Global Environmental Politics*, 6, 1, 23–49.
Benz, A. 2004. "Einleitung: Governance – Modebegriff oder nützliches sozialwissenschaftliches Konzept?", in A. Benz (ed.), *Governance – Regieren in komplexen Regelsystemen – Eine Einführung*. Wiesbaden: VS Verlag für Sozialwissenschaften, pp. 11–28.
Benz, A. 2006. "Eigendynamik von Governance in der Verwaltung", in J. Bogumil, W. Jann, and F. Nullmeier (eds), *Politik und Verwaltung*. Wiesbaden: VS Verlag für Sozialwissenschaften, pp. 29–49.
Beyerlin, U., P.-T. Stoll, and R. Wolfrum 2006. "Conclusions Drawn from the Conference on Ensuring Compliance with MEAs", in U. Beyerlin, P.-T. Stoll, and R. Wolfrum (eds), *Ensuring Compliance with Multilateral Environmental Agreements: Academic Analysis and Views from Practice*. Leiden: Martinus Nijhoff, pp. 359–69.
Blackhurst, R. 2000. "The Capacity of the WTO to Fulfill Its Mandate", in A. Krueger (ed.), *The WTO as International Organization*. Chicago: Chicago University Press, pp. 31–47.

Blackhurst, R. 2005. "The Future of the WTO: Some Comments on the Sutherland Report", *World Trade Review*, 4, 3, 379–389.

Blackhurst, R. and D. Hartridge 2004. "Improving the Capacity of WTO Institutions to Fulfil Their Mandate", *Journal of International Economic Law*, 7, 3, 705–716.

Blackhurst, R. and D. Hartridge 2005. "Improving the Capacity of WTO Institutions to Fulfill Their Mandate", in E.-U. Petersmann (ed.), *Reforming the World Trading System: Legitimacy, Efficiency and Democratic Governance*. Oxford: Oxford University Press, pp. 455–468.

Bogdandy, A. von. and M. Wagner 2005. "The 'Sutherland Report' on WTO Reform – a Critical Appraisal", *World Trade Review*, 4, 3, 439–447.

Bogumil, J. and W. Jann 2009. *Verwaltung und Verwaltungswissenschaft in Deutschland: Einführung in die Verwaltungswissenschaft*, 2nd edn. Wiesbaden: VS Verlag für Sozialwissenschaften.

Bohne, E. 1981. *Der informale Rechtsstaat*. Berlin: Duncker & Humblot.

Bohne, E. 1984. "Informales Verwaltungs- und Regierungshandeln als Instrument des Umweltschutzes", *Verwaltungs-Archiv*, 75, 343–373.

Boisson de Chazournes, L. and M. M. Mbengue 2004. "GMOs and Trade: Issues at Stake in the EC Biotech Dispute", *Review of European Community and International Environmental Law (RECIEL)*, 13, 3, 289–305.

Bronckers, M. C. E. J. 2001. "More Power to the WTO?", *Journal of International Economic Law*, 4, 1, 41–65.

Bronckers, M. C. E. J. and N. van den Broek 2005. "Financial Compensation in the WTO: Improving Remedies in WTO Dispute Settlement", *Journal of International Economic Law*, 8, 1, 101–126.

Bullard, N. and C. Chanyapate 2005. "Ten Years of WTO: Subordinating Development to Free Trade", *International Politics and Society (Internationale Politik und Gesellschaft)*, 2, 21–34.

Casey, B. H. and M. Gold, 2005. "Peer Review of Labour Market Programmes in the European Union: What Can Countries Really Learn from One Another?" *Journal of European Public Policy*, 12, 1, 23–43.

Charnovitz, S. 2002a. *Trade Law and Global Governance*. London: Cameron May.

Charnovitz, S. 2002b. "Judicial Independence in the World Trade Organization", in L. Boisson de Chazournes, C. P. Romano, and R. Mackenzie (eds), *International Organizations and International Dispute Settlement*. New York: Transnational Publishers, pp. 219–240.

Cho, S. 2004. "A Bridge Too Far: The Fall of the Fifth WTO Ministerial Conference in Cancún and the Future of Trade Constitution", *Journal of International Economic Law*, 7, 2, 219–244.

Cho, S. 2005. "A Quest for WTO Legitimacy", *World Trade Review*, 4, 3, 391–399.

Christiansen, T., A. Føllesdal, and S. Piattoni 2003. "Informal Governance in the European Union: An Introduction", in T. Christiansen and S. Piattoni (eds), *Informal Governance in the European Union*. Cheltenham: Edward Elgar, pp. 1–21.

Clark, I. 2006. "Globalization and the Post-Cold War Order", in J. Baylis and S. Smith (eds), *The Globalization of World Politics: An Introduction to International Relations*, 3rd edn. Oxford: Oxford University Press, pp. 727–742.

Clarke, P. A. and G. N. Horlick 2005. "The Agreement on Subsidies and Countervailing Measures", in P. F. Macrory, A. Appleton, and M. G. Plummer (eds), *The*

World Trade Organization: Legal, Economic and Political Analysis: Volume I, vol. 1. New York: Springer, pp. 679–734.
Cohen, J. 1989. "Deliberation and Democratic Legitimacy", in A. Hamlit and P. Pettit (eds), *The Good Polity*. Oxford: Basil Blackwell, pp. 17–34.
Cottier, T. 2007. "Preparing for Structural Reform in the WTO", *Journal of International Economic Law*, 10, 3, 497–508.
Cox, R. and H. K. Jacobson 1973a. "The Framework for Inquiry", in R. W. Cox and H. K. Jacobson (eds), *The Anatomy of Influence*. New Haven and London: Yale University Press, pp. 1–36.
Cox, R. and H. K. Jacobson 1973b. "The Anatomy of Influence", in R. W. Cox and H. K. Jacobson (eds), *The Anatomy of Influence*. New Haven and London: Yale University Press, pp. 371–436.
Cox, R. W. and H. K. Jacobson *et al.* (eds) 1973. *The Anatomy of Influence: Decision Making in International Organization*. New Haven: Yale University Press.
Curzon, G. and V. Curzon 1973. "GATT: Trader's Club", in R. W. Cox H. K. Jacobson *et al.* (eds), *The Anatomy of Influence*. New Haven and London: Yale University Press, pp. 298–333.
Das, D. K. 2000. "Debacle at Seattle: The Way the Cookie Crumbled", *Journal of World Trade*, 34, 5, 181–201.
Davey, W. J. 2005. "Institutional Framework", in P. F. Macrory, A. Appleton, and M. G. Plummer (eds), *The World Trade Organization: Legal, Economic and Political Analysis: Volume I*. New York: Springer, pp. 51–87.
De Bièvre, D. 2006. "Legislative and Judicial Decision Making in the World Trade Organization", in M. Koenig-Archibugi and M. Zürn (eds), *New Modes of Governance in the Global System: Exploring Publicness, Delegation and Inclusiveness*. Houndsmill, Basingstoke, Hampshire; New York: Palgrave Macmillan, pp. 31–51.
De Senarclens, P. 2001. "International Organisations and the Challenges of Globalisation", *International Social Science Journal*, 53, 170, 509–522.
Deese, D. A. 2008. *World Trade Politics*. London: Routledge.
Donaldson, V. 2005. "The Appellate Body: Institutional and Procedural Aspects", in P. F. Macrory, A. Appleton, and M. G. Plummer (eds), *The World Trade Organization: Legal, Economic and Political Analysis, Volume I*. New York: Springer, pp. 1277–1340.
Dunne, T. and B. C. Schmidt 2006, "Realism", in J. Baylis an S. Smith (eds), *The Globalization of World Politics: An Introduction to International Relations*, 3rd edn. Oxford: Oxford University Press, pp. 161–183.
Durán, E. 2005. "Trade-Related Cooperation and Capacity Building", in P. F. Macrory, A. Appleton and M. G. Plummer (eds), *The World Trade Organization: Legal, Economic and Political Analysis: Volume II*. New York: Springer, pp. 457–468.
Ehlermann, C.-D. and L. Ehring 2005. "Are WTO Decision-Making Procedures Adequate for Making, Revising and Implementing Worldwide and 'Plurilateral' Rules?", in E.-U. Petersmann (ed.), *Reforming the World Trading System: Legitimacy, Efficiency and Democratic Governance*. Oxford: Oxford University Press, pp. 497–522.
Esty, D. 2002. "The World Trade Organization's Legitimacy Crisis", *World Trade Review*, 1, 1, 7–22.

Evan, W. M. (ed.) 1976. "The Organization – Set", *Organization Theory*. New York: John Wiley & Sons, pp. 119–134.

Figueres Olsen, J. M., J.-M. Salazar-Xirinachs, and M. Araya 2001. "Trade and Environment at the World Trade Organization", in G. P. Sampson (ed.), *The Role of the World Trade Organization in Global Governance*. Tokyo; New York: United Nations University, pp. 155–181.

Focus on the Global South 2005. *The End of an Illusion: WTO Reform, Global Civil Society and the Road to Hong Kong*, March 2005 http://www.tradeobservatory.org/library.cfm?RefID=69995

Fombrun, E. J. 1984. "Structures of Organizational Governance", *Human Relations*, 37, 3, 207–223.

Footer, M. E. 2006. *An Institutional and Normative Analysis of the World Trade Organization*. Leiden: Martinus Nijhoff Publishers.

Forrester, I. and O. E. Odarda 2005. "The Agreement on Customs Valuation", in P. F. Macrory, A. Appleton, and M. G. Plummer (eds), *The World Trade Organization: Legal, Economic and Political Analysis: Volume I*. New York: Springer, pp. 531–572.

Franck, T. M. 1990. *The Power of Legitimacy Among Nations*. Oxford: Oxford University Press.

Friedrich, C. J. 1963. *The Philosophy of Law in Historical Perspective*. Chicago: University of Chicago Press.

Gabrielian, V., K. Yang, and S. Spice 2008. "Qualitative Research Methods", in K. Yang and G. J. Miller (eds), *Handbook of Research Methods in Public Administration*. Boca Raton, FL: CRC Press, pp. 141–168.

Gallagher, P. 2005. *The First Ten Years of the WTO 1995–2005*. Cambridge: Cambridge University Press.

Gavin, B. 2001. *The European Union and Globalisation: Towards Global Democratic Governance*. Cheltenham; Northampton: Edward Elgar.

George, C. and C. Kirkpatrick 2004. "Putting the Doha Principles into Practice: The Role of Sustainability Impact Assessment", in H. Katrak and R. Strange (eds), *The WTO and Developing Countries*. Chippenham & Eastbourne: Rowe, pp. 315–338.

George, S. 2002. *WTO: Demokratie statt Drakula. Für ein gerechtes Welthandelssystem*. Hamburg: VSA.

Gordenker, L. and P. R. Saunders 1978. "Organization Theory and International Organization", in P. Taylor and A. J. R. Groom (eds), *International Organization: A Conceptual Approach*. New York: Nichols Publishing Company, pp. 84–107.

Gortner, H. F., K. L. Nichols, and C. Ball 2007. *Organization Theory: A Public and Nonprofit Perspective*, 3rd edn. Belmont, CA: Wadsworth.

Grimwade, N. 2004. "The GATT, the Doha Round and Developing Countries", in H. Katrak and R. Strange (eds), *The WTO and Developing Countries*. Chippenham & Eastbourne: Rowe, pp. 11–37.

Gross, B. M. 1968. *Organizations and Their Managing*. New York: The Free Press.

Guzman, A. T. 2004. "Global Governance and the WTO", *Harvard International Law Journal*, 45, 2, 303–351.

Haas, E. B. 1964. *Beyond the Nation State: Functionalism and International Organization*. Stanford: Stanford University Press.

Habermas, J. 1996. *Between Facts and Norms: Contribution to a Discourse Theory of Law and Democracy*. Cambridge, MA: MIT Press.

Halle, M. 2006. "Trade and Environment: Looking beneath the Sand of Doha?", *Journal of European Environmental and Planning Law*, 3, 2, 107–116.

Harbinson, S. 2005. "The Agriculture Negotiations: The Road from Doha and How to Keep the Negotiations on a Positive Track", in E.-U. Petersmann (ed.), *Reforming the World Trading System: Legitimacy, Efficiency and Democratic Governance*. Oxford: Oxford University Press, pp. 121–126.

Hazelzet, H. 1998. "The Decision-Making Approach to International Organizations: Cox and Jacobson's Anatomic Lessons Revisited", in B. Reinalda and B. Verbeek (eds), *Autonomous Policy Making by International Organisations*. London and New York: Routledge, pp. 11–26.

Heady, F., B. Perlman, and M. Rivera 2007. "Issues in comparative and international administration", in J. Rabin, W. B. Hildreth and G. J. Miller (eds), *Handbook of Public Administration*, 3rd edn. Boca Raton, FL: CRC Press, pp. 605–631.

Heinelt, H. 2002. "Civic Perspectives on a Democratic Transformation of the EU", in J. R. Grote and B. Gbikpi (eds), *Participatory Governance: Political and Societal Implications*. Opladen: Leske + Budrich, pp. 97–120.

Heisenberg, D. 2005. "The Institution of 'Consensus' in the European Union: Formal Versus Informal Decision-Making in the Council", *European Journal of Political Research*, 44, 65–90.

Helmke, G. and S. Levitsky 2004. "Informal Institutions and Comparative Politics: A Research Agenda", *Perspectives on Politics*, 2, 4, 725–740.

Henry, N. 2007. *Public Administration and Public Affairs*, 10th edn. Upper Saddle River, NJ: Pearson-Prentice Hall.

Herdegen, M. 2007. *Völkerrecht*, 6th edn. München: C. H. Beck.

Héritier, A. and D. Lehmkuhl 2008. "Introduction: The Shadow of Hierarchy and New Modes of Governance", *Journal of Public Policy*, 28, 1, 1–17.

Higgott, R. 2005. "Public Goods, Global Governance and Private Actors: Learning from the WTO", in G. Fraser-Moleketi (ed.), *The World We Could Win: Administering Global Governance*. Amsterdam; Berlin; Oxford; Tokyo; Washington: IOS Press, pp. 18–37.

Hilf, M. 2005. "How Can Parliamentary Participation in WTO Rule-Making and Democratic Control Be Made More Effective? The European Context", in E.-U. Petersmann (ed.), *Reforming the World Trading System: Legitimacy, Efficiency, and Democratic Governance*. Oxford: Oxford University Press, pp. 413–420.

Hoberg, G. 2001. "Trade, Harmonization and Domestic Autonomy in Environmental Policy", *Journal of Comparative Policy Analysis: Research and Practice*, 3, 191–217.

Hocking, B. 2004. "Changing the Terms of Trade Policy Making: From the 'Club' to the 'Multistakeholder' Model", *World Trade Review*, 3, 1, 3–26.

Holzer, M., V. Gabrielyan, and K. Yang 2007. "Five Great Ideas in American Public Administration", in J. Rabin, W. B. Hildreth, and G. J. Miller (eds), *Handbook of Public Administration*, 3rd edn. Boca Raton, FL: CRC Press, pp. 49–101.

Howse, R. 2000. "Adjudicative Legitimacy and Treaty Interpretation in International Trade Law: The Early Years of WTO Jurisprudence", in J. H. H. Weiler (ed.), *The EU, the WTO and the NAFTA: Towards a Common Law of International Trade?* Oxford: Oxford University Press, pp. 35–69.

Howse, R. 2001. "The Legitimacy of the World Trade Organization", in J.-M. Coicaud, and V. Heiskanen (eds), *The Legitimacy of International Organizations*. Tokyo; New York: United Nations University Press, pp. 355–407.

Howse, R. and K. Nicolaidis 2003. "Enhancing WTO Legitimacy: Constitutionalization or Global Subsidiarity?", *Governance: An International Journal of Policy, Administration, and Institutions*, 16, 1, 73–94.

Hu, L.-T. and D. Olshfski 2008. "Describing and Measuring Phenomena in Public Administration", in K. Yang and G. J. Miller (eds), Handbook *of Research Methods in Public Administration*. Boca Raton, FL: CRC Press, pp. 205–212.

Hufbauer, G. C. 2005. "Inconsistency between Diagnosis and Treatment", *Journal of International Economic Law*, 8, 2, 291–297.

Institute for Agriculture and Trade Policy (IATP) 2003. *WTO Decision Making: A Broken Process*, WTO Cancun Series Paper no. 4, visited on 15 August 2009 http://www.tradeobservatory.org/library.cfm?RefID=25941

Ismail, F. 2005. "A Development Perspective on the WTO July 2004, General Council Decision", in E.-U. Petersmann (ed.), *Reforming the World Trading System: Legitimacy, Efficiency, and Democratic Governance*. Oxford: Oxford University Press, pp. 53–82.

Jansen, D. 1997. "Das Problem der Akteurqualität korporativer Akteure", in A. Benz and W. Seibel (eds), *Theorieentwicklung in der Politikwissenschaft – eine Zwischenbilanz*. Baden-Baden: Nomos, pp. 193–235.

Jawara, F. and A. Kwa 2003. *Behind the Scenes at the WTO: The Real World of International Trade Negotiations*. London, New York: Zed Books in association with Focus on the Global South.

Jones, K. 2004. *Who's Afraid of the WTO?* Oxford: Oxford University Press.

Karns, M. P. and K. A. Mingst 2004. *International Organizations: The Politics and Processes of Global Governance*. Boulder: Lynne Rienner.

Keohane, R. O. and J. S. Nye 2000. "Introduction", in J. S. Nye and J. D. Donahue (eds), *Governance in a Globalizing World*. Washington: Brookings Institution Press, pp. 1–41.

Keohane, R. O. and J. S. Nye 2001. "The Club Model of Multilateral Cooperation and Problems of Democratic Legitimacy", in R. B. Porter, P. Sauvé, A. Subramanian, and A. Beviglia Zampetti (eds), *Efficiency, Equity and Legitimacy: The Multilateral Trading System at the Millennium*. Washington, DC: Brookings Institution Press, pp. 264–294.

Keohane, R. O., A. Moravcsik, and A.-M. Slaughter 2000. "Legalized Dispute Resolution: Interstate and Transnational", *International Organization*, 54, 457–488.

Khor, M. 2002. *Issues of Transparency and Participation in the WTO Decision-Making Process and Procedure*, paper, Third World Network, Geneva.

Kieser, A. and P. Walgenbach 2007. *Organisation*, 5th edn. Stuttgart: Schäffer-Poeschel.

Kirshner, O. 2005. "Triumph of Globalism: American Trade Politics", *Political Science Quarterly*, 120, 3, 479–503.

Klabbers, J. 2001. "The Changing Image of International Organizations", in J.-M. Coicaud and V. Heiskanen (eds), *The Legitimacy of International Organizations*. Tokyo; New York: United Nations University Press, pp. 221–255.

König, Klaus, 2008. *Moderne öffentliche Verwaltung. Studium der Verwaltungswissenschaft*. Berlin: Duncker & Humblot.

Kooiman, J. 2003. *Governing as Governance*. London: Sage.

Koremenos, B., C. Lipson, and D. Snidal 2001. "The Rational Design of International Institutions", *International Organization*, 55, 4, 761–799.
Kouvaritakis, N., N. Stroblos, L. Paroussos, and S. Tsallas 2004. "Trade Policy", in C. Böhringer and A. Löschel (eds), *Climate Change Policy and Global Trade*. Heidelberg: Physica, pp. 21–57.
Krajewski, M. 2001a. *Verfassungsperspektiven und Legitimation des Rechts der Welthandelsorganisation (WTO)*. Berlin: Duncker und Humblot.
Krajewski, M. 2001b. "Democratic Legitimacy and Constitutional Perspectives of WTO Law", *Journal of World Trade*, 35, 1, 167–186.
Krasner, S. D. 1982. "Structural Causes and Regime Consequences: Regimes and Intervening Variables", *International Organization*, 36, 185–205.
Lacarte, J. A. 2005. "Transparency, Public Debate, and Participation by NGOs in the WTO: A WTO Perspective", in E.-U. Petersmann (ed.), *Reforming the World Trading System: Legitimacy, Efficiency, and Democratic Governance*. Oxford: Oxford University Press, pp. 447–451.
Liese, A. and S. Weinlich 2006. "Die Rolle von Verwaltungsstäben internationaler Organisationen. Lücken, Tücken und Konturen eines (neuen) Forschungsfelds", in J. Bogumil, W. Jann, and F. Nullmeier (eds), *Politik und Verwaltung*. Wiesbaden: VS Verlag für Sozialwissenschaften, pp. 491–524.
Little, R. 2006. "International Regimes", in J. Baylis and S. Smith (eds), *The Globalization of World Politics. An Introduction to International Relations*, 3rd edn. Oxford: Oxford University Press, pp. 369–386.
Luhmann, N. 1995. *Funktionen und Folgen formaler Organisation*, 4th edn. Berlin: Duncker & Humblot.
Maier-Rigaud, R. 2008. *International Organizations as Corporate Actors: Agency and Emergence in Theories of International Relations*. Bonn: Preprints of the Max Planck Institute for Research on Collective Goods 2008/7.
Mann, E. 2005. "A Parliamentary Dimension to the WTO: More Than Just a Vision?", in E.-U. Petersmann (ed.), *Reforming the World Trading System: Legitimacy, Efficiency and Democratic Governance*. Oxford: Oxford University Press, pp. 421–428.
Mason, M. 2004. "Representing Transnational Environmental Interests: New Opportunities for Non-Governmental Organisation Access within the World Trade Organisation", *Environmental Politics*, 13, 3, 566–589.
Mathews, J. T. 1997. "Power Shift: The Rise of Global Civil Society", *Foreign Affairs*, 76, 1, 50–76.
Matsushita, M. 2005. "The Sutherland Report and its Discussion of Dispute Settlement Reform", *Journal of International Economic Law*, 8, 3, 623–629.
Matsushita, M., T. Schoenbaum, and P. C. Mavroidis 2003. *The World Trade Organization: Law, Practice, and Policy*. Oxford: Oxford University Press.
McGinnis, J. O. 2000. "The Political Economy of Global Multilateralism", *Chicago Journal of International Law*, 1, 381–99.
McRae, D. 2004. "What Is the Future of the WTO Dispute Settlement?", *Journal of International Economic Law*, 7, 1, 3–21.
Meagher, N. 2005. "So Far, So Good: But What Next? The Sutherland Report and WTO Dispute Settlement", *World Trade Review*, 4, 3, 409–417.
Messerlin, P. 2005. "Non-Discrimination, Welfare Balances, and WTO Rules: A Historical Perspective", in E.-U. Petersmann (ed.), *Reforming the World Trading System: Legitimacy, Efficiency and Democratic Governance*. Oxford: Oxford University Press, pp. 291–303.

Metzges, G. 2006. *NGO-Kampagnen und ihr Einfluss auf internationale Verhandlungen. Das Multilateral Agreement on Investment (MAI) und die 1997 OECD Anti-Bribery Convention im Vergleich*. Baden-Baden: Nomos.

Michalopoulos, C. 2001. *Developing Countries in the WTO*. Basingstoke and New York: Palgrave Macmillan.

Milakovich, M. E. and G. J. Gordon 2007. *Public Administration in America*, 9th edn. Belmont, CA: Thomson Wadsworth.

Moore, M. 2005. "The Democratic Roots of the World Trade Organization", in P. F. Macrory, A. Appleton, and M. G. Plummer (eds), *The World Trade Organization: Legal, Economic and Political Analysis: Volume I*. New York: Springer, pp. 39–48.

Moravcsik, A. 1998. *The Choice for Europe: Social Purpose and State Power from Messina to Maastricht*. Ithaca, NY: Cornell University Press.

Nanz, P. and J. Steffek 2004. "Global Governance, Participation and the Public Sphere", *Government and Opposition*, 39, 2, 314–335.

Ness, G. D. and S. R. Brechin 1988. "Bridging the Gap: International Organizations as Organizations", *International Organization*, 42, 2, 245–73.

Nielson, D. L. and M. J. Tierney 2003. "Delegation to International Organizations: Agency Theory and World Bank Environmental Reform", *International Organization*, 57, 241–76.

Northrop, A. and S. Arsneault 2008. "Sampling and Data Collection", in K. Yang and G. J. Miller (eds), *Handbook of Research Methods in Public Administration*. Boca Raton, FL: CRC Press, pp. 213–239.

O'Brien, R., A.-M. Goetz, J. A. Scholte, and M. Williams 2000. *Multilateral Economic Institutions and Global Social Movements*. Cambridge: Cambridge University Press.

OECD 2003. Policy Brief. Peer Review: A Tool for Co-Operation and Change. OECD, Paris.

Oxfam International 2005. *Africa and the Doha Round*, Oxfam briefing paper 80, November 2005, http://www.oxfam.org/files/doha.pdf

Pauwelyn, J. 2003. *Conflict of Norms in Public International Law: How WTO Law Relates to Other Rules of International Law*. Cambridge: Cambridge University Press.

Pauwelyn, J. 2005. "The Sutherland Report: A Missed Opportunity for Genuine Debate on Trade, Globalization and Reforming the WTO", Duke Law School, Research Paper No. 68.

Petersmann, E.-U. 2001. "European and International Constitutional Law: Time for Promoting 'Cosmopolitan Democracy' in the WTO", in G. De Búrca and J. Scott (eds), *The EU and the WTO: Legal and Constitutional Issues*. Oxford/Portland Oregon: Hart, pp. 81–110.

Petersmann, E.-U. (ed.) 2005a. "Strategic Use of WTO Dispute Settlement Proceedings for Advancing WTO Negotiations on Agriculture", *Reforming the World Trading System: Legitimacy, Efficiency and Democratic Governance*. Oxford: Oxford University Press, pp. 127–144.

Petersmann, E.-U. 2005b. "Addressing Institutional Challenges to the WTO in the New Millenium: A Longer-Term Perspective", *Journal of International Economic Law*, 8, 3, 647–665.

Porter, R. B. 2001. "Efficiency, Equity and Legitimacy: The Global Trading System in the Twenty-First Century", in R. B. Porter, P. Sauvé, A. Subramanian, and A. Beviglia Zampetti (eds), *Efficiency, Equity and Legitimacy: The Multilateral*

Trading System at the Millennium. Washington, DC: Brookings Institution Press, pp. 3–15.

Prévost, D. and P. Van den Bossche 2005. "The Agreement on the Application of Sanitary and Phytosanitary Measures", in P. F. Macrory, A. Appleton, and M. G. Plummer (eds), *The World Trade Organization: Legal, Economic and Political Analysis: Volume I*. New York: Springer, pp. 231–370.

Püttner, G. 2007. *Verwaltungslehre*, 4th edn. München: C. H. Beck.

Quereshi, A. H. 1996. *The World Trade Organisation: Implementing International Trade Norms*. Manchester; New York: Manchester University Press.

Rainey, Hal G. 2003. *Understanding and Managing Public Organizations*, 3rd edn. San Francisco, CA: Jossey-Bass.

Reinalda, B. and B. Verbeek (eds) 1998. "Autonomous Policy Making by International Organizations: Purpose, Outline and Results", *Autonomous Policy Making by International Organizations*. London and New York: Routledge, pp. 1–8.

Reinalda, B. and B. Verbeek (eds) 2004a. "The Issue of Decision Making Within International Organizations", *Decision Making Within International Organizations*. London: Routledge, pp. 7–41.

Reinalda, B. and B. Verbeek (eds) 2004b. "Patterns of Decision Making Within International Organizations", *Decision Making Within International Organizations*. London: Routledge, pp. 231–246.

Reus-Smit, C. 2006. "International Law", in J. Baylis and S. Smith (eds), *The Globalization of World Politics*, 3rd edn. Oxford: Oxford University Press, pp. 349–368.

Rhodes, R. A. W. 1997. *Understanding Governance: Policy Networks, Governance, Reflexivity and Accountability*. Buckingham: Open University Press.

Rittberger, V. and B. Zangl 2003. *Internationale Organisationen – Politik und Geschichte*. 3rd edn. Opladen: Leske + Budrich.

Roethlisberger, F. J. and W. J. Dickson 1939. *Management and the Worker*. Cambridge, MA: Harvard University Press.

Rosenbloom, D. H., R. S. Kravchuk, and R. M. Clerkin 2009. *Public Administration: Understanding, Management, Politics, and Law in the Public Sector*, 7th edn. Boston: McGraw Hill.

Sands, P. 2006. "Non-compliance and Dispute Settlement", in U. Beyerlin, P.-T. Stoll, and R. Wolfrum (eds), *Ensuring Compliance with Multilateral Environmental Agreements*. Leiden: Martinus Nijhoff, pp. 353–358.

Scharpf, F. W. 1997. *Games Real Actors Play: Actor-Centered Institutionalism in Policy Research*. Boulder, CO: Westview Press.

Schreyögg, G. 2008. *Organisation*, 5th edn. Wiesbaden: Gabler.

Schuchhardt, C. 2005. "Consultations", in P. F. Macrory, A. Appleton, and M. G. Plummer (eds), *The World Trade Organization: Legal, Economic and Political Analysis: Volume I*, vol. 1. New York: Springer, pp. 1197–1232.

Schulze-Fielitz, H. 1984. *Der informale Verfassungsstaat*. Berlin: Duncker & Humblot.

Schuppert, G. F. (ed.) 2005. *Governance-Forschung*. Baden-Baden: Nomos.

Schuppert, G. F. 2000. *Verwaltungswissenschaft*. Baden-Baden: Nomos.

Scott, J. 2004. "International Trade and Environmental Governance: Relating Rules (and Standards) in the EU and the WTO", *European Journal of International Law*, 15, 2, 307–354.

Scott, W. R. and G. F. Davis 2007. *Organizations and Organizing: Rational, Natural, and Open System Perspectives*. Upper Saddle River, NJ: Pearson-Prentice Hall.

Shaffer, G. 2005a. "Can WTO Technical Assistance and Capacity Building Serve Developing Countries?", in E.-U. Petersmann (ed.), *Reforming the World Trading System: Legitimacy, Efficiency and Democratic Governance*. Oxford: Oxford University Press, pp. 245–274.

Shaffer, G. 2005b. "Parliamentary Oversight of WTO Rule-Making: The Political, Normative and Practical Contexts", in E.-U. Petersmann (ed.), *Reforming the World Trading System: Legitimacy, Efficiency and Democratic Governance*. Oxford: Oxford University Press, pp. 381–408.

Shaffer, G. 2005c. "Power, Governance and the WTO: A Comparative Institutional Approach", in M. Barnett and R. Duvall (eds), *Power in Global Governance*. Cambridge: Cambridge University Press, pp. 130–160.

Shaffer, G. C. 2004. "Recognizing Public Goods in WTO Dispute Settlement: Who Participates? Who Decides? The Case of TRIPS and Pharmaceutical Patent Protection", *Journal of International Economic Law*, 7, 2, 459–482.

Shaw, Malcolm N. 2008. *International Law*, 6th edn. Cambridge: Cambridge University Press.

Shell, R. 1996. "The Trade Stakeholders Model and Participation of Nonstate Parties in the World Trade Organization", *University of Pennsylvania Journal of International Economic Law*, 17, 359–381.

Short, C. 2001. "Making the Development Round a Reality", in G. P. Sampson (ed.), *The Role of the World Trade Organization in Global Governance*. Tokyo; New York: United Nations University, pp. 59–80.

Shoyer, A. W., E. M. Solovy, and A. W. Koff 2005. "Implementation and Enforcement of Dispute Settlement Decisions", in P. F. Macrory, A. Appleton, and M. G. Plummer (eds), *The World Trade Organization: Legal, Economic and Political Analysis: Volume I*, vol. 1. New York: Springer, pp. 1341–1369.

Skaggs, D. E. 2005. "How can Parliamentary Participation in the WTO Rule-Making and Democratic Control be Made More Effective in the WTO? A United States Congressional Perspective", in E.-U. Petersmann (ed.), *Reforming The World Trading System: Legitimacy, Efficiency and Democratic Governance*. Oxford: Oxford University Press, pp. 409–412.

Slaughter, A. M. 1997. "The Real New World Order", *Foreign Affairs*, 76, 5, 183–197.

Slaughter, A. M. 2004. *A New World Order*. Princeton: Princeton University Press.

Steffek, J. 2003. "The Legitimation of International Governance: A Discourse Approach", *European Journal of International Relations*, 9, 2, 249–275.

Steger, D. 2004. "The Struggle for Legitimacy in the WTO", in D. Steger (ed.), *Peace through Trade: Building the World Trade Organization*. London: Cameron May, pp. 111–41.

Steinberg, R. 2002. "In the Shadow of Law or Power? Consensus-Based Bargaining and Outcomes in the GATT/WTO", *International Organization*, 56, 2, 339–374.

Stokes, B. and P. Choate 2001. *Democratizing U.S. Trade Policy: A Council on Foreign Relations Paper*. New York: Council on Foreign Relations.

Stone, D. 2004. "Transfer Agents and Global Networks in the 'Transnationalization' of Policy", *Journal of European Public Policy*, 11, 3, 545–66.

Sutherland, P. 2005a. "The Doha Development Agenda: Political Challenges to the World Trading System – a Cosmopolitan Perspective", in E.-U. Petersmann (ed.), *Reforming the World Trading System: Legitimacy, Efficiency and Democratic Governance*. Oxford: Oxford University Press, pp. 39–52.

Sutherland, P. 2005b. "Reflections on the 10th Anniversary of the WTO: The World Trade Organization at Ten Years", *World Trade Review*, 4, 3, 341–354.

Sutherland, P. 2005c. "The Politics of Trade Policy Development – the New Complexity", in P. F. Macrory, A. Appleton, and M. G. Plummer (eds), *The World Trade Organization: Legal, Economic and Political Analysis: Volume I*, vol. 1. New York: Springer, pp. 27–38.

Sutherland, P. *et al.* 2004. *The Future of the WTO: Addressing Institutional Challenges in the New Millenium*, Geneva: WTO [also quoted as 'Sutherland Report'], visited on 15 August 2009 http://www.wto.org/english/thewto_e/10anniv_e/future_wto_e.pdf

Tallberg, J. 2002. "Delegation to Supranational Institutions: Why, How, and with What Consequences?", *West European Politics*, 25, 1, 23–46.

The Third World Network, Oxfam International, Public Services International, WWF International, The Center for International Environmental Law, Focus on the Global South, The Institute for Agriculture and Trade Policy, The Africa Trade Network, The International Gender and Trade Network and The Tebtebba International Centre for Indigenous Peoples' Rights 2003. *Memorandum on the Need to Improve Internal Transparency and Participation in the WTO*, 13 July 2003, http://www.twnside.org.sg/title/memo2.doc

Thompson, J. D. and A. Tuden 1959. "Strategies, Structures and Processes of Organizational Decision", in J. D. Thompson *et al.* (eds), *Comparative Studies in Administration*. Pittsburgh: University of Pittsburgh Press, pp. 195–216.

Treib, O., H. Bähr, and G. Falkner 2007. "Modes of Governance: Towards a Conceptual Clarification", *Journal of European Public Policy*, 14, 1, 1–20.

Verbeek, B. 1998. "International Organizations: The Ugly Duckling of International Relations Theory?", in B. Reinalda and B. Verbeek (eds), *Autonomous Policy Making by International Organizations*. London and New York: Routledge, pp. 11–25.

Victor, D. G. 1998. "The Operation and Effectiveness of the Montreal Protocol's Non-Compliance Procedure", in D. G. Victor, R. Kal, and E. B. Skolnikoff (eds), *The Implementation and Effectiveness of International Environmental Commitments: Theory and Practice*. Cambridge; London: MIT, pp. 137–176.

Walker, D. J. 2005. "Pursuing Global Free Trade: A Small Open Economy Perspective", in P. J. F. Macrory, A. E. Appleton, and M. G. Plummer (eds), *The World Trade Organization: Legal, Economic and Political Analysis*, Volume III. New York: Springer, pp. 439–456.

Wallach, L. and M. Sforza 1999. *Whose Trade Organization? Corporate Globalization and the Erosion of Democracy*. Washington, DC: Public Citizen.

Weber, M. 1980. *Wirtschaft und Gesellschaft*, 5th edn. Tübingen: J. C. B. Mohr (Paul Siebeck).

Willetts, P. 2006. "Transnational Actors and International Organizations in Global Politics", in J. Baylis and S. Smith (eds), *The Globalization of World Politics: An Introduction to International Relations*, 3rd edn. Oxford: Oxford University Press, pp. 425–447.

Witte, J. M., W. H. Reinicke, and T. Benner 2000. "Beyond Multilateralism: Global Public Policy Networks", *International Politics and Society (Internationale Politik und Gesellschaft)*, 2, 176–188.

Wolfe, R. 2005. "Decision-Making and Transparency in the 'Medieval' WTO: Does the Sutherland Report Have the Right Prescriptions", *Journal of International Economic Law*, 8, 3, 631–645.

Woll, P. 1963. *Administrative Law: The Informal Process*. Berkeley, CA: University of California Press.

World Trade Organization 2003. *Doha Declarations*, Geneva, visited on 15 August 2009 http://www.wto.org/english/res_e/book SP_e/ddec_e.pdf

World Trade Organization 2004. *WTO Agriculture Negotiations: The Issues, and Where We are Now*, briefing document, updated 1 December 2004, visited on 08/15/2009 http://www.wto.org/english/tratop_e/agric_e/agnegs_bkgrnd_e.pdf

World Trade Organization 2008. *Understanding the WTO*, 4th edn, Geneva: WTO, visited on 15 August 2009 http://www.wto.org/english/thewto_e/whatis_e/tif_e/understanding_e.pdf

Xu, Y. and P. Weller 2004. *The Governance of World Trade: International Civil Servants and the GATT/WTO*. Cheltenham: Edward Elgar.

Zdouc, W. 2005. "The Panel Process", in P. F. Macrory, A. Appleton and M. G. Plummer (eds), *The World Trade Organization: Legal, Economic and Political Analysis: Volume I*. New York: Springer, pp. 1233–1276.

Zippelius, R. 2007. *Rechtsphilosophie*, 5th edn. München: C. H. Beck.

Zürn, M. 2004. "Global Governance and Legitimacy Problems", *Government and Opposition*, 39, 2, 260–287.

Index